AF615702

# America's Institutional Dilemma

# America's Institutional Dilemma

**Ernst G. Frankel**

VANTAGE PRESS
New York

FIRST EDITION



Published by Vantage Press, Inc.
516 West 34th Street, New York, New York 10001

Manufactured in the United States of America
ISBN: 0-533-12534-0

Library of Congress Catalog Card No.: 97- 90993

0 9 8 7 6 5 4 3 2 1

# Contents

# Figures

# Tables

# America's Institutional Dilemma

# Prologue

The American economic system, the envy of the world for a long time, is now attempting to transform itself into a leaner, meaner, world-class, competitive, and outward-looking economy. This is necessary at this time of economic globalization.

Despite many successes and the fact that many sectors of the economy have pulled themselves up to achievc new competence and competitiveness, others and, most important American institutions seem to be unable to change in support of these new requirements. Reengineering or restructuring has been successful in much of American industry, services, and agriculture but has had little impact on improving the performance of American institutions.

The structure and workings of American institutions in education, health care, social services support, and the legal and law enforcement sectors appear to be increasingly ineffective and in many cases are so inefficient that they present a major obstacle to the economic and moral revitalization of the country. They virtually act as an albatross around the neck of the economy and society itself, constraining its rebirth. In fact, the inefficiency of these institutions is largely the cause of government budget deficits and economic deficiencies.

This book asks the question: Is tinkering with our major institutions, like health care, education, and law enforcement, really enough, or do we need completely revitalized and restructured systems for such institutions that work? Do we, in fact, need a reinvention of the American economic and social systems if we are to retain world leadership and a growing standard and quality of life for Americans?

We may have to reevaluate some of our most cherished concepts, many of which a long time ago lost their claim to being principles.

Our concept of individual freedom, for example, has changed from that of a principle guaranteeing individuals the rights to pursue personal legitimate interests and concerns to that of legal loopholes that permit an increasing number of people to trample on the rights and interests of others and thus of society at large. Our laws are often used to protect and coddle criminals, while being used less and less to right the wrongs done to victims.

Society itself is now assumed to have few, if any, rights. The rights of individuals to act, however wrongful, antisocial, or damaging their behavior, are now often interpreted to override those of society at large or of any group of society.

It is about time to do what we know is right and not just what is popular. We must revitalize not just our economy but, even more important, the morality of our nation and thereby reestablish not only military and economic leadership but also moral world leadership. Without the latter the others are hollow and corruption, crime, absurd individual selfishness, religious fanaticism, and a general state of social, economic, and environmental lawlessness may become the general rule. The seeds of this chaos sown in Bosnia, the former Soviet republics, Afghanistan, the Middle East, and many parts of Africa and their influence will grow lest the trend is reversed. In fact, much of Africa is now on the brink of tribal, racial, and religious conflict, and faces an AIDS crisis that may parallel the epidemics of the Middle Ages in its devastation.

Unless leadership is regained by the advocates of society's interests, led by America, not only will lawlessness increase, but the world's economy and its social values will begin to move in reverse. The combination of these two developments is a recipe for the self-destruction of civilization as we now know it.

Preservation of what is left of American values and heritage is up to us. We must ensure that our common interest wins out over the short-term egocentric greed of the few who today lead us downhill.

The impending destruction of our thriving economy and unique society can be placed largely at our own doorstep—not on the doorstep of Japan or our competitors in international trade or other former political and/or military adversaries. The problem now is largely the result of our own ignorance, loose behavior, and lack of consideration for the common good and the selfishness of both individuals and groups. Most important, we have allowed our institutions, once the pride of America, to deteriorate and become largely self-serving, resulting in the loss of their original effectiveness.

We blame others for our trade imbalance, sometimes perhaps rightfully so, yet often do little to restore our competitiveness and even less to achieve a balance of fairness in international trade. We blame others for our drug problems, which contribute at least $30 billion to our trade imbalance, while making no serious effort to curtail the domestic demand for drugs. Similarly, we try to solve a host of other problems either by blaming others or by asking others to take actions that will solve our problems, for example, the reduction of drug importation into the United States and an increase in demand for U.S. goods abroad. As long as we tolerate and even generate a demand for drugs and allow our citizens to pay handsomely for them, suppliers will meet this demand, no matter what we or our friends abroad do. As long as we inefficiently produce goods that are in low demand abroad because their quality, price, or form does not meet local requirements, we will not balance our foreign trade.

Because our social political, and economic problems are largely of our own doing, their solutions begin at home and lie mainly in the fundamental reinvention of the structure of our major institutions—health, education, finance, social services, legal or law enforcement areas, and charities—which have largely degenerated into unbridled, self-serving, inefficient, and often corrupt organizations, led and manned by public or private individuals who have distorted many of the traditional functions of these institutions and have transformed them to serve their narrow self-interests, with only superficial concern for these organizations' stated functions and responsibilities.

America's institutions—once the pride of this country and of the world—have, ironically now become our major problem. The S & L bank failures of the recent past are just the tip of the iceberg of institutional corruption and mismanagement. Institutions such as hospitals, banks, courts, and universities, were once respected because they were untainted and basically untouchable yet in recent years have often been found to be themselves the cause of the problem. Our health care problem, for example, is largely the result of inefficient, wasteful hospitals and greedy health care providers. Our law enforcement problems are often the result of overzealous and greedy lawyers or corrupt law enforcers. Our educational problems, similarly, are often the result of ineffective school and academic institutions.

This book describes how these institutions are quietly undermining the technological and economic leadership of the United States, as well as its very social and political structure.

*There has never been a time when hard choices were more urgently required, when the American economy and society were in deeper trouble, or when Americans felt greater uncertainty about their future.*

*To assure continued growth and leadership of the U.S. economy, to revitalize U. S. society, and reestablish American values and moral standards requires a return to basics, a reinvention of the American system, and, most important, the restructuring of the institutions that have taken over the heart, soul, and resources of the great American society.*

The need for action is imperative now, as America has become the only beacon of hope for the world at large—a world that is in greater disarray now than at any other time, a world that is straining at its seams as social, political, economic, and religious realignments explode to correct historic grievances, social injustices, religious goals, and economic imbalances.

A concrete example is the rise of religious fundamentalism as a social and political force, in many ways quite different from traditional expressions and movements of idealism, yet with even more profound economic impact.

Many who expected the fall of communism in the Soviet Union to bring a new wave of socially responsible capitalism are now astonished at the large-scale emergence of often-corrupt regimes, unbridled nationalism, and fundamentalism as driving forces for change in half the nations of the world. In some these forces have undermined established regimes, while in others they have caused major political, social, and military confrontation or even upheavals and war.

Economic theory and resulting decisions based largely on financial and monetary developments have become increasingly irrelevant as human demands concentrate more and more on social, religious, moral, and nationalistic goals and desires.

## Purpose and Aim

What are the reasons for writing this book and, more important, what do I hope readers will gain from reading it? Like all authors, I would hope that readers enjoy the time spent reading this book and find the insight and information presented useful. They may, and I hope will, challenge some of the ideas, conclusions, and solutions offered here. Yet I would guess that many will find the issues illuminating and cause a greater awareness of them.

The purpose of this book is to review the foundations and fundamental structures of America's institutions. Over the past two hundred years America has evolved from a most perfect political union founded on a unique Constitution of equality and the rights of men, a perfect society of mutual human respect, into a society that is highly institutional, in which the political process is perceived by an increasing segment of the population to exist largely to satisfy the interests of individuals and specialized groups and not as the property of society at large. This perception has skewed, and in some ways distorted or undermined, governance that affects the very structure of American society.

As institutions have become more self-serving, they have come to dominate more of the political process. It is for this reason that health care, education, social services, and criminal justice have become the major focus of our political processes. At the same time, they now consume an unacceptably large proportion of our total output. Scarcely three decades have passed since President Kennedy's inspiring suggestion that we "ask not what your country can do for you, but what you can do for your country." That was still a time when individuals made institutions, a time of idealism. Today many citizens are concerned with narrow personal gain and entitlement and we demand that society, largely represented by our institutions, solve our problems.

This book is intended to show how our institutions have changed from serving to service institutions and from organizations with a focus on serving to self-serving, self-preserving bureaucracies. I hope to provide insight, though some readers may disagree with the views stated. I feel that it is important for us to understand

1. the roles our major institutions play,
2. the resources our major institutions consume,
3. the impact of our major institutions on our way of life and our well-being,
4. the organization of our major institutions as well as the interlocking of their management and interests with those of government at all levels, and
5. the methods used for self-preservation and narrow interest protection by these major institutions, including their built-in conflicts of interest.

Some of the views and solutions suggested may appear extreme, while others may seem politically or economically infeasible or incorrect or appear to violate fundamental principles of democracy and individual rights, such as the right to bear arms. My goal is not to challenge the fundamental values of our Constitution, but to show how misuse of our most sacred principles is leading us toward an inescapable abyss—into a world where human life is dispensable; where leaders in politics, law, education, and health care are primarily concerned with their own self-interest; where individuals are cynical and trust neither government nor institutions; where society no longer serves to bind people together for the common good.

I invite the reader to join me in reflecting on where we are, how we got here, what we have become, and what we must do to revitalize America. This, in my opinion, will, most important, require the reinvention of the American institutions that embody much of the American system. We cannot just decrease the growth of their budgets and hope for the best. We must restructure these institutions and bring them back to their fundamental objectives.

# 1
# An American Dilemma

The concept of Americanism—democracy at the level of the individual, whose rights are supreme—has led the technological and economic development of the world for nearly a century. It has encouraged citizens in America to become tinkerers and inventors, solvers of problems, who improve life. They have used their freedom to experiment socially, economically, and technically and become leaders in these fields. The majority of technical, social, and economic innovations of the last century originated in America. Most were the result of individual efforts encouraged by the freedom of thought and conscience provided in America. However, in the past twenty years these concepts have often been misused. Our unique form of government, which elevates democratic principles beyond those envisioned by the Greek philosophers and later Western European pragmatists, made it all possible. Yet today the United States no longer leads unchallenged in technological and economic advances. Its principles, though still advocated and followed by much of the world as shining examples of an ideal world, are increasingly misused or misinterpreted both at home and abroad.

The freedom of the individual is now often interpreted not as the right to contribute freely to one's own well-being and that of the community but as a right to selfishly drain the community's resources, with no duty to replenish them. Institutions and government have become abstract concepts to be used or misused and not institutions of and for the public. Their resources are thought to be bottomless and without origin, and their responsibilities are expected to satisfy the needs of those very citizens who disdain institutions and refuse to participate in or contribute to them. In fact, we are moving rapidly toward a self-centered, self-serving society devoid of mutual trust, in which everyone, including quite often those who are part of the system, tries to milk the institutions of society, society itself, or the system. They do not consider that they have a duty and obligation to the society of which they themselves are members.

Yet the system—usually represented by our institution—is us. It is not merely a reflection of us but is truly what we have made of ourselves—and it is not pretty. Neither is it moving forward. In fact, it is moving toward abyss of overindulging waste, selfishness, lack of discipline, and irresponsibility and, most alarmingly, toward an increasingly disjointed noncooperating society. We preach to the world that the environment must be protected but dispose of many times more waste into the environment than anyone else does.

Our leaders repeatedly prove unworthy of public trust, yet we continue to elect "charismatic" incompetents. We object to increased taxation but demand unnecessary or wasteful services, many of which contribute little to our well-being and safety or only an isolated few.

We have the world's most wasteful and largely inadequate health care, legal, public safety, and educational systems, which together consume nearly 43 percent of our gross national product. While we object to curtailment of these often inefficiently provided or even unnecessary services, we do not object to the obscene incomes of many executives, lawyers, and physicians who have discovered the secrets of income pyramiding and the benefits of providing unnecessary services at exorbitant costs to an unsuspecting public. In fact, our resources are being drained, on one side, by those who could work but prefer to let the public provide for them and, on the other side, by those who are vastly overcompensated and have made a captive out of our society. Lawyers, doctors, and others have organized themselves into largely self-serving, self-policing cartels that set their own rules and wield an inordinately strong political influence.

The bulk of American society—consisting largely of the often maligned middle class—is squeezed between these two selfish and evergrowing groups and is made to pay for their demands, which will invariably lead our society into an economic, moral, and social never-never land where fewer and fewer contribute productively and where we ultimately will sell each other largely unnecessary services and produce nothing of value.

## Putting People First and Society Last

Americanism, as noted before, is often associated with individualism and individual rights. To many, this philosophy implies the right of people to be self-centered and to act in their own self-interest, along with the assumption that society owes us, but we owe nothing to society. This philosophy and its acceptance as proper behavior in America and by Americans have contributed greatly to the breakdown of the American family, the traditional way of American life, law and order, and, ultimately, the productivity of the American economy. It has caused havoc with American education, which now has few, if any standards, and where students graduate from high school merely by showing up.

There is nothing wrong with putting people first, but this must be done by society, by institutions, and by employers who cater to the needs and interests of individuals. In other words, society owes us and we owe society. Like everything else, it is reciprocal: you give and you get. Yet this Americanism, which over its long history has been renowned for its charity, its compassion, its willingness to accept and help those in need, is now being replaced by an increasingly selfish segment from both inside as well as outside society. Many of these are the very people who have benefited most from society, who have never contributed to it, who have never held a job or, for that matter, have never done anything for anyone, least of all for society at large.

Yes, we should put people first. Many companies have learned that such policies pay off if properly instituted. Many people still recognize that society is not a bottomless pit and that employers do not have unlimited resources. We must learn that only by playing fair and balancing the interests of the individual, society or community, company, and family, can we regain the win-win situation in which both the individual and society come out ahead.

The situation in which we find ourselves today is really a lose-lose situation that is too painful to contemplate, as it invariably leads to an abyss. Yet to adopt a win-win approach requires a willingness to let others also win. This is an approach many of us have not yet learned or accepted. We are too involved with our own success and often assume that our success depends on the failure of others.

As Christopher Nash points out, "America is a society of dangerously self-absorbed individuals, fixated on personal goals, fearful of their impulses, and easily controllable by power elites."[1] Such a society has difficulty seeing the big picture and also the benefits of interpersonal cooperation.

## Public Policy and Personal Indifference

The American concept of personal freedom has great economic impact when it involves public policy both at the federal and local levels and with the resulting decision making. The concept of individual rights transcends consideration of the cost to society in many ways, which if considered together, strongly influence both the cost to and effects on the quality of life in American society.

The following example will help illustrate this point. Delivery trucks double-park and otherwise interfere with the flow of traffic in most U.S. cities. Most deliveries are made during rush hour, usually in the mornings. A single delivery truck double-parked for thirty minutes on a busy road, where the truck reduces two traffic lanes to one, will cause an average of 600 cars, buses, and trucks to be delayed by an average of close to two minutes, causing a social loss of twenty person-hours, as well as the added cost of vehicle operation and pollution, all for the convenience of the truck driver and receiving clerk who prefer not to work before or after rush hour. A simple estimate of the costs and benefits of requiring deliveries to be made before 7:00 A.M. between 10:00 A.M.and 2:00 P.M., or after 7:00 P.M. for a typical city of 1 million inhabitants shows that the cost of overtime of about 1,000 hours/weekday for delivery truck drivers and receiving clerks would save approximately 50,000 driver- and vehicle-hours of people stuck in traffic by double-parked trucks. Assuming that the added costs of overtime and delivery rescheduling are about $26/hour (including helpers), the added daily costs to delivery services would be about $26,800/day, or $0.52 per vehicle- and driver-hour saved, a fraction of the economic cost of vehicle- and driver-time costs. However public policy protects the rights of the truck driver, the road repairman, and others to work when and how they want, independent of the cost to society. Policy makers do not care, as the cost to society is not assumed by them while overtime costs would have to be paid by them. In this example, public policy makers themselves are usually oblivious to the public interest and give preference to their narrow budget interests instead. There are many examples in our daily lives where society is made to pay for the convenience or narrow, selfish benefit of individuals.

## Wasteful Consumption and Environmental Costs

We are similarly oblivious to global environmental concerns notwithstanding our concerns with pollution by smoking and its effects on individuals. Although America comprises but 5 percent of the world's population, we consume 25 percent of world energy. Since the mid-1960s an increasing percentage of the fuel required to generate this energy has been imported. Specifically, 50 to 60 percent of oil consumed in the United States is now imported. Only thirty years ago, the United States was not only the world's largest oil producer but also was among the leading oil exporters. Low consumer prices for oil are the principal reason—Americans pay on average only 30 to 40 percent as much for oil products and energy as do people in other industrialized countries—these are the principal reasons for both wasteful consumption and low domestic production.

Energy conservation and reduced fossil fuel burning have been attempted for many years, but such measures have given way to the pressure of political interest groups. Increased energy taxes and fuel import duties have been proposed by several administrations but have been rejected for lack of political will. As a result, the public assumes that it can use energy or fuel inefficiently, as it costs little and is always abundantly available. Similarly, it is not concerned with the larger environmental effects that make it more hazardous to cross a busy street than inhale the air in a smoke-filled room.

Americans have come to associate cheap, inefficient energy use with the American way of life, quality of life, and standard of living. In other words, they make low-priced, readily available energy a philosophical and moral issue. Higher oil prices and restricted availability are seen as antisocial and, in fact, are promoted as such. More important, they are perceived as developments that would primarily affect lower-income people, as cheap energy use (particularly for transportation) is assumed to give low-income Americans a major advantage over low-income people in other countries, through mobility and extravagant use of the large gas-guzzling automobiles. Only in America are low-income people the principal users of large, used, gas-guzzling luxury automobiles. In a way, this is seen as compensation for the otherwise poor living conditions suffered by the low-income class in the United States. It provides some degree of equalization, no matter what the social and environmental costs, and offers an attractive strategic alternative for politicians. The rest of the world also has problems of inequity and major differences in income, which are often greater and more debilitating. However, few try to solve these in this manner.

## American Economic Decline

Recent books by Paul Kennedy,[2] David P. Cale,[3] and Mancur Olson[4] review the condition of the U.S. economy from different perspectives, but the consensus is that America is now in decline, after reaching a dominant position in the world largely through technological inventiveness, economic prowess, and management ability. The United States reached its pinnacle soon after the end of World War II and since then has devoted an increasing percentage of its output and resources to military or policing actions, strategic positioning, overseas and foreign aid commitments, social development, and the buildup of a service and welfare system unlike any experienced before.

Olson argues that entrenched interests have caused an inability by government to act and that these interests have encouraged self-interested and self-serving decisions that advance narrow personal or parochial interests. Others maintain that the Great Society went overboard by introducing a social welfare system without preparing society for the moral and ethical standards required to allow such programs to work. Others contend that fiscal policies designed to benefit only one sector of society, such as business, have caused the decline of the American economy.

The move toward a postindustrial, essentially service economy from a largely manufacturing producing economy is considered by others to be the major culprit, as it makes the United States more import-dependent.

While U.S. world leadership is increasingly questioned on political as well as economic issues, its moral leadership was unquestioned . . . until recently. America has attempted to maintain its political and to some extent economic leadership by extending foreign aid, foreign technical assistance, liberal immigration policies, and military or security guarantees.

Few of these attempts have paid off, and some have even contributed to U.S. economic and political problems.

There are many who contend that the U.S. problem is largely a lack of focus and national will and inadequate popular unity, which results in a lack of preparation for tackling hard economic problems. At the same time, the United States is the only truly multiracial, multicultural society in the world with no single dominating group, although some groups play larger roles in the economy and government than others, in both absolute and proportional terms.

To cope with problems such as those introduced by social diversity, freedom and tolerance are required. Yet these often bring contradictory results, as greater freedom often leads to diminishing tolerance. In fact, some argue that our dilemma is that we overemphasize the right of the individual without countervailing duties and underemphasize the rights and needs of the community or society at large and the obligation to contribute to society, its laws and resources, to take advantage of its benefits and freedoms.

Economic restructuring of the United States may be desirable in light of a continued economic change. While the American government is not directly involved in most commercial activities it maintains significant control and oversight as well as bureaucratic interference, which causes delays and added cost. Much of this interference is caused by a political process largely driven by special interest groups who assure that the public interest and often even commercial practice do not dominate.

## The Nation's Needs

While the most urgent concerns of Americans include the economy, health care, crime and the legal system, education, the environment, and social welfare, in recent years government has advanced only sketchy plans to address these issues. When government or the legislature does consider these issues, it does so often in isolation or in a disjointed fashion, as with the recently proposed crime bill and health care legislation. These issues are highly interdependent and do not lend themselves to piecemeal or isolated solutions. As an example, health care expenses resulting from gun-related crimes alone are estimated at about $100 billion per year. Similarly, legal contingency fees from health-related cases amount to about $60 billion. In other words, there is a large interdependence between the costs of legal fees, crime, and health care and the resulting impact on the economy. We now spend about 43 percent of our Gross National Product (GNP) for health care, crime, and legal and education systems, a figure that is expected to exceed 50 percent before the year 2002.

This is more than twice the percentage spent on these institutions by any other country in the world, even countries with educational, health care, and law enforcement systems superior to ours. Ours is a very high price to pay, particularly when the quality of the services provided by these institutions appears to be in perpetual decline and when a growing percentage of Americans lack access to any health care, meaningful education or protection under the law.

As late as 1960 the costs of education, health care, and law enforcement were each a mere 5 percent of GNP, or 15 percent total. They reached 25 percent only in 1980. Since then they have grown at an accelerated rate, reaching over 42 percent of the GNP by 1993, as shown in figure 1. Unless something is done to contain these costs, they will consume the bulk of our GNP early in the next century, a development that could bankrupt the nation. The 1997 budget proposed a cutback of Medicare costs but concentrated largely on delivery and not unit or service costs.

The problem is not only that such a huge percentage of the national product is consumed by these institutions, but that human and other resources are used inefficiently by these institutions. These resources are simultaneously prevented from contributing to the productive output of the nation by being used elsewhere. We are the only developed nation in the world in which lawyers and doctors each outnumber engineers, and people engaged in health care, law enforcement, and education outnumber those engaged in manufacture and agriculture.

While it is true that we are increasingly moving towards a postindustrial service economy, total employment in government and institutional services listed previously now accounts for the bulk of nonmanufacturing jobs.

We must develop a more effective balance in the use of human and other resources if we are to regain our leadership. Similarly, we must produce more if we are to maintain the growth in our living standard and the quality of life we proudly associate with being American. Otherwise we may soon find ourselves a society consisting of lawyers and law enforcers, health care providers, educators, bureaucrats, criminals, children, and the aged, with no output of tradable or consumable goods and services.

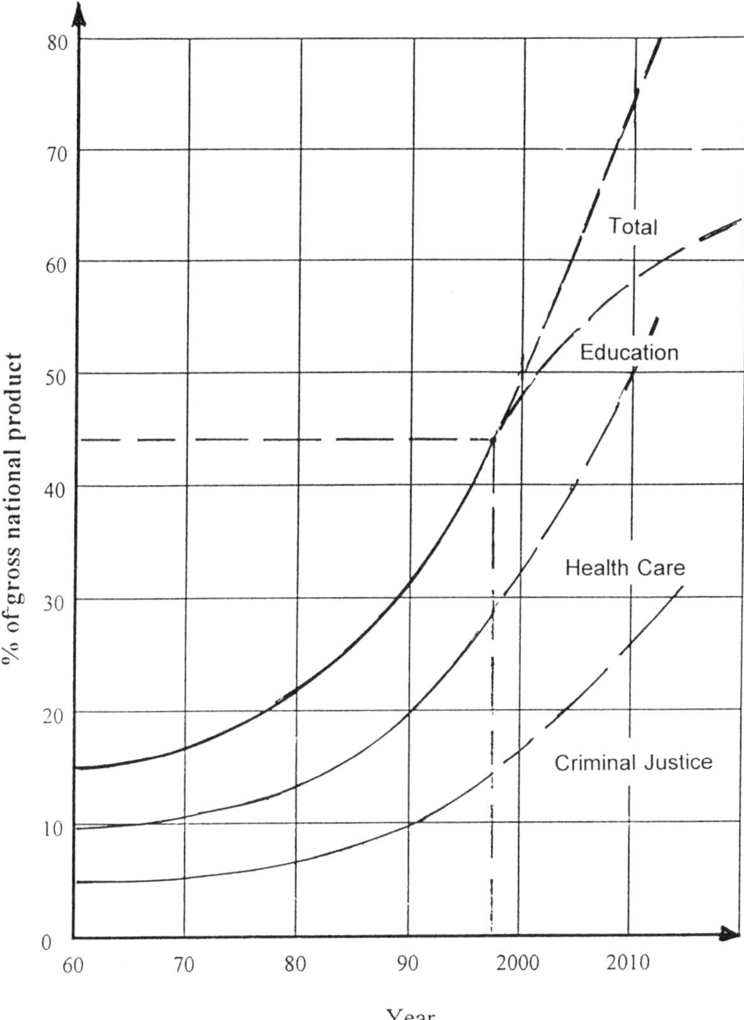


FIGURE 1 Cost of U.S. Health Care, Education, and Criminal Justice as a Percentage of Gross National Product

Source: Authors compilation from U.S. Bureau of Labor Statistics Data - 1996, U.S. Department of Labor

## American Economic Dilemma

The dilemma is that the U.S. economy is in a gridlock of structural constraints that block improvement in U.S. competitiveness and, more important, in economic growth adequate to maintain the standard of living we have come to expect as the American way of life.

It now appears that even a substantial peace dividend, combined with further attempts to improve the productivity of what is left of U.S. industry, will not suffice to correct the serious stagnation of the U.S. economy.

We spend more than twice as much as other industrialized countries on health care, education, and the legal and law enforcement sectors. For this we provide a lower-than-average level of health care, education, and legal protection than that provided by other countries, such as Japan and Germany, each of which spends less than 19 percent of their GDP on these three major institutions or well less than half of the U.S. expenditure in per capita GDP terms.

Not only is the average service quality lower in these three important areas, but in the United States a much lower proportion of the population has access to effective health care, education, and legal services or protection. This lack of access introduces serious inequities that negate many of our democratic principles and at the same time introduces additional costs. As a result, the services are priced at the level of expectation of the middle and upper classes, with the poor and lower middle class by and large receiving substandard—yet expensive—special dispensation of health, legal, and educational services.

A national economy is actually like a business in which required internal services are overhead expenses.

There is an urgent need to make quality health care, education, and legal services universally available and to make these services more efficient, affordable, and responsive to public needs.

The ills of our institutional service sector include lack of access, which is not due to lack of technology but lack of internal efficiency, institutional mismanagement, and outright waste and corruption.

## The New "Not in My Backyard" Idealist

A disturbing development in America is the change in idealism from selfless concern and activism to lack of personal involvement. Hollywood is concerned with environmental and social problems in far away places yet ignores problems in Watts or other blighted areas of Los Angeles.

University presidents and other leaders voice concern about the decline in educational and moral standards in higher education, but few are willing to make the sacrifices necessary to clean their own house. Judges talk about lawlessness in America but are unwilling to tighten the screws of punishment or impose effective methods of rehabilitation and restitution. Police want public support but are unwilling to penetrate the "blue wall of silence" by denouncing or punishing corrupt cops.

As a nation, we still believe in doing good and in justice, work, and equality. We still contribute to causes. We still walk or run to raise money for something worthwhile. But increasingly we do these things in an abstract manner that does not affect our personal life. We have become, by and large, a nation of bystanders and of sociopolitical couch potatoes who watch from the sidelines, unwilling to get involved. We feel less and less responsible for contributing our fair share or adding value in proportion to our consumption. In fact, we have become a largely imbalanced society in which consumption far exceeds production or output.

Honest work produces something useful, something that serves. Under this definition there are many so-called professionals in the United States who do not produce honest work. Lawyers are the most obvious example, but there are many other professionals who match this definition, including bureaucrats who perform no real administrative, policy-making or decision-making function, and still others who contribute neither value nor service to the economy. In other words, we are experiencing an economic breakdown of the American system.

## Breakdown of the American Family

One of the most disturbing aspects of American society today is the breakdown of the traditional family. In America, two out of three black children and two out of five white children currently grow up in single-parent households. The remainder do not experience traditional family life either because both parents work or because parents do not encourage or engage in a traditional family setting.

The reasons for the breakdown in family life and structure are partly economic, as a result of a welfare and support system that either discourages or provides disincentives for family life, and partly cultural, in which family values count for less and less. The system pays more to a single mother with one or two children than she could earn employed as a low-skilled worker. The decline of the nuclear family is a major cause of what ails America—also the decline in educational standards, youth crime, drug addiction, welfare abuse, and more. Overall the institutions designed to address these problems have failed. Social services are inadequate, and the legal provisions originally designed to foster and bind families together have become largely counterincentives. In fact, more often than not, they provide the inertia that drives the break up of families and causes social welfare dependence.

## Who Is to Blame for Our Dilemma?

Let us not assign blame or punish the guilty but work toward restoring an American system that works, that reestablishes the American values of liberty and freedom to pursue life's opportunities, which provide for safety, fairness, and justice for each individual, while providing meaningful incentives for all to contribute to the common objectives of a prosperous society.

Some claim that our predicament is the result of the excesses of the financial community during the last twenty years. Manipulation and tinkering were more profitable than investing and building; speculators', executives', and lawyers' incomes doubled on average every four to six years, while the rest of America barely kept pace with inflation and doubled their income only over an average of eighteen years. At the same time the United States changed from being the world's largest creditor to being the largest debtor nation in an eight-year period, in terms of both domestic and foreign debt. The American economy is out of control not because of any fault in the underlying principles of American capitalism but because many of its citizens have equated democratic capitalism with selfish greed and a right to maximize personal profit with no duty to maintain and contribute fairly to society or the common system. They have interpreted and used capitalism as a one-way street where the system provides protection and opportunity with no resulting obligation by the individual to the system.

In fact, American economic nationalism does not exist. Americans feel no obligation to give preference to local products and services or to exhibit particular pride in using something American. They generally feel a duty only to themselves, a duty to maximize their personal gain or benefit without regard for the impact of their decision. They feel by and large little responsibility toward other Americans or to the national economy, particularly if there is added cost involved. They buy imported products that have American equivalents, for status or because of an assumed difference in quality, even knowing that Americans are losing jobs in that industry, which, in many cases, may even be their own. The parking lots of U.S. car makers and their dealers are full of foreign-made cars. This was justified in the past when American-made cars, and for that matter other products, were often inferior in quality, if not in design. But things have changed. However, these habits remain.

Similarly, staff and workers of U.S. clothing manufacturers often wear imported suits. Equipment used in U.S. ports is usually imported, as are the robots used in U.S. industry, notwithstanding the fact that the underlying technology is often American and similarly good, well-performing U.S. products are available to meet those needs.

These decisions are not antinational, and the blame cannot be placed solely on the purchaser and user of foreign goods. Often the U.S. supplier does produce lower-quality or shoddier goods, does not deliver on time, does not provide effective support services, or expects a higher price and/or profit, particularly from domestic sales. Even so, few Americans have pride in U.S.-made goods or feel any obligation to give preference to American manufacture even if price and quality are equal. By and large we simply carry our freedom of choice as individuals from our social to our economic behavior. We feel no social responsibility for American society at large, so we fail to feel an economic responsibility toward American society. In a way, we are unique in this self-contradictory behavior which is simultaneously nationalistic and antinationalistic. Germans, French, Japanese, and many others, among the people of industrialized countries still maintain a degree of economic nationalism and support their own industry and services, by preferentially buying their products.

## America as a Debtor Nation

America may not appear a pauper or look like the world's leading debtor nation, but this is a fact that will affect not only the standard of living of future generations of Americans but also our future role in the world economy and in international relations or, even more important, our own perception of our position, priorities, and responsibilities toward the rest of the world. Furthermore, the amount of foreign investment in U.S. assets has grown tremendously in the last decade. Today it exceeds the value of total U.S. assets abroad. In 1980 U.S. investments abroad were more than double those of foreigners in the United States but this is no longer so. This means that in the future more profits from investments and ownerships will be exported than returned into the United States development that will make it even harder to balance our foreign exchange and trade.

This will increasingly influence our balance of payments. In the past our merchandise trade deficit was reduced from profits in invisible trade, much of which resulted from profits returned from U.S. foreign investments. This flow has now been reversed, and for the first time in recent history profits from foreign investments in the United States exceed profits from U.S. investments abroad. This trend will accelerate as less of the profits of foreign investors in the United States are reinvested in America.

## From Wealth Creation to Wealth Consumption

Building the foundation of the formation of this perfect union, America became the world's largest wealth creator, with output exceeding its consumption until twenty years ago. But no more! True, we still have many wealth creators. American agriculture and some sectors of American industry and services are efficient wealth creators, but in the last two decades we have become a nation of wealth consumers. It is not just the merger and acquisition artists who enrich themselves by syphoning off wealth without creating new wealth, nor just the new armies of freeloaders who drain our social systems even when they could contribute productively. Our huge and growing institutions of health care, education, and law enforcement have become self-serving, wealth-consuming entities that justify their existence not only on the basis of the value of the services they supply or the wealth they create, but on the basis of need they themselves often established without consulting the public or service consumers. In other words, our institutions have largely become interlocked and interdependent wealth consumers to an extent where they justify much of their activities not on the basis of the needs of the public or of society, but by the need to serve and support each other. The principal responsibility of such institutions is to society and not to themselves, government, or the political establishment, something many do not emphasize enough or often even consider.

Our institutions must become responsible servants of our society and its economy. They must not only work at performing their functions and providing their services efficiently and with the highest quality but at the same time conserve society's resources and minimize their consumption of society's products.

Without a radical change, our major institutions will absorb an ever larger proportion of our national product until we become a net service provider that serves largely itself. We will then consume more and more of our and the world's resources. While this can conceivably be accommodated in isolated cases, such as or Singapore or Hong Kong, with populations of 3.5 and 6.1 million respectively, America is too large and wasteful a consumer. It would result in gross imbalances in our foreign trade and ever larger budget deficits.

# 2

# Institutional Mismanagement: The Principal Cause of U.S. Economic Stagnation

We pride ourselves on being the most successful free market economy where private enterprise plays the leading or even dominating role. However, if we consider the role and size of federal, state, and local government and superimpose on this the role and size of our major institutions in health, education, and law enforcement or criminal justice, we find that government and institutions dominate our society and economy in terms of employment, notwithstanding the fact that many of our major institution's activities are performed by private agencies, firms, or providers.

Our health care system is made up of government agencies concerned with health care, from federal to local regulatory agencies, health care insurers like Medicare/Medicaid to public sector hospitals, laboratories, schools, and services. Private sector participation in health care includes health care insurers, maintenance organizations, hospitals, doctors, nurses, schools, drug manufacturers, diagnostic laboratories, and more.

The law enforcement or legal justice system consists of law courts, law enforcement agencies, prisons, and rehabilitation centers at different levels of government, supported by private sector lawyers and legal service providers, private detectives and protective agencies, and more.

The educational system consists of public and private institutions of learning from kindergarten to postgraduate education and includes research organizations vocational and professional training providers, and more.

These major institutions provide society with its most basic needs and essential services in health care, education, and personal protection. Traditionally, these were provided by simple, locally organized activities. Today they are provided by an array of inefficient, often ineffective, and largely overlapping services provided by ill-coordinated institutions. This situation developed by evolution, with institutions assuming ever greater responsibilities. This often resulted in the usurping of local authority.

Today economic problems dominate public concern and form the agendas of our political parties and their candidates. Politicians promise to introduce various programs that will make America more competitive. Tax cuts and free trade agreements with Canada and Mexico, training or retraining of workers, and a myriad of incentives are offered to the productive manufacturing industry and agricultural sectors, sectors that are already among the most productive in the world. At the same time, little is done to improve the competitiveness of the service sector.

U.S. factory workers and farmers individually outproduce their worldwide competition in per-hour labor productivity. Many manufacturing and farming enterprises have improved their management efficiency and have developed into meaner, leaner organizations capable of competing in the global environment. The problem today is no longer with industrial productivity but with the productivity of our service industry, particularly of our institutions in health, education, and legal services, which together consume nearly 43 percent of our GNP.

These institutions have, in fact, become the most mismanaged sectors of our economy. The costs of health, education, and legal services have increased at more than twice the rate of growth of GNP. Health care costs in 1990 exceeded $760 billion (14 percent of GNP) and are projected to reach $1,000 billion by 1995. Legal services and education are not far behind, and altogether these services—which accounted for over one-third of the American GNP in 1980—are approaching 43 percent of GNP now. Many of these costs are borne by the federal and state governments. Consider what we get for these expenditures, which are among the highest in the world. The quality of our education, health, and legal services is judged to be well below that achieved by most other developed countries, which, in fact, all spend far less for these services than does the United States.

Health, legal, and educational institutions today consume too large a proportion of the U S GNP. This is an unacceptable cost to any society and particularly to one that receives neither quality legal, health, and educational services nor coverage of all the U.S. society in these services. Many educational, legal, and health care services are not accessible to all segments of U.S. society. Similarly, the quality of our health, legal, and educational services is well below those of other developed nations and even of some poorer countries. There are some highlights where such institutions excel in the United States, such as in some basic legal, scientific, and medical research and related education and services. But these are isolated exceptions. Many of our teaching hospitals and research universities are among the best in the world, but they comprise only a small segment of U.S. health care and educational institutions.

Major segments of the U.S. population neither receive nor have access to adequate legal, health, and educational services, notwithstanding the inordinate expense of nearly $10,000 per capita per year for these services in 1992.

In summary, the most worrisome fact is that costs for these institutional services increased from 15 percent to 43 percent of GNP between 1960 and 1990 and are expected to reach 50 percent within a year or two (see figure 2). Even more shocking is the fact that the costs of these institutions have increased from $78 billion in 1960 to nearly $2,680 billion in 1990. In other words, in the period from 1960 to 1990 while the GNP increased tenfold, health, education, and legal institutional costs increased by a whopping thirty-three-fold.

Over the last fifteen years health, education, and legal system costs increased in the United States at more than twice the rate of the growth of the economy and the rate of inflation combined. If this trend continues then by the year 2013 we will theoretically spend all our GNP on health, education, legal system, and government. In other words, we will produce no real products, only services that we ourselves consume. Although this may appear an outlandish possibility, the condition of our nation's education, lawlessness, and health demand continued growth of these institutions. This trend must be reversed if we are to survive as a viable, thriving economy and maintain our quality of life and the world leadership we have enjoyed for so long. But difficult decisions are required to achieve a reversal of this trend that will bring these expenditures back in line to levels of 15 to 20 percent of GNP achieved in the sixties.

American academic, health, and research institutions have experienced some decline in quality, responsiveness, and, most important, ethical standards. In fact, some say that the public indignation over declining ethical standards causes or induces academic institutions to choose contingency and opportunity over value and truth.

The pursuit of research funding, for example, in popular, well-supported areas takes precedence over identifying needed research and selling it. Hospitals, universities, and other research institutions respond to changing interests of sources of support and a new clientele more than to the needs of society.

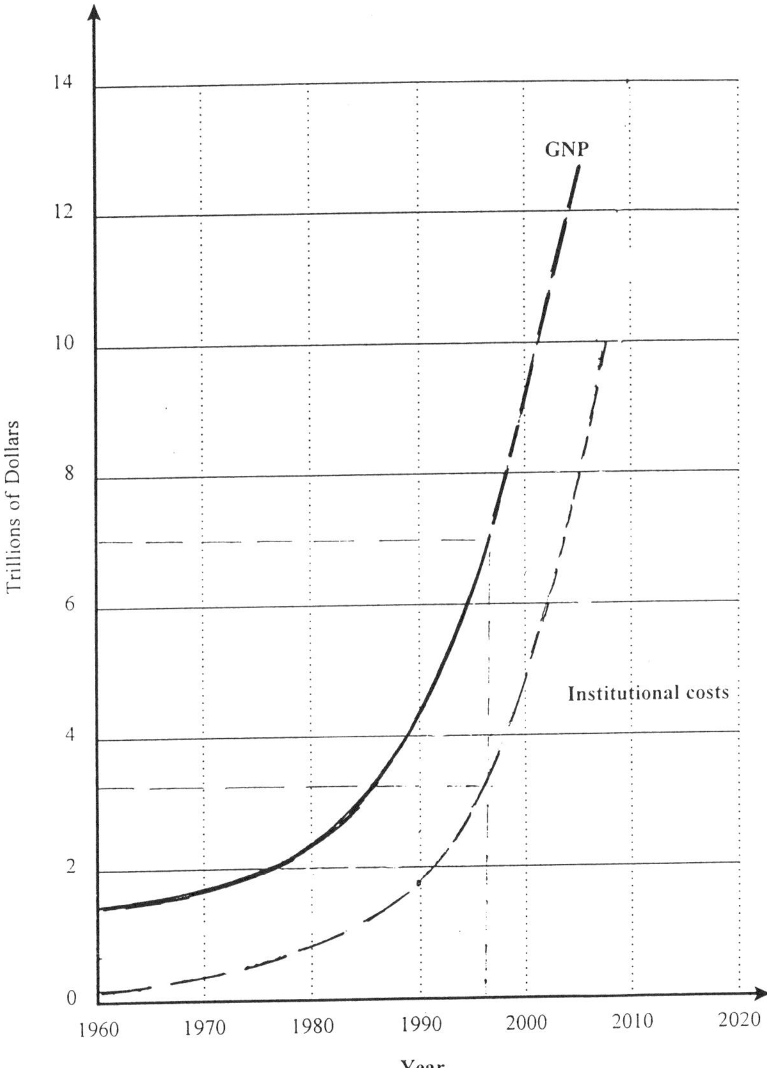


FIGURE 2 GNP and Institutional Expenses

Source: Authors compilation from Bureau of Economic Analysis, U.S. Department of Education

Our institutions were never idealistic, even when organized as real nonprofit institutions, because various participants soon took over and allowed their personal preferences to affect the structure and policy of the institution. As a result, few, if any, institutions have remained true to the objectives or goals of their founders in terms of financial, operational, organization, and work performance.

Most of these institutions, while still managed in the style of the sixties, not by leadership and creativity but by micromanaging, have reduced the role and influence of their professional staff and appointed professional managers to run the institution. Rules for the management of each unit of the organization are now imposed from the top down, supposedly in line with the overall objectives, which are usually quantitative goals in which qualitative and long-term development factors are not considered or are downplayed.

Even office and information technology that, at its infancy, was expected to improve the efficiency of service and primarily institutional management is being used to largely solidify control by management, expand bureaucratic procedures, and infiltrate all aspects of the organization. This, in turn, not only results in loss of efficiency in administration but also in a decline in white-collar workers' morale, as fewer decisions are wholly under their control and the organization becomes more transparent, with micromanagement decisions permeating from top to bottom.

Today—more than ever before—access to and control of information is a sign of power and prestige and in an organizational structure confers position and ultimately rewards, even if the information and the resulting power are misused or used ineffectively. Management and, in particular, management in U.S. service and institutional organizations have turned the advances in office, information, and communications technology around to enhance their control and not improve the efficiency of productivity of their organizations. As a result, instead of improving organizational or white-collar efficiency, it has by and large resulted in a decline of efficiency. Furthermore, it has resulted in an increasing alienation between administrative and production workers, between hospital administrators and nurses or staff, between university administrators and teachers or staff, between administrators of law enforcement and other public safety systems and policemen, jail wardens, etc., and between bank management and bank staff.

Technology that was designed to simplify, integrate, and improve intraorganizational cooperation and incentives has been largely misused in the United States, enhancing the control of management and making it harder, instead of easier, for productive contributions to improve the performance of the organization. New technology is not used for productivity enhancement at the service level or to improve the provision of health care to patients, the learning of students, the safety for citizens, financial services to customers, but is largely used to tighten control and reduce, instead of enhance, the decision-making ability of the productive staff of the institution, which is seen as a potential threat to management of the institution and its prerogatives and rewards.

While Americans in general have accepted, with some concern, the increasing power of management in industry with its increasingly more obscene rewards, a similar trend in both public and private institutions, is a new yet more dangerous, phenomena, as it is not subjected to the usual ownership and regulatory checks and balances under which industry and business operate.

## Institutions of Democracy—Democratic Institutions?

In a democracy public institutions are formed to serve the interests of society and the needs of the people. In theory, they are organized to be accessible to all and to provide services without discrimination. Yet our institutions are largely dominated by interest groups and entrenched management, which consider those who can arrange the financing and licenses as their principal stakeholders and not the people for whom the institutions were formed and whose taxes have paid for them.

Educational institutions do not consider students, their parents, or even society to be their principal stakeholders, nor do health care institutions primarily respond to the desires and/or needs of their patients or communities. Law enforcement institutions are mainly concerned with the needs of the providers of legal and law enforcement services and the rights of the lawbreakers than with the needs and concerns of the people they exist to protect. Yet the principal purpose of these institutions in a democracy is to serve the public or society's needs.

Political considerations usually dominate the governance, management, and operation of institutions, notwithstanding a facade of concern with and for the public. In turn, political considerations are usually responses to narrow self-interests that more often than not are designed to benefit not the stakeholders or people, but the power or the governing elite, who, surround themselves with layers of dependents or beneficiaries who shield them from the bulk of the true stakeholders.

It is interesting to note that in democracies all public institutions and institutions designed to serve the public interest find it necessary to cover themselves with a veneer of democratic organizations where the governing elite is surrounded and supported by a complete establishment of pseudo–democratically anointed peons who provide a popular buffer between the people and the governing bodies of the institution. As we will see, this is the approach used in our educational, health care, legal, and even social assistance institutions, which together have taken over the bulk of our resources and control their distribution or use. This often results in obvious misallocation when total prison budgets exceed school budgets, which is the case in many parts of the country.

## The Growth of American Institutionalism

Institutions have become the mainstay of the American system, while many claim that they *are* the American system: America is its institutions. While this may have been the case for a long time, the nature and role of American institutions have changed radically, particularly during the last thirty years.

Until recently, institutions throughout American history represented and were managed by their members. If an institution was established to render or serve the public with professional services, then the representation and management were carried out by the professionals who provided the services and by representatives of the beneficiaries of that institution. As a result, American schools and universities were run by educators or faculty and their students; hospitals and other health care facilities by medical doctors, nurses, and patients; and legal and law enforcement institutions by lawyers and other legal or law enforcement professionals and the public they protected.

In the last thirty years, this has changed radically. Many of these institutions are no longer run or under the control of the professionals who provide the services the institutions were designed for but are now managed by a new breed of managers and administrators, not all of whom have a professional background in the services they control.

Universities and other educational systems and health care and hospitals, as well as the legal system, have become new and often confused arenas for administrators who, while exerting power and control of these institutions, often have neither the competence nor the integrity for the services these institutions are designed to provide.

It is unclear how we fell into this trap, but the most convincing reason appears to be the increased specialization and focus of educational, health care, and legal professionals, which has made internal communication within specific institutions more difficult, as professionals concentrated more and more on narrowly focused issues. In turn, this has resulted in a breakdown of traditional administrative or management paradigms and allowed a new type of management to gain control of these institutions.

Institutional management in the United States generally does not consider service recipients or the people for whose benefit the institutions are set up as stakeholders. In fact, their needs are not really considered, largely because it is assumed that they do not know them and need guidance to understand what is good for them. Similarly, workers, staff, and professionals of the institution are considered rented factors of production who must be managed to supply the services of the institution.

Although employees are encouraged to feel a part of the institutional team, job security and advancement are used as principal incentives to assure loyalty and job performance. Even though many institutions employ tenure and other systems that, in theory, provide job security, fear of unemployment, career stagnation, and public discredit are used as the major performance motivators. Incentives are usually individualized and do not become team incentives. The reason is that team incentives provide an additional protection layer to individuals who, as a result, would become less dependent on management and the establishment.

## American Equality

American institutions, originally designed to assure egalitarian treatment and opportunity for all, have become increasingly discriminatory. While we still officially maintain equal justice, access to health care, and education for all, the reality is quite different. Justice is primarily reserved for the rich and powerful on one hand and the ardent criminal who manipulates or uses the system to his advantage on the other. The average citizen gets little justice, either because he cannot afford its high cost or because his problems, however painful, are not considered socially important. Similarly, our legal system is more concerned with justice to the criminals than with the rights of their victims.

Similarly, health care is effectively provided to the poor, the aged, and the wealthy and well insured. By and large the independent worker and entrepreneur, the small businessman, the farmer, and similar people, who constitute about a third of the population, are disadvantaged by the three mainstays of American institutions—law, health care, and education. Many have no access or cannot afford their effective use. Most of these institutions are not designed to serve their needs. This notwithstanding the fact that it is this segment of society that makes the largest contribution to the American economy and job creation.

While America degenerates into a self-serving society, the historic foundation of our greatness, with its roots in the independent, entrepreneurial spirit, is rocked and may disintegrate entirely as individualism is discriminated against by being excluded from our mainstay institutions that thrive in an "orderly" environment.

## Institutional Establishments

All institutions attempt to present their professionalism and their concern for the public interest as their primary concern but, sadly, often cloak deficiencies on both counts. Institutional management invariably tries to present an image of virtue and total commitment to the purpose of the institution, while controlling internal activities and external relations through the use of establishment incentives and ties. Only those people who have proven loyalty to the establishment, to the institution, and to its general purpose are chosen for positions of internal control and external representation, no matter how competent or qualified a candidate may be. This practice is designed to ensure that the institutional or establishment interest and image are maintained and advanced and has the added benefit that people in these positions become beholden to the establishment, knowing full well that their position and advancement is a reward not for competence but for loyalty to the establishment. This situation, probably more than any other, is responsible for the decline in the service, quality, and performance standards of our health, educational, and legal or law enforcement institutions.

## Institutions in the Not-So-Public Interest

Our institutions are believed to be the backbone of American democracy. They are designed to provide health care, education, and justice to every citizen, independent of wealth, origin, race, color, or religion. These basic rights provide the foundation of our form of government. We try to believe that our system is the best and most egalitarian, but in truth, we have begun to doubt it, not because of its basic principles and not because our rights cannot be implemented in our richly endowed nation. The reason we have begun to doubt is that we, our institutions, the guardians of our most fundamental rights, suffer from dysfunction, an inverted value system, and the fact that many no longer really work in the public interest but favor narrow interests or special interest groups.

We go through the process of open elections for local, state, and federal political office and institutions. We conduct shareholder elections, though somewhat distorted, to select corporate directors who, in turn, are entrusted with nominating management; however, the system is actually distorted, and the electoral process becomes more a facade than a free and open selection process.

When it comes to institutions, we essentially remove even the trappings of a democratic elective process on the assumption that the public and even the users, staff, and beneficiaries of the institutions are incompetent or otherwise unqualified to decide by whom and how these institutions are to be governed and operate. As a result, institutions and their management have now become largely unaccountable and self-serving organizations that are often captive to some narrow interest group.

## The Functions of Our Institutions

A new development in American universities is that frequently the university administrations do not consider support of the faculty, and thereby education, as their principal function. In fact, education is treated largely as a loss leader, as is preventative medicine in health care institutions and crime prevention in our criminal justice system. The last is actually a revealing concept as it clearly identifies the focus of our legal or law enforcement institutions.

Universities are largely concerned with perpetuating themselves. Tuition normally covers only a small proportion of the budget, and therefore major emphasis is placed on other activities more in line with the institution's goal of effective self-perpetuation by selling itself to supporters and by selling its research ability and the status or prestige it may transfer or convey to its supporters.

Hospitals similarly often discourage preventive and cost-effective medical treatments, as these could reduce the potential revenues from other treatment and services. Similarly, police departments in general spend less on crime prevention than on crime solving and various political services rendered to influential decision makers.

## Institutional Efficiency and Performance

Productivity in manufacturing, agriculture, and mining has increased radically during the last fifty years, particularly in terms of output per unit of labor. On the aggregate, we now produce about 8.2 times as much output per capita in constant value terms than we did fifty years ago. In other words, we require only 12.2 percent of the man-hours to produce an automobile or appliance today that were required just after World War II.

On the other hand, improvements in productivity in the services—a sector dominated by institutional services such as education, health care, and law enforcement—are much more difficult to achieve. Teacher–student, nurse–patient and policeman–citizen ratios have not changed and, in fact, have often moved in the opposite direction as changing conditions or pressures encouraged lower instead of higher ratios.

The same is also true in services such as hotels, restaurants, and transport, even though these are often purely commercial. As a result, the relative cost of services has risen faster than the cost-of-living index, and institutional or service efficiency has declined in both relative and absolute terms over this period, so that institutional and service costs now far outweigh the cost of all productive activities, in America as well as in some other industrialized countries. In fact, we are getting close to becoming an all-service economy, with health care, educational, and law enforcement services consuming the bulk of resources.

Productivity has become a national goal. For years, naysayers have claimed that increasing productivity will result in declining quality. Yet they have been proven wrong. In fact, productivity and quality feed on each other as evidenced first by the Japanese and now by forward-looking American manufacturers. Today the most productive companies are also those that produce the highest-quality products or services.

Yet American institutions such as health care, education, and criminal justice claim that they cannot possibly improve their productivity because it would invariably lead to an unacceptable decline in quality, something neither the U.S. public nor the institutions could accept. It is interesting to investigate these claims not only because they are similar to those made by U.S. manufacturers one or two decades ago, but because these arguments hide a much wider interest in the status quo. In manufacturing, the reasons for the claim were often ineffective organization and fear of job loss; while in institutions, the reasons include fear of the loss of power, influence, and economic or financial gain.

While industrial and commercial entities must perform or die, institutions, be they in education, law, or health care, usually neither are performance-oriented nor have or use performance standards. In fact, it is difficult, and quite often impossible, to measure their performance.

Educational institutions often claim performance ratings based on the success of their graduates, but they seldom relate these estimates to the investment made in education. Does a university's business school, whose graduates start at an average annual salary of, say, $60,000 with an MBA that required an investment of $70,000 over a two-year period, perform better than a school whose graduates attain a starting salary of $50,000/year for an investment of only $30,000 and that for a single year? Standards for measuring success have become even more unclear in health care and law enforcement or legal services.

## Institutional Goals and Objectives

Educational, legal, and health care institutions all claim the public interest as their principal goal. Educational institutions maintain as their objectives the education of their students in liberal arts, science, and skills that will equip them to be effective and well-adjusted citizens, capable of contributing to society and making their lives successful.

As part of this process, our colleges and universities encourage research by faculty and graduate students aimed at contributing new knowledge to the ongoing effort of solving the problems facing mankind.

American educational institutions are failing on both counts: the education of skilled and effective citizens and the advancement of knowledge toward the solution of relevant problems facing society. Many schools have relaxed their standards and are becoming more concerned with satisfying students' (and sometimes parents') as well as politicians' egos than making the hard and unpopular decisions necessary to implement quality education. Students are commonly advanced in primary and high schools independent of their performance, as repeating a grade would cause a student (and parent or parents) mental anguish and is costly to the community. As a result, schools, instead of requiring failing students to repeat a grade, make all students suffer by advancing ill-prepared, failing students with the rest of the class. The process results in lowering the average standards and also greatly discourages the serious student, whose work is being downgraded by being lumped together with that of the inferior students who advance independent of performance. Universities also often allow grade distortions by such methods as outlawing failing grades.

Similarly, research performed in universities tends to be narrowly focused and self-serving, to reflect the particular interest of either the sponsor or the faculty member, yet rarely those of the public or for the solution of relevant problems faced by society, which is the original goal of research efforts.

Institutional management in the United States does not consider service recipients or the people for whose benefit the institutions exist, in general, as stakeholders. In fact, the needs of these people are not really considered, largely because it is patronizingly assumed that people need guidance to understand what is best for them. Similarly, workers, staff, and professionals are considered by many to be rented factors of production, to be managed to supply the services of the institution.

In theory, institutions of health care, education, law enforcement, and social welfare should follow the simple goal of satisfying the needs of the people they are designed to serve. Health care institutions should—to the best of their ability— care for the sick and prevent illness. Educational institutions should provide the best education to the widest range of students they can serve with the means at their disposal. Law enforcement should provide safety and justice for all, by protecting the innocents and punishing the guilty. Social welfare should provide for those who cannot provide for themselves. There is little disagreement that such goals should be the objectives of these institutions, yet the reality is often quite different. Most public institutions, including those privately owned, nonprofit or profit-making institutions in health care, education, law enforcement, or social welfare, have moved away from these goals and now ironically work largely toward objectives that are not oriented to the customers or to these idealistic goals but toward the narrow interests of institutional management.

## The Impact of Lack of Societal Structure on American Institutional Costs and Effectiveness

In most other societies, many of the functions and costs assumed by the American educational, health care, and legal or law enforcement systems are performed or assumed by societal units such as extended family structures. In America the family, as a coherent structure comprised of vertical and horizontal layers, has largely been transformed into a temporary generation-breeding unit that forgoes any continued relationships and, even more important, forgoes responsibility beyond breeding and basic upbringing of the next generation. Once assumed to be self-supporting or to have reached an age where they are judged to be adults, the next generation is now left to their own devices and often return the favor by assuming little if any responsibility for their aging parents.

Ivy League colleges, which pride themselves on their quality education, unbiased fair admission and uncompromising grading or maintenance of standards, are themselves guilty of contravening them. Not only do they habitually admit minority students with SAT scores averaging 150 points below the admission standard required of white students, but they are also more flexible in the admission of children of alumni, particularly of long-lineage alumni who habitually contribute to and support the university financially.

## Institutional Financial Management

Practically all our educational, social, health care, and law enforcement institutions are in financial trouble, notwithstanding the fact that for many years they have annually raised their fees, budgets, and other charges well in excess of the rate of inflation. Their overhead continues to grow well ahead of the rate of inflation, and services or service qualities often decline, directly or indirectly.

These institutions are increasingly pricing themselves out of the market, with the result that they depend more and more on public support, and an increasing number of the people they serve must rely on public financing for the services they require.

The percentage of publicly supported students in institutions of higher learning, patients in hospitals, legal clients, and people requiring social services has increased steadily over the last twenty-five years and is now at a historic high.

The problem is not basic operating costs, such as salaries, which in most cases are well in line with the rate of inflation or general rate increases. The problem is the increasingly high overhead costs, which include administrative costs, fixed cost for capital equipment, malpractice and other insurance, management, public relations, and more.

Institutional management—from health care to education and law enforcement—has become a specialty, a new profession. Entire departments at universities are now training hospital managers, and hospital and health care administration has become a specialized career with a significant reward structure and self-serving objective.

The hospital or health care administrator now controls the hospital even if he or she has no medical training or experience. Similarly, school and university administrators are now being chosen from the ranks of those with pure administrative or management training and with little or no experience in education, research, or medicine.

It is interesting to note that many American institutions, such as primary and secondary schools, state colleges, public hospitals, law enforcement, firefighting, and so on, are financed locally. Their budget, and in many cases quality of service, is therefore a function of the affluence of the local community, county, or state, its fiscal condition and priorities, and local political interests. As a result, the quality and standards of these essential services vary across the land.

The amount of money spent per student differs widely, as does the curriculum. Access to health care facilities and services similarly differ radically throughout the land. Law enforcement and other public safety services, such as firefighting, receive different levels of support and in some places depend completely on volunteers to supply at least a basic semblance of police or fire protection.

In other countries, these essential services are usually based on national standards and are provided through agencies of the central government or at least under central guidance and control. As a result, a more equitable level of education, health services, and law enforcement is provided. In the United States, however, educational standards vary widely, as do the provision of health care and law enforcement, with poorer communities, counties, and states often receiving low-quality services.

## Priming the Legislative Pump

The most politically active sectors of the U.S. are the health, education, and law/legal institutions. Not only do these factions support the largest and most aggressive lobbying organizations in the United States, but they are also among the largest contributors to politicians. Political Action Committees (PACs) provided over $205 million in special interest contributions in 1991/92 (the amounts for the 1995/96 elections were not available at the date of publications) to individual legislators and political parties, 94 percent of this going to congressional candidates. Six of the seven top PACs supported law, health, and educational institution policies, as shown in "Top PAC Contributors." Collectively, PAC contributions aimed at affecting these institutions accounted for over 34 percent of all PAC money. Much of the rest was aimed at influencing special legislative or economic interests, such as subsidies or special interest legislation (for example, abortion).

**Top PAC Contributors***

| | | |
|---|---|---|
| 1. | Teamsters | $11,825,340 |
| 2. | American Medical Association | 6,263,921 |
| 3. | National Education Association | 5,817,975 |
| 4. | National Rifle Association | 5,700,114 |
| 5. | National Association of Realtors | 4,939,014 |
| 6. | Association of Trial Lawyers of America | 4,392,462 |
| 7. | American Federation of State, County and Municipal Employees | 4,281,395 |

*Source: Federal Election Commission (1991/92).

Therefore, politicians are under tremendous pressure to maintain the status quo of the educational, health, and criminal justice or legal institutions, as well as all the government agencies charged with regulating or administrating them. As recent attempts at changing gun control and health care laws have demonstrated, the U.S. legislature is less influenced by public concern than by the interests of institutional supporters and lobbyists. It is not by chance that the law to ban the sale and the import of nineteen assault-type weapons, supported overwhelmingly by the public, barely squeezed through Congress. The same fate awaits legislation on health care and other bills that address the vital interest of segments of the aforementioned institutions.

## Institutional Interdependence

The health, education, and legal or justice systems are highly interdependent, and all, in turn, affect the social support or welfare systems. Lack of drug control, the failure of effective primary education, and our ineffective social systems affect the costs of our health and legal systems. When one fails to provide quality service, the others suffer, because all services provided by these major institutions are highly interdependent.

Little research has been done to study the effects of these interdependencies. This is probably due in part to the fact that most service providers are highly dispersed. In areas, such as health care, the situation is gradually changing as major health maintenance organizations (HMOs) are formed by combining (or absorbing) a large number of smaller health care providers. While interdependent in terms of the effects of their services, few institutions cooperate effectively in providing the services.

## America's Institutional Dilemma

American institutions have grown to a level where they now dominate the American economy (figure 3). They have become the major function of government, and the largest proportion of federal, state, and local government funds are now spent for health care, law enforcement, education, and related and unrelated entitlements.

It is worth noting that institutional functions and responsibilities are shared between government and private industry to a much greater extent in the United States than in most other countries. In health care the bulk of providers are private or so-called nonprofit institutions. To a lesser extent the same is true in college education. The legal system, in turn, is made up of government law enforcement and private legal defense. Incarceration, once solely a government service, is now being privatized, with many prisons operated by private service organizations. Similarly, entitlement programs are partly run by private organizations on behalf of government agencies.

This interlocking of government and private industry in the provision and administration of institutional programs has many implications. In some areas, such as health care and the legal system, the involvement of private practitioners is well established in other countries, but nowhere is it as extensive as in the United States. In few other countries are as large a percentage of health care, educational, and legal or law enforcement services supplied by private interests or as many entitlements, particularly social services, supplied by private firms. The reasons advanced for this difference are that private interests can usually supply these services more efficiently. However, many claim that while this may be correct in theory, it is not necessarily true when the costs of the different levels of government oversight and planning are included in the calculations.

Another issue affecting institutional management is the effectiveness of the structure of institutional service systems when they interlock with government and private enterprise. In many areas the hierarchical management and decision-making structure has become very complex to ensure checks and balances at each level. In turn, these measures are based on the premise that neither recipients nor private providers of institutional services can be trusted and, therefore, effective control must be in place at all levels of the system.

As a result, much of the government bureaucracy, particularly that re-

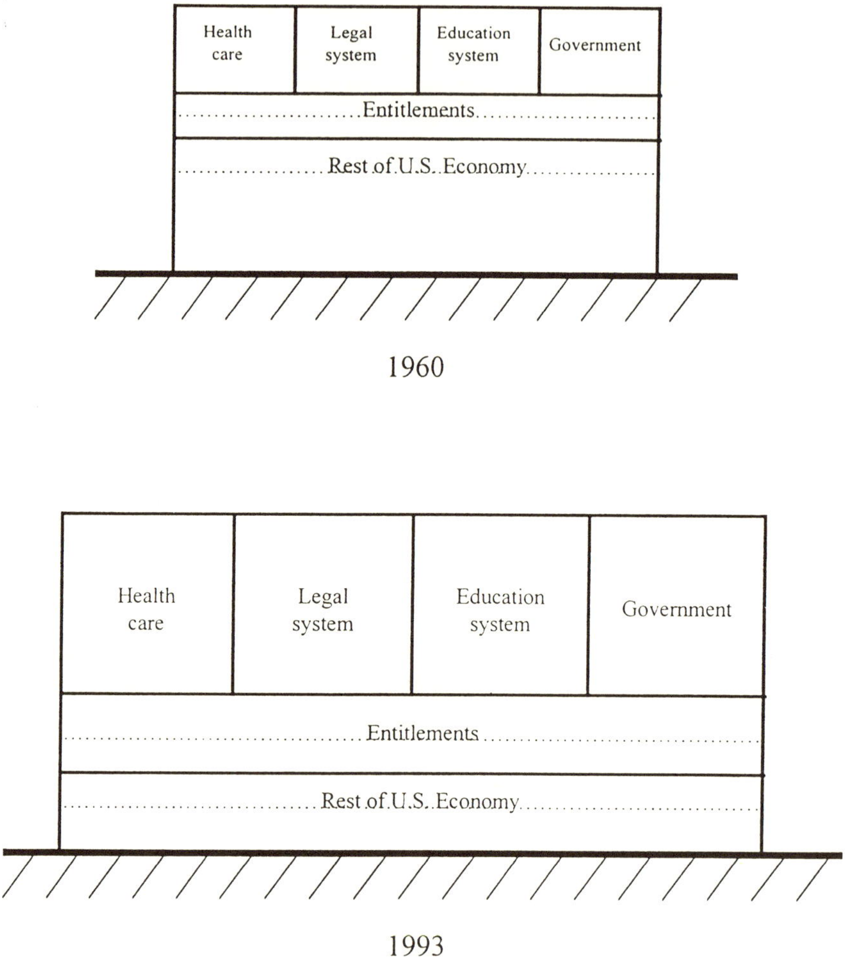

Health care | Legal system | Education system | Government

Entitlements

Rest of U.S. Economy

1960

Health care | Legal system | Education system | Government

Entitlements

Rest of U.S. Economy

1993

FIGURE 3 The Growth of American Institutions

Source: Authors schematic of relative growth of institutional and government expenditures.

sponsible for education, health, legal, social, and related entitlement services, is in place not to provide but to control services and ensure that they are not misused. The paperwork associated with most government-supported institutional services is legendary—now so large that the indirect costs of providing these services often exceed the cost of the services themselves.

This means that costs of these services could be cut by half if only the direct costs had to be paid. The indirect costs are highest in health care, followed by legal, social, and educational services. In addition to the extra costs, the quality and particularly timeliness of these services are undoubtedly adversely affected, as organizations subjected to severe scrutiny are forced to defer their quality of service to the satisfaction of bureaucratic requirements. In other words, institutions, very much like individuals, live up to the expectations of the people or organizations controlling them.

Individuals usually respond positively when given greater responsibility and decision-making powers, as will most organizations or institutions. Yet the system of bureaucratic checks has become so ingrained that most institutions have developed formal procedures to circumvent their effects by assigning charges to unrelated items not subject to strict standards and controls. The situation now requires radical changes to restore not only economic and operational efficiency but also public confidence in our institutions.

The respective roles of government and private enterprise (including so-called nonprofit organizations) in providing institutional services must be formally reestablished. Their roles and responsibilities are currently undefined. It is of the utmost importance that principles of total quality management are introduced into all services. Effective quality service guidelines and standards exist but are commonly neither applied nor enforced in health, legal, educational, or social service organizations. Similarly, methods of monitoring compliance with procedures and standards must not be allowed to continue as solely bureaucratic exercises but must be replaced by real time or periodic checks using advanced monitoring information systems technology.

The dilemma appears when the objectives of service providers differ between government and private organizations as well as among private organizations. Furthermore, objectives are seldom defined in terms of service quality, but more commonly in economic, social or financial terms. While competition among providers, even government and private service providers, may be a good thing, it can be fair only if effective and uniform service quality standards are enforced. Such standards are urgently needed in health care, primary, high school, and university education, law enforcement or legal services, and social support. The large discrepancies now prevailing nationwide are a major contributor to the failure of our institutional (service) system.

There are essentially no educational standards, and high school certificates or university degrees by themselves mean very little. We have functionally illiterate high school graduates and holders of university degrees that qualify them for nothing, not even the qualification of simply being educated. We have huge differences in the methods of law enforcement and criminal judgments.

Differences in the approach to and quality of health care similarly vary widely and make it hazardous to live in certain parts of the country. In addition, the availability of educational, health, and law enforcement services differs to an abnormal degree, with some regions with essentially no access to medical and higher educational services while other regions offer an overabundance of such services.

Institutional services are supposed to be offered on the basis of need but are more often provided on the basis of institutional or professional advantage. Rural medical and educational services are often of low quality and difficult to access because proper services are too expensive or unprofitable. Home visits by doctors have largely been eliminated and severely ill patients must now call an ambulance and use emergency outpatient facilities at hospitals because doctors are unwilling to spend the travel time to call on patients even though ambulance services cost many times as much as the time of the doctor. Doctors are generally unwilling to provide this service because it reduces their opportunity to see more patients.

A major reason for this situation is the way health care, educational, and law enforcement services are financed and administered. Although federal and state governments pick up an increasing percentage of the tab for these services, control remains largely at the local level, with few standards or guidelines provided and fewer enforced by government. Basically, these institutions that have formed the backbone of America and an integral part of its lifestyle are now largely out of control and without focus.

There are many reasons for these developments. Much of it has to do with changes in our society and its priorities. Traits like self-sufficiency and entrepreneuralism, which served the country well for hundreds of years, are now being distorted more toward selfishness and self-centered and narrow goals. These, in turn, have affected many of our institutions. While privatization of many institutional functions or organizations may be a laudable approach toward improved operational efficiency, and while even a profit orientation in many institutions may be justifiable or even attractive to improve their operations, they seem to be losing their focus, and most important, commitment to their basic functions—to provide the public with quality services at affordable costs.

# 3

# The American Health Care System

The United States has long proclaimed its leadership in medicine and health care, with some justification. Many of the most important medical advances of recent years were made in the United States. Most new procedures and diagnostic techniques were developed in America. In fact, much of the new medical and biomedical technology originated in the United States. Notwithstanding the high standards of U.S. medicine, the superior medical research and development, the modern medical technology employed, and the enormous funds expended for health care, quality and affordable medical services are still elusive for many Americans. In fact, recent studies by the U.S. Office of Technology Assessment[1] rank the United States below many developed countries in most health care indicators. For example:

- the death rate for males ages twenty-five through forty-four, 250/100,000 is ahead of all other developed countries, and
- the rate of heart disease deaths for males fifty-five to sixty-four, 630/100,000 is again well ahead of all other developed countries, except the United Kingdom, which is only slightly higher.

For the ten leading causes of death in the United States, America's rates were significantly higher in all but the heart disease death rate of the United Kingdom, as noted previously.

Overall, rates for the ten leading causes of death for U.S. males ages twenty-five through forty-four were twice as high, for example, as in Canada. This is a serious indictment of U.S. health care, whose effectiveness can be measured only by the results achieved.

We have long assumed that while our health care system may lack universality, it is superior in the provision of life-saving procedures, such as transplants and treatments for cancer and other pernicious diseases. A recent study performed for Congress challenges the traditional assumption of U.S. superiority in medicine. For example, the United States was found to rank only sixth in the rate of bone marrow transplants for leukemia, and one-third of these transplants were performed too late to succeed. Canada, which spends only half as much on health care per person as does the United States, actually achieves a generally superior record, with the exception of some specialized treatments.

U.S. health care costs, while high, are uneven. Only 1 percent of the population, for example, consumes over 30 percent of the health care costs, and 30 percent consume over 72% of the costs. This cross-subsidization is aggravated by the fact that the system is largely aimed at concentrated treatment of illness instead of emphasizing health maintenance. In fact, because the approach is generally not to keep people healthy but to care for the sick, health care providers benefit from sick people and extended treatment, not from preventative cure.

To a large extent, the reason for this is the fault of the way the U.S. health care system is set up. It is not a market that offers services for competitive price, but a rigid, closed market where the supplier assumes quasi-monopolistic powers by capturing clients unaware of the price to be charged—which is simply imposed after the fact. Insurance companies often contribute to this situation—though many pay negotiated rates for certain standard procedures. They seldom question the need for the procedures.

Confronted with malpractice claims, insurance carriers tend to pay or settle frivolous claims simply to avoid being drawn into long and costly court procedures. Similarly, lawyers do not operate in a market system. U.S. lawyers are among the greatest proponents of a free market—for everything except legal and health care services.

Further, government and legal defense requirements impose a need for vastly excessive medical record keeping, which today consumes over 8 percent of our health care costs, notwithstanding large-scale introduction of computers and other record-keeping technology.

Health insurers have traditionally paid doctors and hospitals on a fee-for-service basis, with patients free to choose not only doctors and hospitals but also the number and types of services, procedures, and tests. Most patients simply follow their doctor's recommendations or suggestions, ultimately providing incentives for health care providers to simply crank up their charges. We have achieved medical goals that our grandfathers never dreamed of, but too often any number of procedures, services, and tests are ordered, even when their use adds little, if anything, to the quality of health care. They are often not medically or financially justifiable and may, in fact, cause damage to the patient.

When asked if they would request certain complex, nonessential procedures that may add some but usually little information and that they themselves would have to pay for, nearly 90 percent patients indicated that they would not. Medicaid and Medicare impose predetermined prices for 7,000 items, but these controls affect only the price and not the number of procedures.

Some procedures—for example, a bone marrow transplant—cost in excess of $150,000, and many promise only an uncertain probability of success, as well as questionable quality of life—even if "successful."

Many of the expenses of complex procedures and tests are justified by the cost of advanced equipment. However, in most cases the equipment is highly underutilized and its cost, as well as the cost of training and maintaining specialized staff necessary to operate the equipment, is spread over a small number of patients. This wasteful condition exists largely because each hospital (and doctor) wants his or her own equipment, even if another hospital a short distance away already has such equipment with low utilization and, therefore, ready availability.

The Harvard Community Health Plan, a Massachusetts HMO, states in its annual report that as few as a third of all medical ministrations of drugs, surgery, and tests have been shown to help cure disease or preserve health. On the contrary, the ministration may in many cases actually make things worse and in some cases actually endanger a patient.

For years drug companies have routinely offered incentives to doctors as marketing tools. Free samples are only the visible tip of the iceberg. Weekends in luxury resorts, air travel credits, sales meetings at first-class hotels billed as "professional education," and office and medical supplies or equipment provided gratis are just a few of the approaches used to promote the use of expensive drugs.

Finally, under tremendous public pressure, the $900 billion health care industry and, with it the drug companies are at last yielding and trying to contain costs. Yet while the heat is on, for most health insurers, medical suppliers, drug companies, hospitals, and doctors it is business as usual as they ward off criticism by containing annual cost increases alone, thus protecting the long-term increases in fees and charges.

## U.S. Health Care Economics

The nation's health has been continually debated in the United States for over a century, and many approaches have been advocated to assure that U.S. citizens have access to adequate health care. Political debate and, more important, the underlying vested interests have thus far succeeded in preventing a national health care policy and system that could maintain a level of health care consistent with our presumed standard of living, as facilitated by a per capita income close to the top among nations and a health care industry with a research and technology base second to none.

For many years national health care has been labeled socialized medicine or, anti–private enterprise with threatened government control of the provision of health care, which would stymie initiative and prevent the efficiency of the free market from regulating health care access and costs. While these may appear to be valid arguments, experience has shown them to apply only in a truly free competitive environment in which doctors, hospitals, dentists, drug companies, and other sectors of the health care industry compete fairly, do not fix prices, have no conflict of interest (such as interlocking services), and are subject to quality control but not to legal harassment.

**Table 1**

**U.S. Health Care Costs (Billions of Dollars)**

| Sector | 1970 | 1980 | 1990 | 2000 |
|---|---|---|---|---|
| Hospital Care | - | 102.4 | 256.0 | 654.2 |
| Physicians | - | 41.9 | 125.7 | 360.5 |
| Dental Services | - | 8.7 | 31.6 | 75.4 |
| Home Health Care | - | 1.3 | 6.9 | 18.8 |
| Drugs and Medical Supplies | - | 21.6 | 54.6 | 91.0 |
| Vision Products | - | 4.6 | 12.1 | 28.4 |
| Nursing Home Care | - | 20.0 | 53.1 | 130.8 |
| Other Personal Health Care | - | 4.6 | 11.3 | 33.9 |
| Program Administration and Net Cost of Private Health Insurance | - | 12.2 | 38.7 | 85.3 |
| Government Public Health Activities | - | 7.2 | 19.3 | 34.8 |
| Research and Construction | - | 11.3 | 22.8 | 39.8 |
| Total | 108.2 | 250.1 | 666.2 | 1600.0 |

Source: U.S. Health Care Financing Administration

Unfortunately, this idealistic picture is not the case. Not only have health care costs risen more than other costs in terms of percentage of GNP or per capita GNP, but this increase bears no relationship to any real or claimed improvement in health care. As shown in table 1, health care costs

**Table 2**
**Sources of Health Care Costs**
**(Billions of Dollars)**

| | **1970** | | **1980** | | **1990** | | **2000** | |
|---|---|---|---|---|---|---|---|---|
| | $ | % | $ | % | $ | % | $ | % |
| Private Health Insurance | - | - | 73.4 | 29.0 | 216.8 | 33.0 | 507.6 | 31.0 |
| State/Local Governments | - | - | 59.5 | 24.0 | 136.1 | 20.0 | 302.8 | 19.0 |
| Medicare | - | - | 37.5 | 15.0 | 111.2 | 17.0 | 290.3 | 18.0 |
| Medicaid | - | - | 33.2 | 13.0 | 87.3 | 13.0 | 243.8 | 16.0 |
| Out-of-Pocket Payments | - | - | 26.1 | 10.0 | 75.2 | 11.0 | 238.6 | 15.0 |
| Other Private Spending | - | - | 12.1 | 5.0 | 30.6 | 5.0 | 61.6 | 4.0 |
| TOTAL | 108.2 | 100.0 | 250.1 | 100.0 | 666.2 | 100.0 | 1600.0 | 100.0 |

Source: U.S. Health Care Financing Administration

have increased over 150 percent every decade since 1970, an escalation that is expected to continue at least to the end of the century. Similarly, the sources of health care costs have changed in terms of their relative contributions, as shown in table 2.

Health care is the single most important runaway cost in the United States. AccordIng to the "Health Care Financing Administration," total health care costs grew from $250.1 billion in 1980, to $666.2 billion in 1990, and to $898 billion in 1993 and are projected to reach $1.0 trillion in 1995 and exceed $1.6 trillion by the year 2000 unless radical changes in the U.S. health care system are introduced (figure 4). More important, these costs, which constituted 9.2 percent of GNP in 1980, 12.2 percent in 1990, and 14.3 percent in 1993, are expected to grow to 16.4 percent in 2000 and reach 20 percent by 2020. As shown in table 2, an increasing amount of this is paid for by Medicaid and state and local governments. By the end of this century, Medicaid, the fastest-growing cost in U.S. health care, is expected to exceed state/local government costs. Similarly, figure 5 shows the distribution of health care costs and increased expenditures for nursing home care program administration and public health activities.

Considering next the escalation in the cost of drugs: the U.S. Bureau of Labor Statistics indicates that while the U.S. consumer price index increased by just over 50 percent between 1980 and 1990, the price of medical drugs increased by 122 percent and the price of pharmaceuticals increased by a whopping 172 percent over the same period. Overall, the costs of drugs increased at nearly three times the rate of increase of the consumer price index.

Considering next other health expenditures: costs for hospital care, physician services, drugs, and nursing home care dominate, and hospital and physician service costs are growing more rapidly than others, even nursing home costs (table 1).

According to the U.S. Congressional Budget Office, medical costs have increased from $542 billion in 1988, $608 billion in 1989, $652 billion in 1990, and $738 billion in 1991 to over $828 billion in 1992. In other words, U.S. medical costs are increasing at a compound rate of 11 to 12 percent per year, or over double the rate of inflation.

The nation's 615,000 physicians and 6.2 million health care workers, the largest per capita medical establishment in the world, account for over 60 percent of these costs, while health insurance and hospital administration, hospital supply, pharmaceuticals, diagnostic services, and makers of medical devices consume the rest.

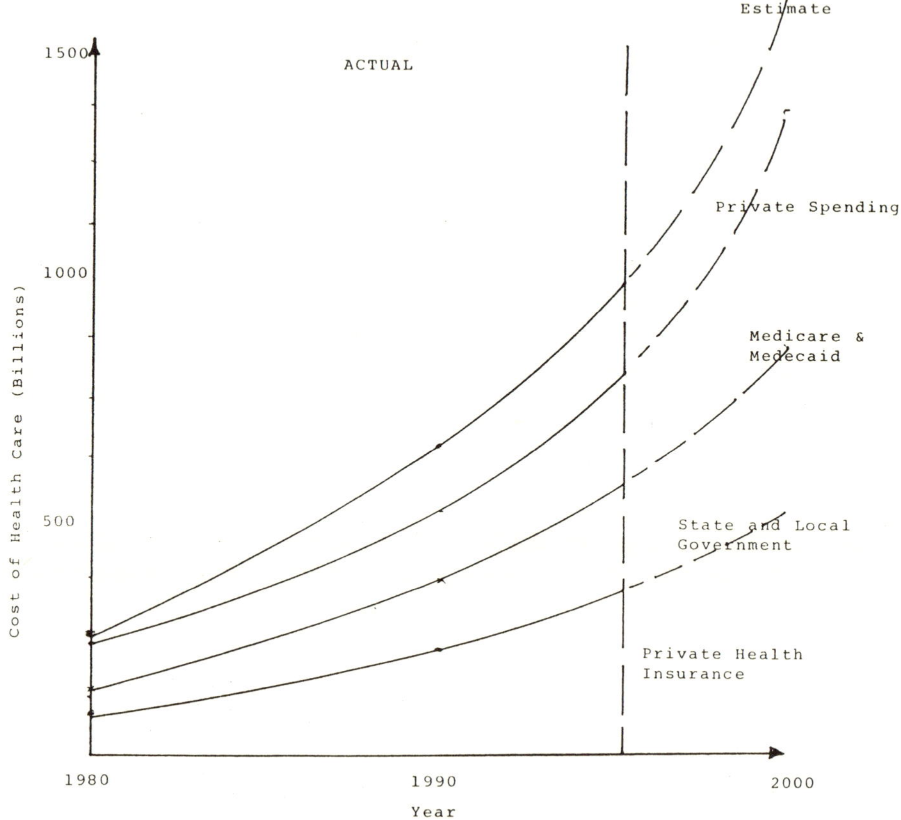


FIGURE 4

HEALTH CARE COST

Source: U.S. Health Care Financing Administration

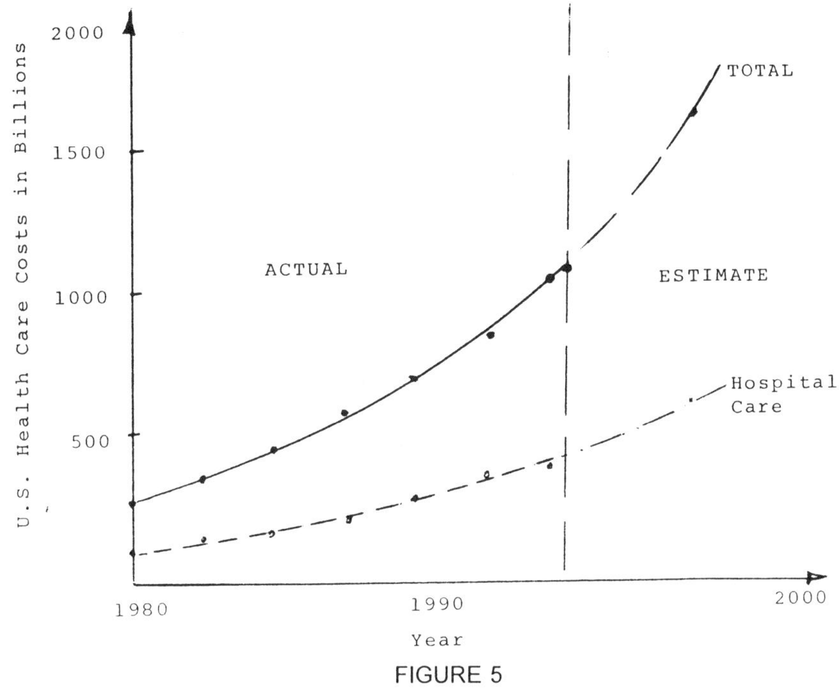


FIGURE 5

PROJECTION OF HEALTH CARE COSTS IN BILLIONS

Source: U.S. Health Care Financing Administration

The U.S. medical professionals have become medical businesspeople whose job is perceived to be not to keep people healthy but to help sick people get well.

No one expects doctors to work for little pay. Society wants doctors to be well rewarded. However, the system has become one that rewards doctors not for how well their patients are but specifically for the number of procedures, treatments, and tests their patients undergo. It is not surprising that even the conservative American Medical Association agrees that an enormous number of unnecessary and often life-threatening surgeries are performed every year.

Doctors like to conform and cooperate closely with other doctors, not because this practice is medically advisable or benefits the patient, but because it increases business cooperation and reduces risk to the doctor.

Lawyers have contributed greatly to this state of decreased quality of medical services at increased cost. Ambulance chasing and malpractice suits have become a major source of legal waste. Frivolous suits are entered into simply because lawyers expect health insurers to settle in order to avoid adverse publicity, however little merit there is in a suit. These lawsuits now account for nearly $100 billion in additional medical cost or waste and a nearly equal amount of ill-earned legal income.

The American Medical Association's 1990 figure for the average annual income of a qualified U.S. medical doctor was U.S. $164,820, or about three times that of a qualified professional engineer or certified accountant, 4.3 times the average income earned in the United States, and nearly 5.1 times the average earning of a registered nurse. In fact, medical doctors averaged only slightly less than lawyers, though it must be considered that a larger percentage of lawyers work for the government, thus reducing their average income.

Similarly, according to the U.S. Bureau of Labor Statistics (1992–93), the average annual income of an American physician was nearly three times that of engineers, accountants, architects, university professors, and senior government officials and about 10 percent above the average income of lawyers. It is not coincidence that both U.S. lawyers and doctors each number about 660,000. They outnumber engineers by a factor of two, and each group has a combined direct income in excess of $100 billion. It is expected that doctors' incomes will increase by another $40 billion before the year 2000 (as shown in table 3).

**Table 3**

**Statistics of U.S. Doctors**

| **Year** | **Number of Participating Doctors*** | |
|---|---|---|
| 1989 | 406,000 | Average Cost $240,000/MD |
| 2000 | 477,000 | Average Cost $406,000/MD |
| MD/Capita 1986 | | 144/100,000 |
| MD/Capita 2000 | | 176/100,000 |

*Total number of doctors in United States, (1992–93) is 660,000 according to U.S. Department of Labor statistics. This includes medical researchers, etc. Direct doctors' income cost escalation alone will add $40 billion to U.S. health care costs between 1989 and 2000.

The question of whether it is exorbitant or justifiable is subject to discussion. Doctors argue that this income (after direct expenses) is justified by (1) the long training period and its high cost, (2) the risk and cost of malpractice claims or similar charges (malpractice insurance itself is a direct cost), (3) the continued need for and cost of retraining, and (4) health risks. While the average income may seem justified, it often masks significant additional income from indirect sources related to the practice of medicine, such as (1) laboratory income, (2) prescription income, or (3) referral income. Adding these, it is readily shown that U.S. doctors' income is often well over $200,000/year.

If our health care costs are allowed to continue to escalate, they will not only consume a fifth of our GNP and employ 6 percent of the U.S. working population but will exclude an ever-increasing population of Americans from adequate health care, as only the rich and those employed by government and major corporations will be able to afford or qualify for health care. The resulting social costs in terms of lost production, declining technology growth, and societal/environmental impact can be expected to add substantially to the estimates of the costs of health care, thus worsening the situation even further.

The number of U.S. licensed doctors more than doubled between 1970 and 1987 from 350,000 to over 600,000 and is expected to reach 720,000 by 2000. This means approximately one doctor for each 312 people, about four times the number of doctors per capita in Western Europe, five times more than in Japan, and as much as twenty times those available per capita worldwide. Doctors' income has increased at a rate of over 10.7 percent per year and at over 6.9 percent per year if malpractice insurance costs are deducted. For example, one-fifth of U.S. heart surgeons made over $600,000/year in 1987.

There are many reasons for the exploding costs of U.S. health care. Among them are:

1. collusion between health insurance providers and doctors,
2. collusion between drug suppliers and doctors as well as hospitals, and
3. billing procedures by U.S. health care providers.

For example, a hospitalized Boca Raton (Florida) woman was recently charged $142.82 for four tablets of nicotine gum $17.59 for one disposable razor, and $17.33 for a breakfast that she found inedible. These are quite common charges.

According to Aetna Insurance, of over $735 billion paid by Americans for health care in 1991, about $145 billion was spent for unneeded testing and treatment.

Managed health care, which includes well-conceived preventative health care, medical services based on need and not greed, elimination of the legal costs of malpractice, and smarter choice of medical services, could reduce health care costs dramatically and reduce their growth rate as well. HMO membership has almost doubled, from 25.7 million in 1986 to over 45.2 million in 1993. This large-scale grouping permits HMOs to achieve huge economies of scale and leverage for cost control. It is interesting to note that HMOs are able to provide expanded medical services for seniors on Medicare without any added premiums. In fact, they often pay many services not usually covered by Medicare.

## U.S. Health Care—What It Buys

Annual health care costs peaked at $3,160 per head in the United States 1992, or a record 13.86 percent of GNP, nearly twice that spent by any other industrialized country as noted before.

A U.S. household spent on average $8,000 directly or indirectly on health care, a ridiculous sum compared to other living expenses. In other words, the average U.S. household spent nearly as much for health care as for shelter and nearly 30 percent more on health care than on education or food.

What does all this expenditure buy? In many areas of health care, we rank well below those of other countries. Using indicators such as infant mortality and life expectancy, the U.S. health care system ranks well below countries such as Japan, Canada, Israel, and most European countries.

The U.S. health care system has become high-tech and elitist in one sense, while compassionate toward the poor in another. It is easy to have complex, high-tech diagnosis prescribed, if necessary or not, but in most parts of the country it is virtually impossible to arrange for a house call by a doctor, even if the patient cannot or should not be moved. Instead of a thirty-, fifty-, or even eighty-dollar house visit by a physician, that patient will be brought by ambulance to the hospital, be hospitalized for a day or more, and then be returned, at a cost of thousands, all for the convenience of the doctor. Our practicing physicians would rather have large sums of public or private money spent unnecessarily than inconvenience themselves and spend half an hour traveling to a patient for a half-hour house visit for which, in good conscience, the doctor can only charge thirty to eighty dollars. In his practice, he expects to be able to see three to six patients (or more) during that hour and therefore house calls are simply not cost-effective. The patient's and public interests are seldom, if ever, considered.

There are few urban areas in the United States where home visits by doctors are available or offered. Doctors still provide such care in some rural areas, but with fewer than 6 percent of U.S. doctors serving rural populations the practice is rare indeed. The United States is one of a very few countries in which home visits by doctors and home care for all but the elderly have been eliminated. As a result, the injured or sick must make their own way or use an ambulance to get to a medical care facility, however far. This can cause critical delay and additional exposure, as well as adding exponentially to the cost of health care.

My wife recently suffered severe back pain and very high temperature, only to be told by our health care provider to visit their emergency room about forty minutes away. There, after a wait of another twenty minutes, she was seen by a nurse, then briefly by an intern who diagnosed her condition as an inflammation of the kidney, prescribed some antibiotics, and sent her home, with no clinical evidence to verify the diagnosis. The long car ride increased her pain. Her condition became worse, and she then visited a nearby gynecologist who determined that her pain had nothing to do with kidney inflammation and required a different type of treatment.

In many cases the lack of home visits, particularly for the elderly and infirm, has not only become a tremendous cost to patients and to their health care providers but in many cases also increases the medical risks as a result of the delay in diagnosis, delay in treatment, and lack of top-quality physicians in emergency rooms, as well as the added strain and exposure of the trip to a hospital emergency room or a doctor's office.

Medicine in the United States has become a business in which time is money, and time that cannot be billed properly, such as travel time to and from a patient, is simply considered waste that must be eliminated. Doctors have followed lawyers, who for years have maximized their billing hours and/or percentage of billable time. American doctors have adopted this approach, but at a cost to effective health care, particularly of the elderly, and obviously at a tremendous additional cost to the health care system. Another price paid for the time-is-money approach is personal care. Medical treatment has now become impersonal, with major reliance on computer records and little on interpersonal contact or communication between doctor and patient.

The approach also adds significantly to the nation's health care bill in many ways. For example, patients, particularly those covered by Medicare or other government-sponsored health programs, will take an ambulance to a hospital and stay there for some days to be checked out even for minor medical problems. A doctor's home visit or the ready availability of a general practitioner or family doctor assigned to each patient could resolve many unnecessary hospitalizations at a fraction of the average cost of $620 for an ambulance delivery and hospital admission. Many HMOs now assign a primary physician or family doctor to each of their members, recognizing that preventative diagnosis can improve service and reduce costs.

## Corrective versus Preventative Health Care

One major problem facing U.S. health care is our lack of general practitioners and primary health providers. The percentage of doctors practicing primary care medicine has declined from over fifty percent in 1960 to now under 30 percent. The age of doctors in general practice is rising, as the percentage of new doctors entering primary care practice is now less than 20 percent, with the majority choosing a specialized medical field, largely because it is more lucrative.

Doctors have become remote and are no longer family health caretakers but providers of specialized services, rendered reactively instead of preventatively. Few doctors know their patients or have a personal relation with them, which is so important for effective treatment. In other words, medicine has become an impersonal service rendered mainly to correct some malfunction.

Eleven million patients are wheeled into operating rooms in the United States annually, about twice as many on a percentage basis as those subjected to surgery in any other country. While mortality rates in surgery have improved significantly, survival is often achieved only by use of exotic auxiliary means that may prolong life marginally but often do not provide the quality of life to make it worthwhile.

Among the American nations, only Haiti and Bolivia have a worse record than the United States in child vaccination. Similarly, considering infant mortality at birth, the United States ranks seventieth among nations, just behind Mongolia. This is blamed largely on

1. the structure of the U.S. health care system,
2. the low percentage of U.S. doctors who practice primary care, and
3. rigid licensing requirements that prevent nurses and qualified technicians from performing basic medical or even preventative treatment.

It is interesting to note that a major New York health care facility will now allow registered nurses to act as primary health care providers on an experimental basis. Another obvious issue facing the health care industry is the overriding interest of U.S. doctors in the use of highly paid specialists and special treatments. Not only do doctors no longer provide home visits; they do not even allow adequate time for in-depth patient diagnosis and care. An average doctor sees three to four patients per hour during office hours and twice or three times as many on hospital visits. Fifteen minutes does not allow adequate time for personal care.

## Defensive Medical Practice

Medical malpractice insurance premiums in the United States account for about 8 percent of personal health costs. Therefore, this is not the crucial cost of the litigative environment in which U.S. health care is provided. It is the fear of litigation, with the associated loss of time, reputation, and money, that has forced the introduction of defensive medicine, with its tremendous waste of doctors' and patients' time. Doctors practice defensively, often ordering many more tests and clinical procedures than they would if they did not fear litigation. In turn, many of these tests are performed in doctor-owned laboratories that provide substantial added income to doctors while driving up insurance premiums.

The practice of defensive medicine then becomes a self-serving and self-perpetuating system. Doctors act defensively to protect themselves from litigation threatened by legal practitioners, using their own laboratories and diagnostic facilities to build defensive walls around their practices. The practice of defensive medicine not only adds significantly to U.S. health care costs but also contributes to the ineffectiveness of medical care. Delays and indecisive medical actions are important factors causing unnecessary suffering. The defensive approach to U.S. medical practice is estimated to account for as much as one-fourth of medical costs. These enormous losses in both material and human terms are entirely avoidable.

## The Business of American Medicine

Contrary to popular opinion, American doctors are by and large businesspeople who use the provision of health care as their business opportunity. In this respect they are no different from lawyers who similarly make the provision of legal support a business. Medicine in the United States degenerated from a profession with a mission to a business with financial goals. This does not mean that American doctors do not strive to practice good medicine or health care but that the overriding objective and driving force for many doctors is, in fact, financial success.

Granted, they face tremendous financial pressures, which usually start with large debts following graduation and licensing. Yet the increasing trend away from family practice into specialized and more lucrative medicine has become a dangerous trend. Not only has it depleted the ranks of general medicine to an extent that today we have less than a quarter of the general practitioners on a per capita basis than were available just twenty-five years ago, but major segments of the population no longer have access to a personal physician.

Peer pressure on doctors and increasingly narrow specialization result in over-investment in expensive equipment and techniques, and also increasingly in the prescription of unneeded procedures and services to utilize unnecessary equipment, laboratories, and services. While a fee-for-service approach may be fair and reasonable to providers and patients alike, standards must be employed to prevent misuse of such a system.

Recent studies indicate that as much as 30 percent of nonelective surgery is unnecessary. This includes hundreds of thousands of unnecessary cesarean sections (*Washington Post*) hysterectomies, bypass surgeries, and numerous other procedures that either are not needed or do not serve the patient's welfare.

In 1993 over 760,000 major heart operations were performed in the United States at a cost of over $50 billion, or about 6 percent of the total cost of health care (about $66,000 per procedure). Among these were 400,000 bypasses, 300,000 angioplasties, 58,000 repairs to damaged heart valves, and 2,000 transplant operations. This is 3.8 times the number of such operations performed in 1980. While heart surgery has increased in part as a result of improvements in technology, procedures, and training of surgeons, there is increasing concern that many of these operations

- are unnecessary
- do not improve the patient's condition,
- add unnecessary risks to patients, and
- are readily replaceable by drugs or changes in lifestyle.

Efforts to control the excess of unnecessary procedures and treatments have been largely unsuccessful in the United States. Cesarean sections were used in 25 percent of U.S. births in 1990, up from 5 percent in 1968. Dr. J. M. Terris concluded in 1990 that eliminating unnecessary medical care and procedures could save one-quarter of health care costs ($125 billion in 1990) without affecting the quality of health care.[2]

Dr. Arnold Relman, former editor of the *New England Journal of Medicine,* maintains that commercialization has distorted the U.S. health care system to an extent that it is difficult for doctors to practice medicine with the patient's interests uppermost in mind.

## The Distribution of Doctors in America

There were 586,715 doctors licensed to practice in America, or a doctor for each 433 people, according to the 1990 U.S. Census. This is one of the highest number of doctors per capita in the world. On the other hand, the distribution of doctors by professional area and geography is quite uneven. As we have noted, the number of physicians in general practice is small and growing smaller. Similarly, black and Hispanic doctors make up less than 8.5 percent of the total or less than one-third of the percentage of blacks and Hispanics among the U.S. population, as shown.

Over 80 percent of all doctors practice in major urban areas that contain less than 40 percent of the total population. As we can see, access to doctors is distorted among medical specialties and areas of residence. Doctors are concentrated in mainly white areas of population, while in rural areas, in general practice, and in largely black and Hispanic neighborhoods there is gross underrepresentation of doctors.

| Category | Number of Physicians 1990 | % of all Physicians 1990 |
|---|---|---|
| White | 472,351 | 80.5% |
| Black | 20,874 | 3.6 |
| Hispanic | 28,781 | 4.9 |
| American Indian | 868 | 0.1 |
| Asian/Pacific | 63,552 | 10.8 |
| Other | 289 | 0 |

Source: U.S. Census

## Doctors' Income

As noted, the average income of U.S. doctors in 1992 was $166,000 to 179,000, depending on whose survey is used. While many among the public claim that this is excessive, doctors defend these incomes as justified by the high cost of medical training, the high cost of malpractice insurance, and the cost of maintaining medical skills.

The question is what would be a proper mean income for doctors if the costs of medical education and malpractice insurance are covered from other sources or somehow eliminated. The debt accumulated during medical training is obviously higher than that incurred by other professionals, such as lawyers or engineers, largely because the training of doctors takes longer and is usually more expensive. The difference in the cost of training and resulting debt is probably $60,000 to 90,000 (1995), which by itself would justify an additional income of $5,000 to 10,000 per year to pay off the difference in outstanding debt, as well as the loss of several years of income while serving as interns for a very nominal remuneration.

Similarly, while doctors today are affected more than other professionals by malpractice insurance, other professionals must also maintain such coverage. Therefore, only the added cost of such insurance should be considered in justifying additional income requirements by doctors.

In 1992, the average net pay of an HMO or hospital staff physician was $139,732, while a self-employed doctor's income averaged $179,000. Staff doctors are usually allowed to maintain private practice 33 percent of their time. Median salaries of staff physician specialists are as follows:

| | |
|---|---|
| Reproductive endocrinology | $259,750 |
| Cardiothoracic surgery | $259,700 |
| Radiology | $183,150 |
| Anesthesiology | $179,900 |
| Obstetrics/gynecology | $166,100 |
| Emergency Medicine | $121,000 |
| Psychiatry | $108,150 |
| Family Practice | $100,600 |
| Internal Medicine | $100,000 |
| Pediatrics | $ 98,037 |

Source: U.S. Department of Labor Statistics

Doctors' pay has risen at an annual rate 2.8 times that of inflation since 1985, just slightly ahead of the annual increase in U.S. health care costs overall. Although doctors' net pay constitutes only about 13.8 percent of the $819.9 billion in total U.S. health care costs (in 1992 figures), it is the single most important factor driving up overall health care costs. Furthermore, the additional nondirect income of U.S. doctors (after expenses) derived from ownership in health care facilities, services, or equipment is estimated to exceed $68 billion, which adds nearly 80 percent to their direct income and constitutes another 8.9 percent of health care costs. Total doctors' income then becomes 22.7 percent of total U.S. health care costs, after expenses.[3]

## The Role and Cost of Nurses

Nurses' pay in the United States has improved in recent years. A full-time registered nurse with about ten years' experience made $26,000 in 1987 and now makes $42,300. Nurses have become the mainstay of most hospitals and, in fact, of the health care system, particularly as many doctors do not work full-time at a hospital except during their intern and initial years. Therefore, nurses provide the necessary medical continuity and are, to a large extent, also responsible for quality control. In other words, nurses and medical technicians represent the productive or service side of the health care industry. Yet curiously, nationwide earnings of these direct health care service workers account for less than $55 billion, less than 7 percent of the health care expenditure of the nation.

Yet now, when the health care industry is under pressure to reduce costs, much like educational, financial, and legal or law enforcement institutions, it is the number of nurses and the cost of nursing that hospitals try to reduce—this at a time when health care administration, indirect support services, pharmaceuticals, and diagnostic or testing costs are rising at more than twice the rate of the cost of nursing. Much like we did ten years ago in manufacturing, the U.S. health care industry now tries to contain escalating costs by reducing the productive or service output. It will similarly fail and ultimately be forced to reduce its waste in paperwork administration, unnecessary diagnostic and lab services, underutilized medical technology, and unnecessary procedures, while increasing productive medical service.

## Drug Approval

The government, as the guardian of drugs and treatment whose use must be authorized by agencies of the U.S. government, has unwittingly become a collaborator not only in preventing proven drugs and remedies to be applied, but also in supporting delays in their use. Many drugs, hydrazine sulphate for example, have been found to be remedies for certain phases of cancer called cachexia. Yet more than twenty years after the discovery that it was able to arrest cancer and shrink tumors, the government, particularly the National Cancer Institute, is still trying to prevent its use, notwithstanding the fact that it has been approved in other countries after extensive testing. Were other competing drugs or treatments available, one could argue that concern with public safety or possible side effects has led the government to this position, but no other drugs or treatments exist, and thus far serious safety or side effects have not been identified, though the drug has been used over extended periods by hundreds or thousands of patients in many parts of the world.

There is the unavoidable suspicion that the government's concern is not with the safety or side effects of the drug but with the politics of cancer research and competing drug developments that would not be able to reap large profits, even if successful, if an inexpensive drug like hydrazine sulfate were on the market. In an earlier chapter we had a look at the strength of pharmaceutical lobbies.

The unnecessary health care costs that result from withholding approval of hydrazine sulfate and many other drugs and treatments are in the billions of dollars, as well as the resulting heavy tolls in human suffering and lives lost.

## Drug Costs in the United States

Drug costs in the United States are significantly higher than in other countries. This applies particularly to prescription drugs, which have outpaced other medical costs since 1980 (figure 6). Drug prices are often justified by the high cost of research and development, but recent studies show that

1. a major part of R&D costs are underwritten by government agencies, foundations, and others;
2. today's world market is so large that R & D can be easily underwritten with reasonable unit prices;
3. drug companies could reduce their prices significantly if they would reduce the enormous and often only self-serving advertising and marketing on which they spend nearly as much as on research; and
4. competing drugs are often developed not because they serve a medical purpose but to circumvent patent and licensing restrictions.

It is for these reasons that the prices of drugs are significantly out of proportion.

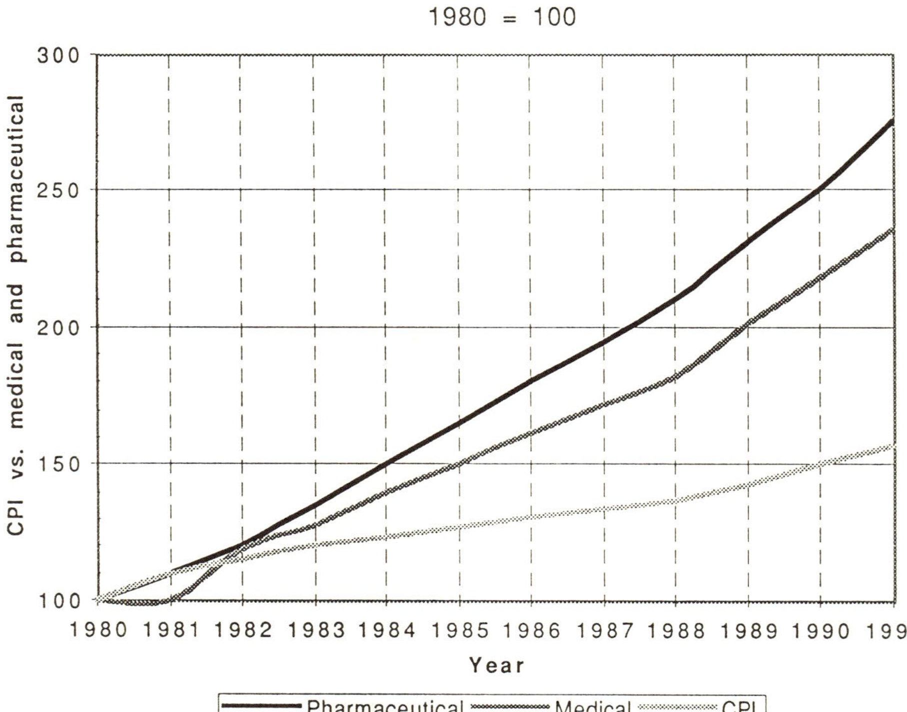


FIGURE 6 - Prescription Drug Prices Outpace Medical Prices

Source: Bureau of Labor Statistics

## U.S. Health Care Waste

According to Aetna Insurance, of the $735 billion that Americans paid for health care in 1990/91, almost 20 percent ($145 billion) was spent for unneeded tests and treatments. Others clams that an additional 20 percent ($160 billion) could be saved by improving hospital efficiency, through reducing the massive investment in highly underutilized, specialized diagnostic equipment, improving hospital management, simplifying hospital procurement and billing operations, and reducing paperwork in general, as well as eliminating the huge waste in material use.

U.S. health care overhead, defined as the nondirect health care costs, are estimated to be two-thirds (66 percent) of direct health care costs. As an example, medical paperwork costs are conservatively estimated at $66 billion per year, of which $14.8 billion is attributable to hospitals, $33.9 billion to medical insurance, and $18.2 billion to doctors. Similarly, the added cost of unnecessary prescription drugs, including the difference in cost between prescription and identical generic drugs, is estimated to be about $13.2 billion per year.

Next, the annual costs of unnecessary procedures, specifically tests performed by use of expensive equipment or laboratories, either as a pure defense against lawsuit or because of a conflict of interest, are estimated to exceed $48 billion.

Another problem is the excess personnel in U.S. hospitals. An average U.S. hospital employs nearly twice the number of indirect (nonmedical) personnel of similarly sized (bed) hospitals in other high-medical-service-quality countries, such as Switzerland, Japan, Germany, Israel, and Sweden. While part of the excess employment is the result of restrictive work rules, narrow job definitions, and inefficient hospital design, the largest contributing factor appears to be ineffective hospital management.

## Health Cost Sharing

The cost-sharing literature reports unequivocally that people will be more selective in their choice of health care services when they have to pay directly for such services, a basic tenet of human behavior. A recent Office of Technology Assessment (OTA) report brief summarized how patient cost sharing affects use and costs of health care services and ultimately health outcomes.[4] Patient cost-sharing plans can be designed as follows:

1. *Initial deductible:* the patient pays a fixed sum or percentage of the cost of every service or for the cumulative cost of services in any specified period, up to a predetermined amount.
2. *Co-insurance:* a percentage of covered expenses must be paid every time a health service is rendered.
3. *Copayments:* the patient pays up to a maximum dollar amount per period on covered deductible and co-insurance incurred by the plan.

It is clear that cost sharing reduces health care costs significantly. Even single-payer systems can eliminate abuse by requiring a minimal payment by the patient.

## Administrative Costs of U.S. Health Care

According to a recent survey, American doctors spend on average 33 percent of their time on record keeping and paperwork. This percentage is surpassed by the time nurses spend on paperwork and administrative functions, which are conservatively estimated to consume 50 percent of their time. In addition, hospitals and other health providers (HMOs, private clinics, and doctors' offices) employ approximately two office workers or administrative staff for each health care professional (doctors, nurses, medical technicians, etc.). In other words, the administrative costs of U.S. health care can be conservatively estimated at over $146 billion, or about 17 percent of total health care costs. Most of these costs are expended on dealing with complex record keeping and the filing of forms for hundreds of insurance companies and government agencies, all of which impose their own specific requirements. Because of the complexity and the lack of uniformity, even sophisticated computer network systems have not been able to reduce the bureaucratic burden of the U.S. health care system.

## Equipment and Technological Costs in U.S. Health Care

The proliferation of complex medical and diagnostic equipment in U.S. health care is out of control. For example, metropolitan Denver hospitals were recently found to have a total of nineteen MRI machines, a number greater than the total for Canada, a country with a population roughly twenty times larger and a service area that is 100,000 times greater.

Nationwide the problem of overinvestment in expensive medical equipment is equally grim. This situation is magnified because each such investment immediately triggers a need for building space and associated services and staff. Therefore, the costs are not just financial capital and amortization, but overhead costs that triple the cost of equipment. Gross underutilization of equipment space and staff, in turn, causes a drive toward both (1) use for unnecessary or marginally useful procedures or investigations and (2) overpricing for the use of the equipment and related staff.

Cursory investigation of MRI and similar equipment use indicates that the cost in American hospitals and institutions is four to eight times that in Canada and Europe.

Emphasis in medical research and development has in recent years been placed on high technology such as gene therapy, diagnostic imaging, laser surgery, and CAT scans. Not only has a disproportionate amount been spent on these technologies, but many hospitals invest inordinately large amounts to acquire these technologies without benefit of a proper or effective cost-benefit study or any type of economic evaluation.

On the other hand, less flashy, more fundamental, and in most cases much more urgently needed medical technology is ignored by investors and goes unfunded. Among these are diagnostic methods, medical decision support systems, and multimedia communications, all of which could assist in preventing health care problems, as well as improving the efficiency of the health care process.

It is obvious that the wasteful U.S. health care colossus needs a reorientation of priorities. Information technology and multimedia communication are probably among the most important developments that can be used to guide the U.S. health care system to becoming a lean, effective, and efficient provider of essential services with no loss of quality and an improvement in accessibility.

## Controlling Health Care Costs

It is obvious that health care costs must not only be contained but actually reduced if the United States is to achieve universal health care coverage while maintaining an adequate level and quality of affordable health care.

Some have suggested institutional controls, such as the use of managed competition. States would form insurance-purchasing cooperatives or similar institutions for the people of their state. Insurance companies would compete for customers in the pool, an approach thought to force insurers to keep their costs down and thereby indirectly lower health care costs. Others feel that additional cost controls may be required—for example, a limitation on the amount insurance companies can charge. Some also believe that cost controls should be imposed at the supplier level, by requiring hospitals, doctors, and laboratories to publish their rates and also by introducing a cap on rates of typical services and procedures.

Investment in medical equipment is often quoted as an issue in health care. It is generally assumed that Canada underinvests in sophisticated medical equipment, while there appears to be gross overinvestment in such equipment in the United States. Countries such as Germany, Switzerland, and Israel appear to have adequate, yet not excessive, medical equipment and equipment accessibility.

Doctor availability is another issue in health care costs and is closely related to patient demand for doctors. While the per capita number of doctors' visits per year in the United States is 5.3, in Canada it is 6.6 and in Israel 11.5. On the other hand, ready accessibility and covered costs of doctors' visits can result in demand for unnecessary care or treatment.

A recent survey of physicians found that U.S. doctors are highly dissatisfied with both the health care system and their work. They see fewer patients and spend less hours on administration than their Canadian and German counterparts, and fewer practice primary care (table 4).

The United States leads all developed countries except one in number of doctors per thousand population:

| | |
|---|---|
| Sub-Saharan Africa | 0.12 |
| Other Asia and islands | 0.13 |
| India | 0.4 |
| Middle East | 1.04 |
| Latin America/Caribbean | 1.25 |
| China | 1.37 |
| Developed countries | 2.52 |
| Formerly socialist Eastern Europe and USSR | 4.07 |
| United States | 3.98 |

Only formerly socialist Eastern European countries and the former USSR lead the United States by a small margin. However, this statistic may be misleading, as many "doctors" in these countries are equivalent to medical technicians by U.S. standards, with only four years of undergraduate medical training. In recent years health care institutional investors have had a major impact on slowing medical and health care inflation. By combining large numbers of hospitals into large hospital enterprises—such as Columbia/Hospital Corporation of American Health Care, an $11 billion a year provider of managed care controlling about two hundred hospitals nationwide—medical costs rose only 5.3 percent in 1993, the smallest increase in twenty years.

Many American companies now enroll their employees in managed care plans for which large health care providers compete. The $360 billion U.S. hospital industry is now under tremendous pressure to reduce its costs. Until the mid-eighties nearly all of the 6,000 U.S. hospitals were run as tax-exempt nonprofit operations, with few incentives for efficiency while contributing little in taxes and few services to their respective communities.

Because they were nonprofit, private, or public service organizations, their procedures and charges were seldom questioned, and public agencies as well as insurers paid their charges without question. With no motive for cost reduction, no accountability, and a driving force for prestige and status, these institutions invested in unnecessary equipment, facilities, and services. The result was a complete breakdown of health care economics, with $18 aspirins and $500 X rays. It was just a matter of time before profit-oriented organizations took over hospitals and transformed them into cost-conscious, efficient, and effective business operations.

Private for-profit hospital corporations have demonstrated that effective, cost-conscious, profit-motivated hospital management can provide quality care at substantially lower costs than nonprofit hospitals by simply cutting waste and streamlining operations. Similarly, medical costs such

TABLE 4

Doctors' Attitude and Job Satisfaction

1. Only 37% of American doctors provide primary care versus 54% in Germany, 62% in Israel, and 48% in Canada.

2. Doctors see 70 to 170 patients per week and contrary to popular opinion U.S. doctors see fewer patients than German, Israeli, and Canadian doctors.

3. American doctors are least satisfied with the way the U.S. health care system works. They also feel more strongly that changes are needed.

4. American doctors overwhelmingly contend that patients require more care than they can afford or are provided.

5. Doctors everywhere complain about the shortage of competent nursing staff.

6. Doctors spend 15-25% of their time on administration.

7. American doctors have greater access to well-equipped hospitals than most other doctors.

Source: U.S. Department of Health and Human Services

as doctors' fees, drugs, diagnostic tests, and rehabilitation are highly overpriced, inefficiently provided, and often performed unnecessarily. On top of it, unbridled fraud has recently been reported in health care provision, with little, if any, formal enforcement or punishment on discovery of such misconduct.

Only if reform includes transforming health care into an efficient, businesslike operation nationwide will it have a chance to improve the system into an effective, affordable service, available to all, that does not bankrupt the economy.

## Health Care Fraud

A recent General Accounting Office (GAO) report estimates that 10 percent of our health care expense is due to fraud in bogus and unneeded tests, services claimed but not performed, kickbacks to patients who submit phoney bills to insurers, kickbacks to doctors, drugs paid for by Medicaid or insurers that are resold to pharmacies, inflated bills, and more. One recent case in California involved mobile medical laboratory operations that bilked Medicaid, insurers, and patients of $1 billion in unnecessary tests.

Seniors, drug addicts, and the poor are the usual targets of many of these scams. Major fraud also involves unneeded or no longer needed psychiatric care. In addition to outright fraudulent charges, there is a gray area of overcharges for needed service performed but charged at an exorbitant rate.

Frequently doctors are now financially involved in peripheral activities such as ownership of test laboratories, expensive diagnostic equipment, and pharmacies. Equipment suppliers will supply equipment with no money down, to be paid for by a share in the patients charges. Doctors cannot lose—they build up an expensive plant and are then under pressure to maximize its use.

Doctors' charges have escalated at an average annual rate of more than 10 percent in recent years and therefore more than twice that required to keep up with inflation. However, doctors are involved more and more in collusion, fee splitting, and other practices to increase their income, at enormous added cost to the system.

Fraud in health care was estimated to have reached $100 billion in

1993, according to a study by the Republican staffers of the Senate Subcommittee on Aging, which performed its investigation with the assistance of the GAO. Most of the fraud was perpetuated on Medicare, Medicaid, and health insurers by doctors who filed claims for services not performed or certified untrue patient conditions so that patients could claim various compensations, prescribed unnecessary medication or orthopedic appliances for colluding suppliers, etc.

These direct frauds are in addition to prescription of unnecessary tests or treatments, many of which are performed under the guise of defensive medicine, although again, much of this is also driven by a profit motive as a result of ownership, by the same doctors, of laboratories and suppliers.

Together waste and fraud easily account for $160 to 200 billion/year now or 20 to 25 percent of our total national health care costs. This amount alone is more than adequate to cover all uninsured Americans and expand the health care system to include home visits and other presently excluded care. It is interesting to note how little attention is being paid to the effectiveness and honesty of health care provision, with all the attention placed on health care demand and concern for new sources of financing the added costs of universal coverage.

The cost of health care has escalated due to

1. increased demand for medical services generated by Medicare and Medicaid,
2. malpractice insurance costs and practice of defensive medicine,
3. overinvestment in often largely underutilized high technology,
4. medical costs of services demanded by third-party insurance,
5. medical fraud,
6. fraud by health care, and
7. unnecessary indirect service demands.

Other issues are the inordinately high charges of doctors and hospitals for medical services and procedures. These, in turn, are largely influenced by the controlled supply of new doctors. As a result of Flexmer Report 1910, medical schools were restricted "to assure greater quality," and as supply declined, the cost of doctors' services went up. It has been going up ever since.

One of the fallacies of many of the health care studies is the assumption that demand for medical services is constant per capita. Yet statistics prove that like other services, it is very much a function of price. As a result, Medicare costs many times as much as initially estimated. This carries also into drug and test prescriptions. For example, doctors now order as many and at least as expensive tests for Medicare patients as they do for their richest patients.

Without co-payments or deductibles, demand for medical services will always soar if price is no factor. Since Medicare, demand for medical services by people over sixty-five has escalated with a substantial part of that demand doctor-induced, fraudulent, or hypochondriac. Although the number of doctors is now increasing at a larger rate as a result of a larger number of graduates as well as a wave of immigrant doctors, the price spiral for medical services continues to escalate as doctors specialize in increasingly narrow specialized fields and maintain their mutual support by referral.

Medical referral used to be purely professional advice given by doctors to their patients. In many cases today referral involves financial payoffs, a practice that corrupts the system and again adds to its costs.

Fraud in health care is also practiced by some hospitals and in some cases by insurers. The total cost of fraud is probably well above the $80 billion (1991) estimated by the GAO and at its current rate of growth may well overtake the cost of waste in the U.S. health care system.

## Managed Competition in Health Care

Managed competition in health care has been suggested as an approach that could resolve the U.S. health care dilemma of inadequate coverage and excessive cost. It would involve sweeping changes in the organization and delivery of health care and would affect doctors, hospitals, and insurance and drug companies. This system would introduce major new incentives and is aimed at producing:

1. government guidance of the market forces,
2. competition among and accountability of health care providers,
3. national standards for the provision of health care and elimination of wasteful procedures,

4. greater cost-consciousness by providers, employers, and individuals, and
5. elimination of discrimination by insurers against high risk individuals.

Managed competition is designed to encourage partnerships or HMOs for doctors, hospitals, and insurers, who would then compete on the basis of price, quality, and patient satisfaction.

Small providers could set up cooperatives to compete with larger HMOs. A combination of employer contributions and government subsidies would cover the uninsured.

Tax breaks would be limited to only the lowest authorized costs, and a national board would establish basic benefits to be offered. While managed competitive health care looks like a step toward a more efficient and inclusive health care system, many potential problems exist with this approach.

It will be difficult to achieve consensus on basic benefits and costs, as well as on what procedures or technologies are wasteful. Assembling groups of major players who once colluded to freely compete will be very difficult in the medical field, where doctors are trained to cooperate with and protect their colleagues' as well as their own economic and professional interests. This approach could conceivably drive bureaucratic and overhead costs through the roof and thereby negate any cost savings in the delivery of medical services.

## Influencing the Health Care Debate

For years the health care industry has contributed generously to key congressional committee members and others who influence U.S. health care policy. Contributions by doctors rose (according to the Federal Election Commission) from $590,073 in 1990 to $1,459,611, in 1992; by pharmaceuticals from $119,400 to $235,600; by hospitals from $134,948 to $142,786; and by insurers from $458,098 to $487,568.

These direct and indirect campaign contributions to seventy-eight key members of the House and Senate from twelve PACs concerned with health care legislation were in addition to private contributions. Total 1992 contributions of $2.33 million were unevenly distributed, with some legislators receiving significantly more than the average $29,353.

## Health Care Financing

The health care programs proposed by the Clinton administration had laudable aims. They were an attempt to guarantee basic health care coverage for all Americans but fell short of realism in their proposed method of financing. They appeared to grossly underestimate both costs and cost savings in the existing system, because these were obtained mainly from savings in bureaucratic procedures, paperwork, regulations, and approvals. These savings would be offset in part by new administrative costs.

The cost of Medicare has doubled every four years since 1984, and these costs now grow at nearly two to three times the sum of the increase in percentage of people covered and the increase in the cost of living. In other words, the costs of Medicare are out of control and if their growth rate is allowed to continue will consume 100 percent of the federal and state budgets by year 2004. Savings in Medicare paperwork and other nondirect costs could at best introduce a one-time cost reduction of about $68 billion, without slowing the growth of other costs. In fact, these savings would only buy us a reprieve from two to three years of cost escalations. Similarly, we note that total U.S. health care costs have grown as follows:

1929 $ 4.0 billion total costs
1965 $40.0 billion total costs
1980 $200.0 billion total costs
1992 $700.0 billion total costs
1996 $920.0 billion total costs

As shown in figure 7, these costs are fast approaching $1 trillion and if allowed to continue to grow at the present rate will exceed $2 trillion soon after the end of this century and theoretically exceed the GNP of the United States by year 2020. Obviously this cannot happen in practice, but the problem of the cost of the system cannot be solved just by reducing bureaucracy and paperwork, even though these consume a hefty $120 billion (in Medicare, hospitals, and insurance), or even by reducing or eliminating malpractice, liability, and defensive medical practice costs, which by 1996

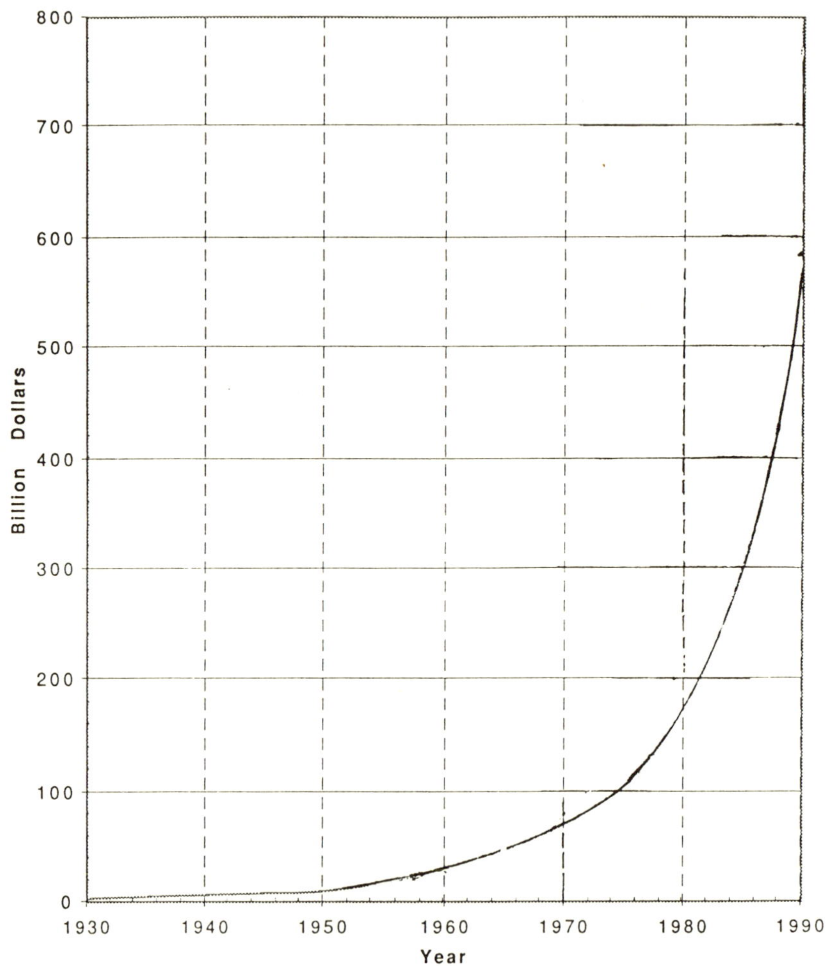


FIGURE 7 - U.S. Medical Costs

Source: Health Care Financing Administration, 1992

will probably reach $100 billion. The goal can be met only by eliminating the overall waste in the system of excessive medical procedure costs, many unnecessary medical procedures, sometimes obscene charges of doctors, unnecessary use of medical services by patients, and, most important, just bad administration and management of the health care system in all its components.

Preventative medicine is not effectively pursued in the United States and even where available is not really encouraged, largely because hospitals and other medical service providers want to sell the use of their facilities and their staff and not reduce the need for their services. It is curious, for example, that in an exercise-mad country like the United States health programs and hospitals have only recently started to recommend preventative methods and exercise. Yet few of those who need exercise and preventative medicine—mostly the young, the old, and the poor—are encouraged to participate in such programs, which are often available only at high cost, at a workplace or as part of an educational program. Some HMOs, recognizing the cost-saving impact of exercise, now offer free weight control and exercise programs to their members.

Additional factors important in U.S. health care costs are (1) teen pregnancies, (2) drug abuse, and (3) AIDS as well as other immune system diseases. These factors, which accounted for a scant 3 percent of U.S. health care costs in 1968, now readily absorb 16 percent with costs growing at a rate of 8 percent per year. At this rate, their annual cost by the end of the century will exceed $200 billion.

A third issue in health care costs is that of increasing longevity. The size of the population over sixty-two is growing at an annual rate of over 1.5 percent and is projected to reach 26 percent of total population by the end of the century.

Historically, health care costs increase with age, and today nearly 38 percent of total health care costs are incurred by people sixty-two years of age and older. In other words, per capita health care costs of older people average more than twice that of younger people, if we exclude infants, the chronically ill, AIDS victims, drug abusers, etc. Yet this does not have to be so. Greater emphasis on healthy lifestyle and preventative medicine can greatly reduce the costs.

## Patient Cost

Although the literature on patient cost sharing is still sparse, it reveals that cost sharing decreases the use of health care services effectively designed by reducing performance of unnecessary tests and procedures without affecting the quality of essential services. The issue at hand is effective design and monitoring of cost sharing. However, there is no proof that people make better decisions about demand for health care under cost sharing.

One approach to ensuring improved decisions would be to lower or even eliminate cost sharing in preventative and primary care, while increasing it for certain tests, cosmetic procedures, and so forth. The design of effective cost sharing must consider the differences in health, environment, age, education, and social environment. One cost-sharing system cannot be designed to fit all situations, and although cost sharing can save unnecessary health care costs and assure that doctors' decisions are monitored, individual plans must be designed to cater to specific groups.[5] Health care is among the least efficient service sectors, in which the consumer (patient) has little, if any, market power, and where charges are paid by third parties. This results in an imperfect market that cannot be regulated simply by cost control.

A fourth issue in health care cost is the large variation in the cost of specified health services. For example, the cost of surgical procedures differs widely among regions of the country. A hysterectomy costs on average $5,123 in New York City and $1,746 in Denver.[6] There are similar discrepancies in procedures such as coronary bypass, cesarean section, appendectomy, and vasectomy. While some of this margin may be the result of differences in overhead and equipment used, the major factors appear to be competition and anticipated income.

## Quality Control in Health Care

Rampant viral attacks such as HIV and resulting contraction of fatal AIDS have brought quality control in health care into the limelight. Recent statistics on hemophiliacs in the United States show their numbers to have been decimated by the use of HIV-tainted blood. This occurrence, along with unacceptable levels of tainted blood in our Red Cross and other blood banks and the commercially used blood products of viral or other contami-

TABLE 5 - Blood and Plasma Errors

- Blood and Plasma Errors and Recalls

| | Errors and Accidents | Number of Recalls | Units Recalled |
|---|---|---|---|
| 1989 | 1,100 | 100 | -- |
| 1990 | 1,600 | 84 | 28,200 |
| 1991 | 3,600 | 200 | 308,800 |
| 1992 | 10,400 | 248 | 20,400 |
| 1993 | 9,080 | 204 | 10,300 |

January 1, 1990 to April 7, 1994 the Food and Drug Administration received 29,586 reports from blood banks of 'errors and accidents' with donated blood. The most important problems occurred in storage and shipping followed by inadequate testing for hepatitis, wrong blood types, as well as inadequate tests for HIV, syphilis, etc.

Source: U.S. Food and Drug Administration

nation imported (table 5), raises the question of the effective management of quality in our health care industry. Other industries manage quality to a 5 to 6 sigma level and thereby assure users levels of less than one in a million cases of deviation from acceptable safety standards. Surely health care and health care providers, whose lapses in quality control are often life-threatening, should be able to maintain similar or higher standards. There is no excuse for hospitals using tainted blood in surgical procedures and thereby sentencing a patient to death following a successful surgical operation.

Today mislabeling of blood, plasma, and other products is common in U.S. hospitals and, although effective procedures are available to check their safety, tests are often bypassed in the interest of time or economics. We place the patient at risk rather than waste cost or operating room time. Similarly, few health care professionals have been trained in quality management procedures. In fact, the majority of such "accidents" can readily be traced to human error and lack of quality management.

While tainted blood and blood products and their role in spreading AIDS are the most publicized examples of lack of effective health care quality control, many other examples exist in which users of health care services or products are put at risk because of the lack of total quality management. It is curious that decades after total quality management was shown to improve the safety, performance, and reliability of products and services without increasing their cost, and after most manufacturers and other service providers introduced effective total quality management systems and trained their staff at all levels in the use of quality management concepts, the health care industry still lacks a formal commitment to total quality management.

One reason for this laxity may be an absence of effective enforcement procedures that would penalize health care providers for misconduct. While there are, obviously, legal procedures by which doctors or hospitals can be charged for malpractice, the medical profession's own watchdogs, which may be state medical or other professional bodies and which are generally contemptuous of risks and of patients' rights, appear to consider their role largely one of protecting the profession and maintaining its status.

Most states have health departments and health commissioners whose function is to maintain professional standards. These bodies would obviously be well advised to become proactive in selling and enforcing quality standards, not just behaving reactively to excuse failures in the industry.

While medical liability costs increased from $15 billion in 1970 to $45 billion in 1993, this appears to have had little corrective effect on quality management in health care, as much, if not all, of these costs are simply passed on to the public. The problem is that many who sue for malpractice are not really injured. On the other hand, doctors who perform badly and are a hazard to their patients are seldom identified by the system.

A recent study of malpractice in New York State headed by Dr. Howard H. Hiatt of the Harvard Medical School found that of 2.6 million patients discharged from New York hospitals in 1984, medical treatment had injured 100,000 of these patients, or 4 percent. A third of these cases were the result of negligence by doctors, nurses, and/or others. Similarly, half of the 14,000 deaths caused by injuries sustained in the hospital were the result of negligence and thus had been easily avoidable!

Medical malpractice and quality management are closely related. The first is usually the result of

1. ignorance,
2. lack of skill,
3. inadequate or wrong equipment use,
4. inappropriate procedure,
5. lack of knowledge of patients condition or history,
6. lack of adequate and/or trained staff,
7. improper medication, and
8. lack of sobriety or mental alertness of doctors and nurses.

These are similar to the issues addressed in effective total quality management. Yet few hospitals or other health care providers have total quality management systems in place, and where they are installed their standards are irregularly enforced. What is needed is a Baldwin or ISO 9000-type quality standard administration enforced on the U.S. health care industry by independent bodies.

We must also have agencies that enforce accountability. The issue is one of moral and ethical values and professionalism, in which doing what is right becomes the only driving force and money, status, and similar rewards assume a subordinate role. We must bring professional standards and pride in doing the best and providing the most effective treatment back to the health care providers, from doctors and nurses to all support staff.

The working environment of the health care industry is another area for improvement. Studies of differences in health care quality and costs among similarly sized hospitals or provider companies in the same field and geographic location have shown that job satisfaction, knowledge of worth by workers, effective recognition, and delegation of responsibility and decision-making can have a strong, positive effect on worker attitude, depression, interpersonal relations, and attendance records.

In fact, satisfied workers who enjoy their work and working environment are significantly less likely to fall sick or require medical services themselves. The benefits are higher quality and lower health care costs, and also greater productivity and more on-the-job time.

As in other industries, quality management is effective only if it involves everyone and receives personal commitment at every level of an organization. This is particularly important where provider–patient contact and relations play a large role in the ultimate quality of the service.

## Where Do We Go from Here?

The problem of developing a new approach to health care or, as we now say, "a new health plan," is that everything that affects health care is continuously changing. Any solution to health care problems will not necessarily solve the problems we face tomorrow. An effective plan must therefore be flexible and dynamic, and it must be designed to respond to changing requirements and conditions. Merely copying single-payer systems such as used in Canada and elsewhere will only solve part of our problem.

All proposals currently under discussion have four common shortcomings.

1. They address only the supply side of health care, its accessibility or universality.
2. They do not aggressively approach issues of health education, preventative care, and lifestyle.
3. They assume that costs are inviolate and cannot be controlled without price and/or service control as well as rationing, both of which are politically unacceptable.
4. They assume that waste in our health care system can be re-

> duced only by rationing and do not consider introduction of real incentives to reduce waste in services, investment, and resource use without sacrificing quality.

Health care providers by and large want to do the right thing but are often driven toward waste, such as defensive medicine or technological overinvestment, by social and legal pressures. These must be removed. Society must be reeducated, and the legal risks reduced for honest health care providers who do their best to provide conscientious quality service.

The problem of cost control really lies with the reactive incentives already in place that make referrals, excess laboratory work or tests, overinvestment, and depreciation of large technology investments so attractive.

While economic incentives are needed, they should be active and associated with efficiency and quality of service. There should be economic incentives to prevent people from getting sick or requiring health care, on both the providers' (supply) side and patients' (demand) side.

Wellness incentives are used in other services and in manufacturing and could be applied to the health care industry area as well. Similarly, morale status and social incentives may be found more effective than purely economic ones, as experienced in other fields.

The lack of efficient communication between health care providers is a major contributor to service inefficiencies. As long as providers consider themselves simply service providers and get paid per unit of service delivered, prices of services will continue to rise even in a competitive environment. In fact, in our fee-for-service arrangements we maximize the use of services and often of provider revenues, independent of patient needs and health care costs.

What we must be concerned with is how to maximize the health of the nation and then consider cost savings that do not affect the maintenance of the health of all Americans. In other words, we must define health care in terms of patient health needs. If some measures are more cost-effective, then these should be chosen, given that they have the same health effects. Similarly, preventative measures should be emphasized. But methods must be introduced to allow meaningful rewards for health care providers for use of preventive and not just healing procedures.

Some single-payer systems in which revenues are prepaid are designed to minimize costs by preventative methods and effective weighing of each procedure to achieve high-quality efficient health care. As noted, this requires the elimination of communication barriers and a reduction in the fragmentation of health care provision.

As doctors decide on the amount and type of service patients are to receive and doctors are usually paid on the basis of fee-for-service, a potential for conflict of interest is inherent, unless salaries and other methods of remuneration for doctors are introduced. One step in this direction is to pay attractive salaries to all general practitioners. This method works fine in Canada, where over 50 percent of physicians are in general practice.

Quality assurance of medical care will remain a major issue and cost factor in any health care plan. Our traditional approach has been to use malpractice suits or the threat thereof as an incentive to ensure quality service, but this method is an expensive counterincentive approach that does not address the fundamental issues of the problem. Not only are lawyers and uninjured patients the prime beneficiaries, but as doctors are able to simply pass on the costs of malpractice insurance, there is no particular incentive for bad doctors to improve. No-fault insurance has been suggested and may lower legal and administrative costs, but it will not provide an incentive for doctors to improve quality. Recent studies show that up to 90 percent of medical errors are preventable by

1. improved quality control,
2. greater discipline,
3. use of computerized record and expert systems to check procedures and treatment steps,
4. instant access to updated information,
5. up-to-date doctor skills, and
6. well-maintained facilities and equipment.

With regard to the final item, it was found that equipment that is not used extensively is often less well maintained and operators are less skilled in its use. To improve, quality HMOs, hospitals, and institutions in general should be liable and therefore be forced into effective total quality management of their medical services.

Recent polls indicate that in general the U.S. public feels that doctors are doing a good job and are well trained but charge too much, do not take adequate interest in their patients, make patients wait too long, and have too little time for their patients. Family doctors usually rate higher in patient satisfaction than other doctors, those associated with HMOs, and local hospitals. On the other hand, doctors feel under attack and are concerned with their status in society—this not only because of sometimes unfair criticism of exorbitant charges (or income) but more often because of the lack of self-policing or even self-criticism of medical practitioners by their association or peers. Public perception is that doctors have largely become businesspeople who ply their trade primarily for monetary gain and for whom patients are simply a demand for service they specify and provide at their price.

As general practitioners are much less inclined to use expensive diagnostic equipment, they could serve as a barrier to unnecessary treatment, and many HMOs now use this approach. Yet in the United States, where the number of general practitioners is only 20 percent of physicians, versus Canada with 50 percent, their influence is small. On the other hand, with 33 percent more surgeons in the United States, we perform 40 percent more operations per capita than are performed in Canada (as reported in *Technology Review,* 1990), and direct fee-for-service payment system procedures and operations are often performed without consideration of medical necessity.

The most important step to be taken to reform the U.S. health care system is the removal of the control of costs from medical doctors and health care providers. One way this may be achieved is through use of salaried group practices, community health centers, and similar organizations. This method assures better communication and cooperation among health care providers and facilitates a close relationship between primary health care providers and specialists. At the same time, quality standards can be effectively enforced.

## It Is the Waste in the System, Stupid

The health care debates range in topics from quality of care to freedom of choice and universal coverage. Few are willing to address the core of the problem, which is waste and, in part, the corruption of the system. Waste is the unnecessary or ineffective use of medical resources. To identify waste requires a clear definition of the health care goals that we lack. We argue about the shell of the system, about coverage, payment, method of delivery, and government control. However, the basic issues remain waste and ineffective management, which in turn are affected by the structure of the system. We have seen that we pay nearly twice as much on a per capita basis for health care as most industrialized nations and we receive neither universal nor the most excellent of care. Even high medical technology, once touted as the American medical care advantage, has been shown to be less accessible in the United States in cancer treatment and bone marrow transplants than in other industrialized countries. Furthermore, expensive treatments are also less accessible on average.

One of our health care system's greatest problems and source of inefficiency, waste, and resulting high cost is inadequate information and communication systems. Information technology (IT) can improve the efficiency and also the quality and reliability of health care provision.

An effectively designed IT system has all the relevant information on patient history, condition, allergy, tests, and more on record and is available in an easily usable form which improves effectiveness and safety of treatment. It also allows procedures to be efficiently planned, facilities and resources to be efficiently used, and their utilization to be greatly improved. IT can be a major key to cost reduction and safety improvement. While IT and electronic expert (diagnostic) systems are readily available and their costs moderate, their use is still low. The waste in the U.S. health care system falls into six broad categories:

1. *General Administrative Costs:* 5.6 percent of total health care costs in the United States versus 1.2 percent in Canada (where medicine is administered by private insurance companies at most state and local levels).
2. *Insurance Costs:* Waste includes enrollment costs, the cost of reserve maintenance, and profit.
3. *Administrative Costs:* Incomprehensibly detailed paperwork at the provider, government, and insurer level. This is largely the result of lack of trust, but the way it is now administered actually encourages fraud.
4. *Excess Facility and Equipment Costs:* Although there is a shortage of hospital beds in some rural areas most urban areas are vastly oversupplied. High technology investment, particularly for diagnostic equipment, is two to four times higher per capita in the United States than in other industrialized countries.
5. *Malpractice Insurance and Preventative Medicine:* This adds 8 to 16 percent to the cost of health care provision in direct and indirect costs.

6. *Manning Inefficiency:* In hospitals and other health care facilities, employment is often two to three times larger than in similar-quality and -size facilities in other high-quality health care delivery countries.

Conservative estimates of waste in the U.S. health system place the figure at an alarming 25 percent to 40 percent. Equally important is the fact that waste in health care costs grows at a much higher rate than do legitimate costs and therefore is the major cause of the seemingly out-of-control cost spiral of our health care system.

An active contributing factor to waste in health care is medical collusion among doctors in the provision of services, treatments, and tests, which, as discussed elsewhere in this chapter, is sometimes driven more by greed in the interest of payoffs or profit than by medical necessity.

Rules regulating conflict of interest must be rewritten and compliance strictly monitored—not by medical professional associations but by independent bodies. This same caution applies to procedures governing licensing, registration, repetition, and misconduct. Unless the medical profession cleans its own house, its reputation and status in society and professional effectiveness will continue to decline. An effective program of the following improvements will not only eliminate a major part of the present waste in health care costs but will also make the system more affordable and accessible and will improve its quality, reliability and safety. It would also go a long way toward reestablishing public trust in the system. Without the initial improvements listed, discussion of universality and who is to pay for what is moot. What is needed is

- waste reduction or elimination;
- effective quality management;
- elimination of conflicts of interest and collusion, including referral fees;
- complete reorganization of malpractice procedures and inclusion in quality management systems to eliminate the need for defensive medicine;
- independent setting or review of need and justification of facility and medical technology investment, which include cost-benefit evaluation before such investments are made;
- efficient management of health care providers and elimination of excess employment; and

- introduction and use of modern information and communications technology, including expert diagnostic systems and elimination of unnecessary clerical and accounting procedures.

Once the fat is cut, corruption and collusion eliminated, and the quality of and trust in the system reestablished, questions of accessibility, universality, and cost of services will largely resolve themselves. It is not effective enough to replace the roof and widen the doors of a rotting house with gold-plated fixtures. Let us first get the rot out, and we will see that the rest of the problems are much easier to solve.

We should be able to reduce the cost of American health care by 25 to 40 percent over a short period of time, without any reduction in the quality and accessibility of service. In fact, we may be able to continue to pay doctors, nurses, and other medical professionals at least as well as they are paid now—by simply cutting out all the waste described above and eliminating or greatly reducing medical fraud. Better management and quality control should also help in improving the quality of medical services provided.

## Patients Are Also Responsible

America has one of the best medical systems and introduces more medical advances than the rest of the world combined. Its medical and pharmaceutical research laboratories have developed the most advanced medical technology, techniques, and medications. We can now replace most organs with donor organs and, in some cases, artificial organs. We can unclog arteries, study brain functions, and perform the most complex of operations. Yet the average health of Americans is lower than that of people in many other countries. Lower life expectancy, higher infant death rates, and a larger number of sick days by the average American worker are just some of the symptoms. While some Americans devote themselves to exercise, diet, and general health care, most do little or nothing to assure their physical and mental well-being. Sports are largely spectator events, even in schools and universities, where a selected few represent the institution while all others watch. We must educate, particularly that physical exercise is essential for well-being. This may require a change in the way sports are organized in many of our schools, where sports have become largely elite exercises and only the most competent are encouraged to actively participate, with the rest of the students simply becoming supporters. We should not spend 50 percent or more of our schools' budget on a football or similar team to enhance the prestige of the school, with most students simply acting as spectators. Participatory sports only should be encouraged and all students encouraged to take part throughout their school life. Only this way will sports and students' other health-providing activities become part of our life.

The renewal of our health care system not only requires cleaning up the system in terms of abuse, misuse, and corruption, but a new mind-set by both providers and the public. The public must assume a much greater responsibility for its health. It must learn what contributes to health problems, take preventative measures, and most important, live a healthier lifestyle. Our eating is largely unhealthy. We live too stressful a life and, by and large, get too little physical exercise and mental relaxation. Most important, we lack adequate interpersonal support and live subject to constant competition.

The providers must get their act together and, as pointed out before, really clean house and provide the public what it needs—honest, compassionate, and quality health maintenance.

# 4
# The Dilemma of U.S. Education

Many claim that we in the United States have the worst-educated kids in the industrial world and that this problem is not getting better, this not only in terms of children's abilities in math, science, writing, and social sciences but also in behavioral and social skills. In other words, they do not learn to function well in society.

In the past, societal skills were largely the responsibility of the family, who trained their younger members to get along and to function in various social environments. The breakdown of the family structure in major sections of U.S. society has eliminated this part of the education process for many of the young, particularly the economically disadvantaged who need it most.

Spending more on education and child care is advocated by many as the solution. However, I disagree with the notion that pumping more money into an ineffective and inefficient system will solve anything. In fact, I would argue that increasing educational budgets will actually reward an already obscenely uneconomic and incompetent educational system and encourage further waste. True, many school systems, schools, and most certainly teachers and educators are competent and committed, but these are, unfortunately, in the minority. By and large, U.S. education has grown into a huge, self-serving, inefficient bureaucracy at all levels—from kindergarten to college—which is ruled and run not by educators but by professional and often unprofessional administrators, for most of whom our children are just one, and not necessarily the most important, focus of the enterprise.

Teachers, professors, and child care providers are in the minority in this educational bureaucracy and in most cases have little, if any, say on how the education is to be provided and the educational institution is to be run—and most important, they rarely control the budget. In most cases the direct costs of teaching or education bear little relation to tuition or the growth in the cost of education.

Considering typical U.S. educational institutions from primary to graduate school, the bulk of expenditures go for noneducational purposes. For example, in a typical U.S. university, the teaching staff comprises less than 25 percent of the total salary budget and the direct cost of teaching consumes an even smaller percentage of the total operating budget.

## The High Cost of American Education

America spends a larger percentage of its GNP and a much larger amount per capita and per student on education than does any other country in the world—yet the results are disappointing. The standards of the average graduate of a U.S. grade school, a high school, and often even a university are well under those of graduates of similar institutions in most developed countries and even fall below those of graduates in some developing or newly developed countries such as Korea, Singapore, and Israel.

The United States spent $295 billion on public schools, or an average of $5,920 per student, in 1992. Adding the cost of private schools, two-year and four-year colleges and universities, and full-time technical training schools, the total cost of U.S. education approaches $730 billion. Government and industry spent an additional $35 billion for training such as skill upgrading, in-house courses, and technical education.

College costs ballooned between 1980 and 1990 by a staggering 146 percent for private and 109 percent for public colleges, a rate over double that of inflation. Total college costs have now reached $326 billion. The principal causes for the high cost of tuition or per-student costs are:

- high salaries for faculty “stars”;
- inefficient and costly administrations and high administration salaries;
- “prestige” investment in often unneeded infrastructure, buildings, and equipment;
- unreasonable entitlements for student, staff, and faculty;
- proliferation of disciplines, departments, courses, and programs;
- wasteful bureaucracy and excessive paperwork; and/or
- lack of quality management.

Few universities or departments within universities share facilities, equipment, or faculty, even where they are neighbors or where these resources are underutilized. This isolationist approach has been known to lead to ludicrous developments where universities, departments, or individual faculty/staff build up space, equipment, or human resources to meet a temporary need—say the requirements of a large one-year research project—but never relinquish the added resources after completion of that project. As a result, space and other needs of the university continue to grow, independent of the number of students, staff, and faculty or even research load.

While in some cases permanent additions are justified by new research, most are not. Many American universities have introduced new office, computing, and communications technology at a tremendous cost, based on the justification that these will improve efficiency and reduce costs. The reverse has actually happened. The new technology required new and higher-paid staff, while the original staff and facilities were left in place. This duplication now causes not only additional costs but in many cases also loss of productivity.

## Cost of Student Aid

The increasing cost of education, particularly higher education, has put tremendous pressure on the student aid system. Although much of the aid comes from public sources, most student aid programs are administered by universities and private financial institutions.

Student aid has not kept pace with the increase in the cost of education. In 1980 total student aid was equal to about 26 percent of tuition costs; by 1990 it had increased only another 4 percent, during a period when federal and total student aid increased by 47 percent and 70 percent respectively. This was largely the result of dramatically rising tuition costs. Another reason appears to be the terrible performance of student loan collections. Defaults of student loans average 7 percent at public and private four-year colleges, 17 to 18 percent at two-year colleges, and a whopping 41 percent at for-profit vocational schools.

The major reason for these abuses is general laxity in both the granting and collection of loans, no effective pursuit of deadbeats, government reimbursement for bad loans, which reduces the incentive to pursue the perpetrators, overstatement of loan needs, and basic fraud.

Considering the cost of U.S. education in more detail, it is noted that we spend on average just over $5,920/year per student in primary and high school and over $12,800/year in college or technical/vocational school. With nearly half of all high school graduates going on to college for whatever reason or for no reason at all, the average number of years a child spends in U.S. educational institutions is now nearly 14.8, at an average cost to the public of just under $100,000 per child. This inordinate cost in dollars, and similarly in students' time, should buy an education second to none, yet recent studies indicate that our students on average trail those of every other industrialized country as well as those of many poorer countries in most skills and fields of knowledge, although we spend nearly 40 percent more on education on a per-student basis than does any other industrialized country.

The skills of the average U.S. student in reading, mathematics, science, and liberal arts are inferior when compared with those of their foreign counterparts in industrialized countries, nor do our students acquire essential cultural and moral values or interpersonal and communication skills. They simply spend 2.1 more years (12 to 20 percent) in school, reducing both their career opportunities and lifetime earning capacity. The additional years an American student spends in school or college also reduce his or her productive working life by over 6 percent. At the same time, our educational system is not effectively designed or focused to meet the needs of our society and economy in terms of skills. There is little focus on the career requirements of society as a whole, and students are left to an unenlightened freedom of choice, often to the stage in the students life when it has become too late to choose.

The United States cannot be competitive without a well-trained, well-balanced workforce. Although fundamental reform of the educational system is essential, this will take time to accomplish. More near- and medium-term priority should be given to post–high school job training. A large improvement in vocational training will require coordinated action by the federal, state, and local governments and by U.S. business. Career and continued job training is urgently required, as few jobs, if any, can now be performed proficiently with basic preemployment education and training.

There is a good deal the federal government can do to improve the scene, even with the existing training resources. The armed services spend very large sums on training; some of this training is redundant, and little has been used by private industry, although much could benefit private industry, which is called upon to absorb redundant or "retiring" military personnel.

Middle-level technical training is neither effectively organized nor easily accessed in the United States although the bulk of well-paying jobs fall into this category. One reason for this lack appears to be the social ("blue-collar") stigma associated with middle-level technical persons, particularly if not college-trained. As a result, a significant proportion of skilled technical people who hold positions in manufacturing, office, legal, medical, and administrative work are college-educated, something that rarely contributes to their job proficiency. For example, nearly 40 percent of secretaries and office clerical personnel hold a university degree and another 20 percent have had two years of college or similar higher education. This is not because these people failed to obtain a professional education, but because they see a college degree as a sign of education, culture, and proficiency. These expectations are rarely met, because most U.S. colleges do not offer broad-based cultural programs but emphasize a more focused education not necessarily aimed toward or useful for technical jobs.

As a result, many technical personnel in the United States are, in a way, overeducated and underskilled for their jobs. Not only does such unnecessary college education cost large sums of money and a substantial amount of time, but it also delays the attainment of experience in the technical skills and often leads to unjustifiable expectations.

For example, a British or German secretary, age twenty-two, would have had a one-year secretarial training course and four years of experience as an entry-level secretary, while a similar secretary in the United States usually has six months of secretarial training in addition to four years of liberal arts college and little, if any, experience. As a result, the secretary in the United States will be less proficient and have lost four years of earnings in addition to the cost of his or her college education, a total cost roughly estimated at between $120,000 and $150,000, or about 10 to 15 percent of life earnings. This imposes a heavy social cost and also affects living standards, without contributing appreciably to the secretary's job, society, or quality of life.

## The Funding of American Schools

American public schools are funded primarily by local authorities, such as cities, towns, and counties, whose main source of revenue is real estate taxes. The result is a wide disparity in per-student funding nationwide and, therefore, also in quality of schools and education. All citizens are supposed to obtain equal education, and attendance at school is mandatory in most jurisdictions until at least the age of fourteen. However, differences in the standards and quality of education have evolved, independent of the fact that resources devoted to primary education have increased and the per-student cost in U.S. schools is greater than in any other country. As we have seen, educational achievements nevertheless lag far behind and average among the lowest of developed or industrialized nations.

Many feel that equity must be brought into the classroom and that money spent per student should be uniform nationwide and independent of a student's domicile. Of course, money alone does not determine the quality of education. To the contrary, some of the wealthiest school districts in the United States produce some of the poorest-educated students. One reason for this irony is the huge amount of money spent on public school administration, overhead, and bureaucracy. In addition, sports, prestigious programs, and various other nonacademic activities often absorb a large percentage of the capital and operating budgets of schools, without contributing proportionately to education. In fact, the amount spent on administration and what may be called extracurricular activities today exceeds 50 percent of the total budget in many school districts and is growing. Furthermore, incentives for staff and teachers of extracurricular activities, particularly sports, are usually superior to those offered to teachers of basic educational subjects.

## The Cost of the Illiterate American

Five to 6 million working Americans are functionally illiterate. While about 3 million have never learned to read or write, an equal number are unable to do so because they do not use their reading and writing skills on a regular basis. An additional 5 to 6 million do not consider these skills necessary for employment, while a further 8 to 10 million have reading and writing skills in only a foreign language, predominantly Spanish. This means that a full 20 percent of the total workforce and over 40 percent of those in service industries are essentially illiterate in English, a fact that will affect the future direction of our economy, particularly as the country moves toward increased use of technology and higher total quality management (TQM) in the products and services supplied.

This lack of literacy skills has a wide impact on communications, training, and morale on the job, as well as on the ability to improve productivity and quality of performance. On-the-job communications and information transfer or handling are now of importance in both the manufacturing and service industries. Communications skills are an important prerequisite to effective performance at all job levels, including the most basic ones. Illiteracy and lack of communications skills, in addition, prevent or diminish intellectual and skill growth, reduce teamwork and feedback, and make it difficult to enhance job performance through training.

Low levels of literacy and communication skills reduce interpersonal contacts and limit interpersonal relations in the workplace. Both job direction and performance reporting become rather ineffective, as a significant number of directives are poorly understood and the job is poorly or incorrectly performed. Similarly, feedback from the job is often delayed, if offered at all, and then is frequently misrepresented.

As a result of various degrees of illiteracy, nearly 20 percent of the U.S. workforce is stuck at the bottom of the job ladder, performing nonsatisfying low-level and low-income jobs that present no opportunity for advancement. Although public agencies and even some employers attempt to alleviate this problem through training, the success of such programs has been very low, as the issue goes well beyond skill training and job enhancement. It involves moral, cultural, and social issues that cannot be resolved by the workplace alone.

The cost of illiteracy to the U.S. economy is complex and staggering. It involves the cost of decreased performance by up to 20 percent of the workforce and the cost of remedial literacy training that could otherwise be more effectively channeled—for example, used for skill enhancement. It also forces the illiterate workforce to grapple with technological change.

This problem is evident on the manufacturing shop floor, where workers lack the basic language and interpretive skills to allow the introduction of such state-of-the-art technology as robots, automation, and quality testing equipment. The same situation often appears in service industries such as banking, logistics services, and even food processing. The introduction of advanced technology would increase the value added per worker, which in turn affects the wages that companies can afford to offer. This vicious circle has forced many U.S. industries to see their competitive advantage slip away. Ultimately, it also affects U.S. unemployment, as the companies that traditionally employ illiterate Americans will become non-competitive and go under.

## K-12 and Primary Education in the United States

In 1993 we expected to spend close to $300 billion on primary education (K–12), in the United States, of which less than $2 billion (1 percent) was spent on technology such as computers and information systems and their applications. Less than half of the public expenditures for primary education go for teaching and education-related activities, even after the cost of facilities, services, and supplies, while only half of the remaining amount goes for actual teaching.

Primary education has not only become heavily bureaucratic but is overcontrolled. Teachers are being asked to do the most creative work that we have. In most school systems the number of nonteaching staff (administrators, custodians, security personnel, and more) far outweigh the number of teachers, teacher's aides, and others with a direct impact on education. Teachers are told what, when, and how to teach. Their contact with students is largely confined to the classroom, and contact with parents generally occurs only at PTA meetings and other "official" forums. Teachers spend an inordinate amount of their time on administrative functions. In fact, paperwork in most U.S. schools has doubled every ten years for the past several decades.

Another issue standing in the way of quality education is the approach to teaching. Even with the abundance of administration, there is really little feedback or accountability in the U.S. educational system. According to Lou Gerstner, CEO of IBM, "We are the only nation that does not measure the output of our public schools."[1] We are concerned with how much we spend on education without much idea of what it buys. We are unwilling to set even minimal national standards and are not prepared to measure the productivity or performance of our educational system.

We bend the rules—where they exist—and graduate the least motivated students, thus penalizing the hardworking and talented students with inferior programs and with standards designed for the lowest common denominator. Today's information technology provides the tools for separating students and for satisfying their individual needs at the proper level. This system could motivate all students, not only the more talented, but the institutional structure of our schools does not allow this. Instead it forces students and teachers into a straightjacket. It considers use of technology only for its own sake—not to allow the use of technology to revamp the educational system, but only to improve teaching efficiency. Computers are used as tools, to teach what has always been taught but with less teacher involvement. These miraculous new tools are not generally used to expand students' intellectual horizons, their competence as workers, or their general learning ability.

Clearly, we have failed miserably in making use of technology to advance the standards and quality of American basic education. This may be our last chance to ensure development of an educated, motivated, and productive new generation, capable of reversing our mistakes of recent years and restoring America to world leadership not only in a military but also in an economic, technological, and moral sense.

We are doing an injustice to our young generation by not revamping our basic education system, and future generations will rightfully hold us accountable for this omission—unless we quickly correct the situation.

## Standards of Education

A major factor contributing to the low average level of elementary, secondary, and college education in the United States is the lack of standards. Most other developed and many poorer developing countries impose uniform, usually national, standards of achievement on the different segments of the educational system. In the United States, where basically all primary and secondary schooling is funded at the local level by a school department or by a private or parochial organization, standards are imposed locally. In turn, these standards are affected by

1. school budgets, funded largely by local real estate taxes and as a result a direct reflection of the average income level of the community;
2. educational standards of the community, which ensure that

farming and working-class communities will have generally lower educational aspirations and expectations than do the more affluent communities inhabited by more educated professionals who pay much higher property taxes;

3. political pressures, which influence the composition of school boards and educational budget committees at the local (and state) levels and, in turn, tend to emphasize or prefer politically attractive budget allocations, hiring practices, and educational policies to satisfy their narrow political objectives;
4. perceived social and democratic equality, which ironically caters to the lowest common denominator in educational standards. Our schools are unique in allowing students to advance from grade to grade independent of performance, notwithstanding the fact that these students pull down the rest of the class and, ultimately, such a process pulls down the school's overall rating. We somehow abhor burdening ill-performing students with the stigma implied by repeating a grade, ignoring the implications and impact of such a policy. While the brightest student may still perform close to potential in such an environment, the bulk of good and average students who must now work harder for good grades are turned off by a countermotivating policy that rewards the nonperformer with the same promotion and ultimate high school certificate.

High school certificates have now become virtually meaningless, and our average expenditure of over $5,600/year per high school student is not only a waste of money but a disgrace. Consider the average achievements in reading and mathematics by, say, thirteen- and fourteen-year-olds as compared to those in other countries (table 6).

### Table 6

**Average Achievements in Reading and Mathematics in Thirteen- and Fourteen-year-olds (1991)—Percentage above/below Average**

| Reading | | Mathematics | |
|---|---|---|---|
| Finland | +10 | Switzerland | +19 |
| France | +6 | France | +8 |
| Sweden | + 5 | Italy | + 7 |
| Switzerland | + 4 | Canada | + 2 |
| USA | + 4 | Britain | + 1 |
| Germany | + 1 | Holland | 0 |
| Denmark | 0 | Spain | - 7 |
| Portugal | 0 | USA | - 7 |
| Italy | - 2 | Portugal | - 16 |
| Holland | - 3 | | |

Source: U.S. Department of Education

Few top universities consider high school performance records in their admission decisions, and private testing organizations had to be developed to provide performance measurements that lead to a common standard.

Universities and other institutions of "higher" learning similarly lack any uniformity in standards. While it is shameful that a significant number of high school graduates are functionally illiterate and do not possess basic communications skills, many college graduates with first degrees are found to have remained functionally and professionally illiterate as well. In fact, nearly half the U.S. college-educated bachelor degree holders demonstrate only elementary communications skills and no marketable professional skills. As many as one-third of the graduates of liberal arts programs (which constitute nearly half of college placements) work as secretaries, receptionists, and store clerks and doing similar jobs for which they could have qualified and probably been much better prepared for by taking a short vocational program, saving themselves at least two years in time and the economy tens of thousands of dollars. In addition, they would contribute two additional productive years to the economy and themselves.

Some justify a first degree and particularly a liberal arts education on the grounds that it raises the standard of education for a significant proportion of the population, yet those who have reviewed liberal arts programs are skeptical that this is really achieved. On the contrary, it appears that many college programs are, in fact, remedial programs to make up the deficiencies of high school education. The costs of this educational deficit are staggering in economic terms, including lost productive output when college graduates enter jobs that should be filled by vocational school graduates, as they are in other industrialized countries.

## Effectiveness of American Education

As discussed, U.S. educational institutions in general and universities in particular have not displayed responsible attention to the spiraling costs of education. The annual growth rate in per-student costs for primary education is estimated as between 6.4 and 10.8 percent, with higher education costs growing even more rapidly during the last twelve years. According to a recent Organization for Economic Cooperation and Development (OECD) study (1992), U.S. college/university expenditures in U.S. dollars (converted using purchasing power equivalents) was $13,890 per student or 2.6 percent of GDP versus $7,140 per student and 8 percent of GDP in Japan and $6,550 per student and 1 percent of GDP in Germany.

At the same time the quality of education at all levels continues to decline, notwithstanding the fact that most increases in expenditures for education have been justified on the basis of needed improvements in educational standards and achievements. The United States now ranks among the lowest in math and science skills among advanced industrialized nations and lags well behind newly industrialized nations such as Korea, Singapore, and Taiwan, as well as some developing countries.

As Thomas Sowell points out in his book, *Inside American Education,* American students are made to feel good about themselves while American institutions stress self-esteem more than knowledge and standards. In fact, standards have become generally lower and more lax. Students seem to care less about studies and more about social status and self-perception. With graduation from school practically guaranteed and quality control largely absent, the U.S. educational system has become a jungle of schools, each maintaining separate standards and using its own approach. The educational establishment has become a largely self-serving network of institutional empires with their own, often narrow, local or even political agendas. Much school time is spent catering to instead of teaching students.

Universities expect the public to foot the bill, no matter what the cost—this at a time, as we have seen, when the quality of American education is declining by world standards. Yet there is little that can be done under the present system. Complaints, if they arise, tend to be dismissed under the guise of lack of understanding by the public, and particularly by parents, of the process of education.

On the other hand, as pointed out, American educators are fascinated with making students feel good about themselves, even when their academic performance is severely lacking. They emphasize self-esteem, personal recognition, and, at the primary level, trappings such as graduation exercises for toddlers and primary school candidates, independent of the education or lack of education received. At the secondary level all students are graduated without consideration of achievement or standards attained.

Educational experimentation in American schools and universities never ends. The educational leadership is most concerned with publicity and with "innovation," which is often nothing more than playing around with simple-minded tests and reducing students to the role of social guinea pigs. Instead of education in basic knowledge, American students spend much of their time in social and psychological reviews and sensitivity sessions that they neither need nor understand. The result is an excess of staff for special needs and of social experimenters, as well as of "educators" who are concerned with the feelings but not the intellect or true education of their students. The ratio of administrators to teachers in schools and to professors in universities has more than doubled in the last twenty-five years, a period that parallels the fall in educational standards.

By and large, the American educational system is more concerned with perpetuating its power structure than improving the performance of its basic functions, which are education and, in the case of universities, also research. Today their primary concern is social and political correctness and only, to a much lesser degree, scholarship and quality of education.

## The Economics of U.S. Elementary and Secondary Education

The U.S. elementary and high school population tripled to 45.6 million between 1900 and 1970 and has since fallen to a level of 41 million. Total school population has since remained fairly constant at about 20 percent of the population. Over the same period, the average age of the population increased, thus decreasing the segment aged five to seventeen from 28.4 percent in 1900 to 18.2 percent in 1990.

The percentage of five to seventeen-year-olds enrolled in school has climbed from 71.96 percent in 1900 to over 89.1 percent in 1990, with the scant 3.4 percent who continued to high school in 1900 growing to 30.4 percent by 1990. The percentage of all students graduating from high school is now approaching 60 percent, an abnormally high number that reflects the present educational and training requirements of the economy.

The percentage of high school graduates who continue to college has risen nearly 10 percent over the past decade and now exceeds 61 percent. Yet of the 1.12 million (39 percent) high school graduates who do not enroll in college, only about 100,000 (8.3 percent) were enrolled in any vocational (secretarial, trade, or technical) education courses.

Federal funding for education was comparatively modest in the eighties. The amount grew from about $14.1 billion in 1980 to $25.7 billion in 1991 and was designated chiefly for primary and secondary education. The total cost of primary and secondary education, however, was nearly $181.1 billion, of which the federal government supplied about 13.6 percent with the remainder funded by local, state, and private sources. The cost of higher education has grown at an even faster rate. While the average cost of elementary and secondary education grew from $2,272 to $4,243 per student per year between 1980 and 1988 (an annual rate of about 8.5 percent), higher or university education costs grew an average of over 11.8 percent per year during the same period. This same trend continued until now—1997.

## Investing in Human Resources

While the educational level of professionals and management personnel in the United States is usually high, that of the lower-skilled or unskilled workforce is quite low. Furthermore, little, if any, of the investment in training and education by companies, public agencies, and government is spent on lower-level workforce training. This perpetuates educational mediocrity as well as locking workers into low-paying, low-status jobs. In fact, it makes this largest segment of the U.S. workforce an economic liability, unable to effectively use modern technology and, as a result, often employed only on an hourly basis. These workers are not part of the company or other establishment and, in fact, are considered just another economic input factor much like capital or material. It is not surprising that labor, by and large, does not associate itself with the interests or objectives of industry or other economic enterprises they serve. Labor is not and does not consider itself part of the company or corporate family. It does not, in most cases, partake in the benefits of company or in corporate success.

Incentives provided to workers, if any, are often meager and sometimes meaningless. Job security and social and health care benefits for this segment are usually deceptive.

Workers are normally given only minimal on-the-job training, adequate enough to perform the assigned function. As a result, their career or advancement opportunities are limited. The personnel departments of most companies manage workers just like other resources and are often organized more like a procurement than a human resource department.

This approach is quite different from that taken by companies in the two other most successful world economies—Japan and Germany. In both, the management of human resources is considered the most important function of management and is given priority above all other functions. Career paths are wide open, and many senior executives emerge from worker ranks. Workers at all skill and educational levels are expected to participate in periodic training, skill upgrading, and educational programs.

For example, German companies, small or large, generally use apprenticeship programs in which young graduates of high school or a two-year post–high school trade school are trained in the necessary physical skills and educated in the statistical and other theoretical requirements of their chosen field. Apprenticeships usually extend over two to three years, and apprentices are given salaries and benefits. The majority of skilled workers in Germany have undergone formal apprenticeships that are followed by periodic training as a person advances in skill levels. As a result, the German manufacturing and service industry workforce is, as a result, significantly more skilled than its U.S. counterpart.

Accordingly, the status of and respect for skilled German workers are high, barely distinguishable from that for other professionals, particularly as many of them have risen through the ranks. In other words, skilled workers and other professionals engineers, accountants, lawyers, managers, etc.) not only respect each other but share in a common concern for the success of the company. Their working conditions, incentives, and benefits are similar, and salary differentials are reasonably small. There are none of the obscene executive salaries as in the United States, where a chief executive officer or vice president of production may make a hundred times more than a skilled worker.

German workers' unions play a much greater role in the management of a company, and workers are often represented on the board of directors. Worker/management relations are usually cooperative and nonconfrontational. Japanese companies do not employ formal apprenticeship schemes but continuous on-the-job training, by which young workers are added to groups of experienced employees who undertake to train the new members.

In both Japan and Germany and to a lesser extent in other European and Far Eastern industrialized countries, training of workers is taken very seriously and is done formally. A typical German corporation may have an apprentice force of 4 to 6 percent of its total workforce and spend 5 to 8 percent of its budget on its apprenticeship scheme. Apprenticeship schemes in Germany and some other European countries and in the Far East often go beyond basic skill training to include general education, statistical method, quality management, and other subjects that assure skilled workers adequate preparation to move up the responsibility ladder and not be left behind as technology advances.

Training and human resource development budgets, which in U.S. companies seldom exceed 1 percent of annual sales, are traditionally double to four times as large in these countries and are devoted to a large extent to the training of lower-level workers. By comparison, in the United States 80 percent of the training budget is normally devoted to executive or management training. Furthermore, such training in the United States is often tied to planned advancement. In other words, only employees selected for advancement are offered training.

With major U.S. manufacturing and service companies devoting 80 percent of their training budget to executive/management training and 20 percent to workers, the argument is advanced that a company should invest only in career staff who are expected to remain with the company for a long time. This position is not persuasive: U.S. Department of Labor statistics indicate that the workers actually stay longer with a company on average, and make fewer job changes, than do professionals, managers, and executives working for the same firms.

Training by U.S. companies is often used as an incentive or fringe benefit, particularly to attract bright, well-educated young professionals and managers, though it is also used to retain senior staff. Little attention is given to training the skilled workers who form the backbone of a corporation.

A major problem now faced by U.S. industry is the lack of the well-trained and motivated workforce so necessary for U.S. competitiveness in a high-tech world where technical skills are as important as management. In the emerging technological environment, skilled workers will be required to perform independently, without guidance or control by management. Considering the sorry state of human resource development at that level, the future looks ominous. This problem is magnified by the low level of high school preparation, as we have seen.

A large percentage of the U.S. workforce did not finish high school, and even those who did generally lag behind their foreign (Far Eastern and Western European) counterparts by at least two years in mathematics, statistics, and the physical sciences. They also often lack training in communication and interpersonal skills, subjects rarely addressed in U.S. high schools.

As technology advances, there is an escalating demand for entrance-level skills. Job opportunities for basically unskilled workers are declining as the functions they perform become mechanized or automated. This occurs on the manufacturing shop floor as well as in sales, materials handling, financial transactions, and more. The reasons for this trend are often not to save labor costs but to improve quality and flexibility.

Human resource development is arguably the greatest challenge now facing the country, because future economic development and maintenance of the U.S. standard of living will depend heavily on the technical capability of our human resources. Unless the proper investments are made in this area, the United States risks losing not only its economic but its technological leadership and with these, any pretense to world leadership.

The rapid changes that technology now imposes on our workforce are unique to our time, and an infrastructure of training and standards to judge competence is not yet in place. Our workforce has not kept pace with our technology. In an effort to address this problem, the Clinton administration has proposed a school-to-work program ($1.2 billion over five years). The program is designed to improve the marketable skills of non-college-bound high schoolers, create a national skill standards board, create apprenticeship openings by employers, and establish proper skill credentials for such students, to enable employers to judge competence and experience. The program combines on-the-job training with high schools and community colleges to permit apprentices to maintain their options for skilled jobs and college degrees. This program is a step in the right direction, but it will require much industry involvement and commitment in order to succeed.

Another issue is the need for lifelong education and training. While many U.S. universities offer continuing educational programs, often designed particularly for mature midcareer students, these programs tend to be highly specialized and provide participants with only narrow improvement in their skills. What is needed is a formal system of lifelong training and education that assures that workers maintain their skills and that these skills are upgraded as technology, technology use, society's requirements, and the economic/ecological/societal systems evolve and advance. People must be able to continually hone their present skills and acquire new ones as technology and work environment change.

It is important to maintain skills, but also to make sure that experience, often as critical to success as up-to-date skills, is not lost when older workers and professionals are replaced by younger, more technologically proficient and up-to-date employees. To achieve this goal American universities must become more practice-oriented; they must "learn to learn" from the experience of their continuing education program students.

An issue affecting the young is flexibility in our human resource development to allow an individual who has chosen vocational training later to advance, if he/she is competent, toward a professional or managerial position by university training or vice versa. We are unfair to our young to require them to make their largely irrevocable education and career decisions when they have no job experience and know little about their aptitudes or preferences.

Institutions of higher learning consume huge amounts of public resources, which can be justified only if they meet the needs of society. Greater effort must be made to reconcile the often-conflicting interests and objectives of individuals and of society.

## American Universities

Universities stand in special esteem in American public opinion. As the only country in which the majority of high school graduates go on to college (61 percent 1993), we essentially consider universities a public service, accessible to all. It is not that students opting for a college education necessarily know what to do with it. It is difficult to understand why someone who will work as a secretary, technician, or nurse for life requires four years of undergraduate education. Americans, as egalitarians, assume a college education to be an essential preparation for life and an opportunity that must be open to all. In fact, the reason such a large percentage go on to college is that they do not know what else to do. We have not educated them in their options; in fact, little career training is usually provided in high school.

Although the majority of American universities are private, they are expected to be affordable and thereby accessible to all. This assumption, deeply embedded in the American culture, has in recent years been subjected to severe shock and rising public resentment as annual tuition increases have greatly exceeded the rate of inflation, making many private colleges unaffordable except for the few, even on scholarship.

Now in 1997 tuition is increasing at an average annual rate of 7.8 percent, a reduction compared to previous years. Student aid offered by colleges and government agencies is simultaneously becoming more difficult to obtain. College costs are becoming a political issue that will not go away as they continue to escalate and as research funding, private contributions, and tuition support programs decline. In addition, colleges have been unable to clean up their administrative inefficiencies. They are surprisingly often among the worst or least effectively managed institutions, even those who train administrators in effective business management. Colleges are among the few U.S. enterprises whose overhead and administrative costs have consistently increased, even after massive investment in advanced technology designed to reduce administrative costs.

## Universities as Cradles of Education and Leadership

Our colleges have largely become a jungle of academic bureaucracy. Educators are quite frequently creating a vacuum of leadership by self-serving academic exercises that do not foster creative innovation, unorthodox discovery, or the extension of knowledge but instead induce students and faculty to follow the well-trodden path of their academic superiors.

Universities have lost much of the excitement that made them an adventure and not just a step in a career path. Students and faculty once flocked to the best institutions of higher learning, not just because of the value of the credentials conferred in career building but because that was where the excitement and the challenge were to be found.

Academic honesty was the norm—not the exception—and trust was assumed. No more! Today's universities are concerned with status more than with quality of education, with their influence more than with the leadership skills imparted to their students, and are more committed to donors and sponsors than to academic and scholarly principles.

A great university recognizes its people—its greatest asset and the source of its strength. Stone walls and a well-paid administration do not ensure academic excellence. Unfortunately, at many major American universities image has become more important than accomplishment or contribution to science, knowledge or society. Perception has become a powerful tool, surpassing and now often supplanting the underlying reality. Many of our best institutions live more on their past than for their future.

## Running the U.S. University

Increasingly the role of the university has become not education or research its contribution to the solution of the problems facing society, but the narrow self-gratification of a non–democratically elected few who set themselves up as the arbiters and representatives of the faculty and students, those who are, in fact, the university but have little, if anything, to say about its policies. The lack of meaningful representation and control by faculty has become fairly universal in American universities, most of which are now run by professional administrators with little teaching or research experience or who have forsaken teaching and research for the glory, power, and fat salaries of university administrators.

University administrators, once as poorly compensated as faculty, have emerged toward executive affluence in terms of not only direct salary but also an array of direct and indirect perks. In 1965, the presidents of Ivy League colleges earned salaries and perks valued at less than 2.5 times those of an average full professor at the same institution. By 1993, this ratio had risen to well over five times. In other words, the salaries of university executives have risen more than twice as fast as those of faculty.

In addition, the number of senior executives in university administrations (provosts, vice presidents, deans, and department heads) more than tripled during the same period. As a result, senior executive costs have increased nearly tenfold in many major U.S. academic institutions. While some of this expansion was the result of new government regulations or requirements, such as equal rights and environmental laws, most increases in the senior executive ranks can be traced to:

1. empire building,
2. infiltration or takeover of functions or responsibilities traditionally assumed by the faculty, and
3. administrative inefficiency.

The problem is now acute because of the slowdown or actual decrease in government funding and stepped-up government surveillance of the spending by universities.

## Empowerment of the Faculty

By definition, universities are collegia of scholars organized to further education, research, and other scholarly activities for the purpose of advancing knowledge. Their faculty, who are the scholars, have historically made all relevant administrative, educational, and research decisions in such universities. In recent years, though, faculty has been increasingly disempowered, and the resulting feeling of loss of control has had a detrimental impact not only on individual faculty but also on the collegium of faculty who make up the university.

Decisions in most American universities are no longer reached through discussion by faculty and students but are largely made by professional administrators whose stake is their own job and related career interests and not necessarily the advancement of scholastic activities unless it also improves the financial and operational performance of the university.

## Academic Freedom and Intellectual Honesty[2]

Over the years, academic freedom and rights of expression, however controversial, have been upheld as important factors in academic life. At the same time, it may be argued that such freedoms are associated with the responsibility for accuracy, honesty, and fair accreditation.

For example, it is now common practice for thesis supervisors to place their name after—often even before—that of their student who actually carried out the research and usually wrote the paper or report, particularly when such "joint" publications are based mainly, if not exclusively, on a student's thesis research. It seems highly inappropriate to appear as author or coauthor of research which was not performed and often not even instigated or supervised carefully by such a faculty supervisor. A name on a paper or report implies not only responsibility for but also significant contributions to its contents. In a way, this is tantamount to stealing part of the credit from the author of the research. The argument is often advanced that as faculty provides initial guidance in the selection and later performance of the research that forms the thesis, they deserve credit for the results, even though they have often performed no more than the function of guide, supervisor, sounding board, or reviewer.

I have a great deal of trouble with this argument. Does an investment adviser get credit or profit from investments he or she suggested and transacted for an investor? Can an art teacher cosign student paintings even though he/she guided the work? Can an editor claim coauthorship of a book he/she suggested, helped plan, and edited? I think not. Faculty are paid to advise and direct students in their research work. They are paid to help students select research topics, advise them on the methods and approaches to be used, and supervise and review their work. Although they may, as a result, contribute intellectually, this contribution is in the form of ideas, criticism, and guidance. It is not usually a substantive contribution to the research process, unless the faculty member actually performs some of the research, performs the analytical and other work, or otherwise substantially participates in this process.

Some argue that the student, particularly when employed as a graduate research assistant, actually assists the faculty in the research, working for and under his or her supervision, and therefore the results are the bona fide research results of the faculty member. This argument assumes that the student performs only as an assistant to the faculty member, a situation rarely experienced, and certainly not in cases where the student submits his or her research as the pivotal graduate research consideration, for example as a doctoral dissertation. In the case of a thesis, in fact, the supervising faculty certifies that the research and analysis presented is the sole and original work of the candidate yet often soon thereafter claims coauthorship and credit. While not plagiaristic in the legal sense, this is certainly inconsistent.

In addition to attaching their name as coauthors to reports on research supervised by them yet performed by graduate students or researchers, faculty commonly base their own papers on the result of student research, with or without credit to the "original" researchers.

Other lapses of integrity, such as subtle or outright plagiarism, are on the rise as "publish or perish" continues at most American universities as the principal criterion in tenure and promotion decisions. Some faculty fill their résumés with papers authored jointly with graduate students and based largely on thesis work. This certainly presents less than a fair record of a supervisor's contribution.

Research is often performed jointly by faculty and students, and while all members of a research team should share credit for results, it is important for faculty to record the honest degree of their contribution in such cases. Even if academic rules are lax on this issue, intellectual honesty and personal integrity demand no less.

## Academic Fraud and the Self-Policing of Science

Dishonesty in scientific investigation and research is not new; to some degree it has always been with us. However, the new and disturbing aspect is that once discovered, such fraud (often in the form of plagiarism) is now not only tolerated or even covered up, but in many cases the discoverer of the fraud (the "whistle-blower") is penalized or otherwise discredited in order to protect the reputation of a government, academic, or research institution and/or the officials who have directly or indirectly supported the research. Two federal (NIH) researchers, Walter Stewart and Ned Feder, became well-known as the discoverers of scientific fraud. These men were leading participants in the investigation of work done by Harvard cardiologist John Darsee and of a paper by Nobel laureate David Baltimore (MIT) and Thereza Imanishi-Kari (Tufts) that was found to be forged. Stewart and Feder have been restrained from continuing their work by administrative action within the NIH.

Theirs is not an isolated case. Many who have dared to expose scientific fraud have been severely reprimanded by their own institution or by the institution whose name and reputation may be affected—which may be one and the same. Public image is too often valued over truth or integrity, and scientific and research institutions in government, industry, and academia have been known to go to extraordinary lengths to cover up scientific fraud or misconduct when such action may protect their reputation.

## Universities as Ego-Driven Institutions

American universities are increasingly driven by personal and institutional egos. The trend is for status and reputation to be the important measures of performance, not substance, quality of research, or educational standards. While many claim that the status and reputation of universities are earned by their commitment to research and education, there are signs that many institutions go to some length to achieve or maintain status and reputation by other than these stated means. In fact, many spend inordinate amounts of effort and money on status or image building, funds that would well be better employed in advancing research and education—this at a time when universities are criticized for financial mismanagement.

With the cost of a university education now increasing at more than twice the rate of inflation, there is a serious question as to whether they really deliver an education that justifies the expenditure of twice as much (in real terms) as only twenty years ago. In other words, today we spend twice the percentage of per capita income on a university education as we did in 1975. The question is: what are these additional funds used for? Faculty salaries at U.S. universities have barely kept pace with the rate of inflation, so we must look elsewhere for the inflated expenditures.

### Collegial Colleges

In theory, universities are scholarly institutions of learning and research where collegiality is encouraged. Yet in practice, they tend to foster cutthroat competition. While intellectual competition is obviously a desirable challenge, more often than not it forces interpersonal relations to deteriorate into personal conflicts, confrontations, and "dirty tricks" that undermine effective and collegial cooperation, fair exchange of ideas, a scholarly environment, and cooperative relationships conducive to good teaching and research.

While these conflicts may sometimes be the result of personality clashes or other differences, the problem is that university administrations seem to do little, if anything, to encourage greater intrafaculty cooperation. In fact, it often appears as though administrators may even encourage confrontational and divisive relations in order to "divide and conquer" the faculty and thereby gain greater power for the administration.

### Education Revisited

American university educational programs often try to cram information, knowledge, and techniques into students without teaching them intellectual initiative, thinking processes, or creativity. Similarly, the "real world" and its relationship to knowledge and methods are seldom covered effectively, primarily because few of the teachers or professors have experienced the real world with all its problems. For them, life therefore becomes a hypothetical environment that can be represented by an array of theories.

## Cost of Academic Administration

Academic institutions were once relatively efficient, with much, if not most, of the budget channeled into their primary function—teaching. The emergence of the research university substantially increased revenues for funded research to an extent where, in some cases, funded research income now far outweighs tuition and endowment incomes combined.

Even more startling is the vast increase in the cost of administration, due partly to the sharp increase in the number of high-salaried administrators. For example, the current number of administrators per faculty member in some institutions more than doubled during the preceding two decades (figure 8). Equally disturbing is the fact that over this same period, on average but more significantly, top salaries paid to university administrators increased at a rate substantially greater than that of the faculty. In the mid-1960s universities had only senior administrative titles such as Dean, Provost, Vice President, and President. Their number has now increased with new titles such as Deputy and Assistant Dean, Provost, and Vice President.

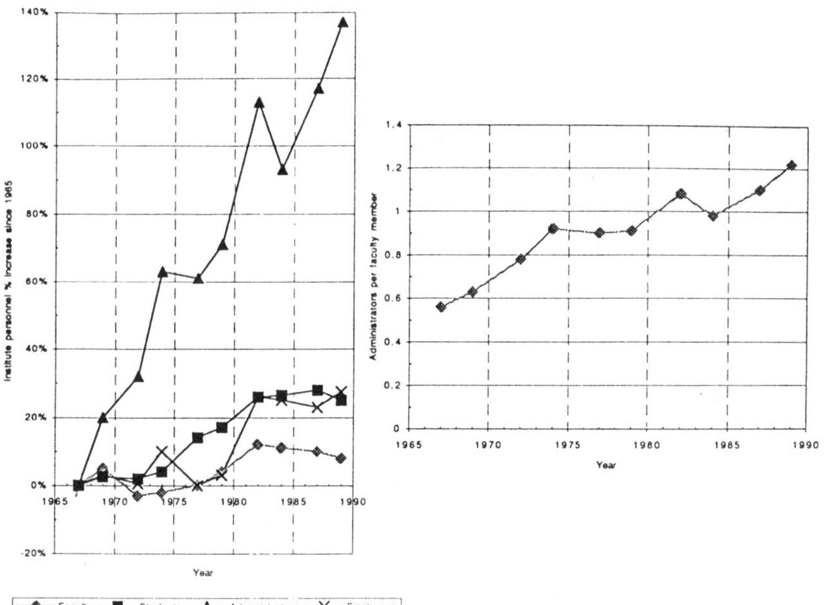


## Total On-Campus Employees

| | FY1969* | FY1974* | FY1979* | FY1984 | FY1989 |
|---|---|---|---|---|---|
| Faculty | 962 | 894 | 952 | 1,031 | 988 |
| Other Academic | 1,070 | 1,465 | 1,389 | 1,694 | 1,837 |
| Research | 814 | 869 | 799 | 1,019 | 1,011 |
| Medical | | | | 150 | 152 |
| Administrative | 622 | 841 | 884 | 1,000 | 1,217 |
| Support | 1,612 | 1,490 | 1,322 | 1,628 | 1,691 |
| Service | 1,323 | 1,100 | 1,029 | 1,193 | 1,019 |
| **Total** | **6,403** | **6,659** | **6,375** | **7,715** | **7,915** |

*Does not include part-time employees

Source: **MIT Factbook**; Prepared by the Planning Office, June 1990

All figures reprinted from The MIT Faculty Newsletter, Vol.III No.4, January/February 1991

FIGURE 8 - Typical University Administration

Considering salaries, we find similar distortions. Administrators now make several times as much as similar-rank faculty. The alarming irony is that the capital investment made to improve administrative efficiency can be shown to have failed to improve administration costs—this because economies in these investments tend to necessitate the hiring of additional personnel to maintain and operate the new technology, while the old system remains in place. This redundancy can be seen in accounting, personnel management, student registration, research project management, and more.

University administrators often claim the added burden of research administration to explain the new additions. In reality, though, research projects are invariably managed by the responsible faculty member, with central administration performing only simple contracting and accounting functions.

## The Academic Year in Major American Association of Universities (A.A.U.) U.S. Universities

American academic calendars have a comparatively small number of instruction days per year, which both lengthens the time students must attend an institution and results in gross underutilization of university resources. The days of instruction per year vary from a low of 118–23 (Harvard) to a high of 162–65 (University of Chicago). Excluding official holidays, there are 246 to 249 weekdays in a normal year. This means that some institutions use only half of the available weekdays for instruction.

Universities using a quarter system, such as the University of Chicago, actually achieve a higher number of instruction days, as their summer quarter is one month shorter than the summer semester of the majority of universities using a three-semester calendar.

Few schools use Saturday instruction on a regular basis, and in the majority of universities summer semesters or quarters are considered vacation period, when the bulk of students and faculty do not participate in formal instruction. At most, summer sessions are used for special programs and make-up classes, with the content of subjects falling well below that offered in the regular terms semesters or quarters). As a result, administration treats summer as a vacation period, and additional tuition is charged students who stay for the summer term.

Similarly, faculty salary is normally assumed to be remuneration for instruction, research, and academic administration during the nine months of "regular" term, with special pay offered for teaching or research carried out during the summer session. During this period the overhead of these institutions, obviously, continues, which adds disproportionately to operational expenses as facilities and administrative resources are being underutilized. This distortion has forced overhead and benefit costs at many U.S. universities to now exceed salaries for faculty and research staff and, for that matter, salaries of profit-making corporations.

These long breaks therefore add significantly to the costs of U.S. academic education and research. In fact, if a typical U.S. university were to increase its days of instruction to possibly 214 by treating summer terms as regular terms, the average cost of instruction covered by tuition and research would decline by nearly 26 percent. In addition, the average student could complete his or her program in 70 percent of the time (three instead of four years for a typical bachelor's degree program) and can then begin to contribute to the economy sooner and at a higher level. The total cost to the student for a bachelor's degree education could probably be lowered by more than 25 percent and graduates would contribute to the economy and tax revenue an additional year. Many countries in Europe, such as the United Kingdom, now offer three-year bachelor degree programs, without any perceivable effect on the quality of the education.

## The New Academic

I have often been struck by my faculty colleagues' lack of curiosity about the "real world," its problems and triumphs. They appear interested mainly in themselves and their narrow and usually abstract world. They care about little beyond this and are not curious to find out what ails the average being or what causes ills in today's society.

The world ends at the self-imposed bounds of their specific field of expertise. If the model or concept does not fit the world, then the world is to blame. If the solution or result does not resolve a problem, then the problem must be reshaped into something unreal that fits the solution.

Sure, we make scientific progress, but we do not really understand in what direction it will take us. Academics truly believe that they have the answers, but they do not usually know to what. They tend to behave as if problems are not their responsibility and, further, are too simplistic to be considered. In fact, *application-oriented* has become derogatory in academia.

University research has become largely an academic exercise performed for goals usually defined as the advancement of knowledge. This would be fine if we were able to define what constitutes knowledge—and therein lies the dilemma. What is knowledge is knowledge to one academic is to another simply an intellectual exercise to add life or depth of understanding to some theory.

Investigation is too often horizontal and not vertical, in which some phenomenon or method is considered from a new perspective. One can argue that this endeavor may add insight, but in most cases it merely demonstrates that the phenomenon can be explained or derived in yet one more way. Far too many fundamental research results contribute nothing to the advancement of mankind, to an improved quality of life, a cleaner environment, safer society, a more nutritious and abundant food supply or more effective distribution of essential needs to people worldwide.

They lack that unappreciated quality—application.

## The Role of the University in Research

U.S. Universities perform about 30 percent of the basic R & D and employ an equal percentage of the total number of U.S. scientists and engineers. Their role in research is perceived largely as that of basic science and technology developers who lay the scientific and sometimes also the technological base but who seldom get involved in the application or the technology or in making the technology work. Their relations with government, industry, and society have been tenuous in the past, because their role, function, and even working approach are not effectively understood. Universities have a culture of their own, distinct and unique, which has difficulty communicating with the rest of society not because they feel privileged, but because they view themselves as intellectually and morally superior.

As with health care and legal professionals, academics and, most important, academic administrators feel that their services to society are unique and must be judged by different norms, and that they must be allowed freedoms not otherwise acceptable, from self-regulation to self-supervision and the setting of standards. This perception of special status has been widely questioned in recent years, particularly by those who feel that universities have failed to effectively transfer technology and diffuse knowledge in a meaningful, effective way and therefore have failed in their obligation to contribute to the U.S. economy and society in solving "real-world" problems.

The conversion of the U.S. university from a place of learning, instruction in the arts and sciences, and diffusion of knowledge, whose objective was to improve the education and skill of citizens so that they could better serve and advance society, may have improved their science base but has not always satisfied their original objectives. In fact, the faculty of our major research universities, which not by chance comprise all major universities in the United States spend most of their time on research and graduate education, activities that too often degenerate into training research assistants and future academic researchers. As a result, U.S. universities have lost their ability to recognize and study real-world problems, but even more important, they are no longer able to apply knowledge in an effective manner.

This condition is now perpetuating itself, as universities inbreed generations of new faculty who see the university as their world and their life—a world unto itself and unconcerned with the realities and problems outside its walls. This convoluted situation has only a short history, as the universities led the computer revolution in the 1960s, following the earlier semiconductor and electronics revolution so well chronicled by Harvey Brooks[3] and others.

The brightest university graduates, particularly Ph.D.s, are now aggressively recruited by universities. This inbreeding obviously reduces communication between academia and industry, as fewer and fewer faculty spend time working professionally outside the university or are hired on the outside. Among those who do leave academia, many seek refuge in government laboratories.

As a result, industry has been forced to train their own researchers, particularly as their problem-oriented research was often berated by academics as too applicable to be intellectually challenging or pure. As a result, the gap has been widening, leaving a serious question as to whether U.S. universities are still on track in fulfilling their function and objectives or have become narrowly self-serving and highly academic institutions that are increasingly unaware of the outside world, its problems, and its needs.

## University Research by Foreigners in the United States

At a time when substantial research at U.S. universities was funded by the government, including significant funding by the Departments of Defense and Energy, foreign students could not participate if the research was deemed to be classified. In the last twenty or so years, U.S. research universities have not accepted classified research. In fact, many have maintained fully owned, yet separate, research facilities that can perform classified work, as these are not directly related to the main university teaching facilities. This arm's-length relationship provides the opportunity for foreign graduate students and faculty to work on classified programs.

At the same time, large percentage of open, on-campus research, funded by government, industry, foundations, or internally, attracts and supports foreign graduate students and researchers. As research becomes more commercially oriented and as even traditional defense-oriented laboratories redirect their research to make it more economically attractive by identifying and transferring commercial payoffs, open industrial research begins to address issues of product and process competitiveness. In fact, the issue is then no longer defense classification, but industrial or commercial propriety and competitive advantage. Here U.S. universities are at an unfortunate disadvantage because they have little experience in commercially valuable technology and their experience in working with commercial firms is very limited.

Unlike defense-related research, sensitive industrial research cannot readily be removed from campus by an arm's-length relationship, because it is much more integrated in the educational process, involves open relationships, and cannot legally be removed from campus under justification of national security.

Considering that over 38 percent of graduate students at U.S. research universities in "solid" subjects, such as science, engineering, and biology, are foreign nationals (mainly from Japan, China, and Korea), most of whom return to their home country (and former employer) on completion of their graduate degree, a major technology transfer is now under way. The effect of this outward flow of our technology is expected to grow as U.S. university research (including arm's-length labs) moves its focus to potentially commercial science and technology.

U.S. government and industry, on the other hand, are handicapped by the fact that government must transfer its funding to university research, while industry depends largely on these universities because of inadequacy of their own internal research facilities. Major U.S. industrial firms, except the electronics and pharmaceutical industries, do not usually support large in-house research facilities, relying instead on research carried out in university or government laboratories and funded by the government or private foundations.

Industrially funded research, particularly at universities, is still rare. Completely new relationships and methods of identifying, performing, and implementing or transferring research, as well as funding it, must be devised if we are to attain effective use of the U.S. research establishment in furthering American economic and commercial objectives and thereby competitiveness. This challenge addresses the difficult question of how to balance the traditional openness of U.S. academic institutions in admitting all qualified students, with the need to build up U.S. commercial competitiveness and its comparative advantage. Graduate research assistantships are now beginning to be funded by industry, government, and private agencies for the purpose of advancing U.S. scientific and technological competitiveness. Much of this support funding, however, is absorbed by foreign students (the percentage of foreign Ph.D. students in U.S. research universities is expected to top 50 percent by year 2000), meaning that the United States loses the professionals we have trained as well as the opportunity to apply the research results. U.S.-trained foreign researchers can and do transfer the technology developed to their home companies, particularly as foreign companies are usually very effective in applications development in both products and processes. They are also much more astute than we are at hiring competent graduates for positions where their training can be used immediately.

This paradox puts U.S. research universities in a bind. To attract industrial research funding, a U.S. university must demonstrate that its research contributes to U.S. competitiveness, and also that this research activity results in training a new and qualified cadre of U.S. scientists and technologists who can carry the knowledge forward. The U.S. research university may, as a result, face the difficult choice of restricting participation of foreign nationals in research of prospective competitive value or forgoing its major role as a contributor to U.S. industrial and economic revival.

As the worldwide economic competition heats up, U.S. universities will become a center of controversy not only because they employ large numbers of foreign researchers, but also because they themselves are often also recipients of some foreign grants and sometimes conduct research funded by foreign firms.

## Total Quality Management (TQM) in University Education

While many American universities are on the bandwagon of the Quality Revolution and now offer a proliferation of courses that deal with TQM and Quality Function Deployment, few have used quality management tools to evaluate themselves, to identify and implement required change, and to advance the quality and relevance of their programs and of education in general. While the TQM approach has proved successful in improving Japanese and more recently American corporate, and particularly manufacturing, performance, few service organizations or government agencies, and even fewer universities and schools, have applied these methods for self-improvement. True, they have given TQM enthusiastic verbal support and have developed many TQM examples for show, but successful application in academia is rare indeed.

It is recognized that university programs will have to change if they are to contribute or even to survive the challenges of the future. Universities, and schools in general, have assumed that their special needs and characteristics inhibit effective application of TQM methods. They have often claimed that the need for academic freedom, the lack of a clear customer definition and base, the lack of customer knowledge of their needs, and the lack of customer sophistication are unique to the environment in which educational institutions work. This, it is claimed, makes it difficult—if not impossible—to employ or apply TQM principles. If institutions admit the need for changes in programs and curriculum, then changes must be planned as concurrent efforts that permit the dovetailing of new and old programs.

## Technological Education

While the absolute number of students in U.S. institutions of higher education increased by 2.8 percent (.8 percent of the population), the number of students majoring in science and technology has actually decreased, in both absolute and relative terms. Fewer undergraduates study science and engineering, and a smaller percentage of graduate students than ever before now specialize in science and engineering. Furthermore, the percentage of foreign students who are studying science and engineering in the United States has grown substantially.

At some of our great research universities, such as MIT, foreign graduate students now comprise over 28 percent of the total and 38 percent of the doctoral-level students. If this trend continues, by the end of this century more than 50 percent of our doctoral degrees in science and engineering will be awarded to foreign nationals.

Considering that the most important nonmilitary basic research in the United States is done at universities and that a researcher can apply this knowledge anywhere, much of the research performed in the United States is invariably transferred abroad. This may not be a bad idea, considering that it was the foreign students who performed the research, especially if this is understood to be a reciprocal arrangement. But as it stands, few Americans do research at foreign institutions, and any other U.S. access to foreign research is highly restricted.

Furthermore, although the transferred technology may have been performed largely by foreign students, the basic research idea and approach were developed, or at least suggested, by a U.S. scientist or engineer. The result is significant knowledge and experience transfer, as well as the loss of U.S.–trained (and U.S.–financed) researchers to our foreign competitors.

As discussed earlier, the trend of U.S. students away from science and technology is driven by:

1. inadequate science and mathematics education at the high school level, which causes the bulk of U.S. college entrants to choose other educational programs;
2. lack of prestige, status, and reward offered to science and engineering professionals; and
3. an overemphasis of the role of the generalists in management, marketing, public relations, and communications, which discourages concentrations in science and engineering.

Students in science and engineering are perceived as "nerds"—strange, weird or incapable of dealing with the real world. This perception is often magnified by a lack of communication and interpersonal skills on the part of scientists and engineers whose education has been narrowly focused on their professional interests.

In a 1986 editorial in *Focus,* a journal of the Mathematics Association of a America, Prof. Morris Kline, a renowned mathematics educator (New York University, 1938–75) said: "On all level—primary, secondary, and undergraduate—mathematics is taught as an isolated subject with few, if any, ties to the real world." To the student, mathematics appears to deal almost exclusively with matter that is of no concern at all to mankind. "At the same time," Kline contended, "mathematics is the key to understanding and mastering our physical, social, and biological worlds."

Kline has also argued that useful applications should be stressed and should be used to present basic principles. Unfortunately, today this is true not only of mathematics but of many subjects in the engineering sciences. These disciplines are intended to lay the foundation for effective engineering, but instead they serve to turn young engineers away from solving real-world problems and encourage students to isolate themselves in a world of ideal assumptions and unrealistic theorizing.

Many of the problems now being addressed by engineering students and faculty do, in fact, have little practical relevance. This is due in part to the fact that an ever-increasing percentage of the engineering faculty has little, if any, real engineering experience, with a vast majority of new engineering faculty stepping directly from ethereal doctoral research to engineering faculty positions. Few have ever applied their work or experienced engineering problem-solving situations at the practical level.

Therefore, it is not surprising that graduating engineering students find it difficult to adjust to the industrial engineering environment and, as a result, often end up in organizations that are oriented toward research or technology development. This limiting situation has caused many sectors of U.S. industry to suffer under slow and ineffective transfer of technology at a time when rapid technology development is essential for competitiveness.

Engineering education, therefore, in my opinion shares a major part of the blame for the declining dominance of U.S industry. I consider it essential for engineering faculty, and for that matter management faculty also, to spend time in real-world engineering and management environments before assuming the lofty position of teaching unsuspecting students who believe that what they are learning in the classroom will make them competent problem solvers and engineers. Nothing is further from the truth. I propose that sabbatical leaves or other periodic intervals be used to get the faculty "wet" by exposing them to real-world engineering and problem solving. Only then will we be able to boast a true engineering (and management) faculty capable of training future professionals to make a real contribution to this nation's and the world's progress.

## Management Education

In recent years American management education in general and business schools in particular have been judged in terms of their real contribution to business and industry. The verdict is universally negative.

Business schools are found to be out of touch with real needs. They teach what they want and make the arrogant claims that they know what is good for business and industry, even when just a very small minority of business school faculty have ever functioned outside a business school and shouldered responsibility for real decisions. Few, if any, practical business skills are taught. The emphasis is on assertiveness, arrogance, and self-gain. Most techniques in which students are indoctrinated are untested theories or fancy models based on unrealistic assumptions. All this is done under the guise of sophistication.

While MBAs from U.S. business schools often acquire reasonable skills in various management techniques, the most successful are graduates who have concentrated largely on acquiring an ability for assertiveness and single-minded selfishness. They learn early that the game of successful management is played as a cutthroat competition which is not designed to further the objectives of the workers or those of the company or even the owners or shareholders. The personal goals of the manager become supreme, in this non-zero-sum game where most of the other players lose so that our student can win.

While cooperation is sometimes preached in the management ranks and in the executive suites, the training and goals of the U.S. manager allow operation to be no more than a convenient facade to be assumed if and only if it advances the individual's goals, themselves too often cloaked under the mantle of corporate or shareholder interests.

## Is There an Epidemic of Academic Fraud?

In recent years, academics in various fields have been accused of dishonesty, plagiarism, and fraud in their publications and research reports. It is possible that this phenomenon is not new and that ready access to and distribution of information have contributed to it; but many believe that these developments have been caused at least in part by the following conditions:

1. increased intensity in academic competition;
2. decline in academic congeniality and cooperation;
3. greater specialization and therefore fewer experts in any one field, particularly at one institution;
4. overall decline in ethical standards;
5. greater demand for academic research performance;
6. striving for status by academics, among themselves and in society; and
7. financial ambition: competition for lucrative consulting, industrial, and government jobs.

Questionable academic behavior takes many forms and is often more subtle and sophisticated than direct falsification or plagiarism. It often involves third parties and a variety of methods designed to cover the track of the perpetrator.

American universities emphasize research more than most and make research performance and the resulting publication the major criteria for faculty advancement and tenure. Of course teaching is paid lip service, but in reality it plays a small role in the career or advancement of a faculty member. In fact, excessive dedication and particularly effective teaching may win a few accolades but little, if any, recognition toward advancement. This is not just hypocritical but actually has a more sinister motive—the disempowerment of the faculty.

Burdened with the demands of research, faculty are inclined to leave decisions to the administration. Until today all but basic academic decisions, such as degree approvals, are made by the administration.

A public that contributes heavily to institutions of higher learning and research has a right to excellence in scholarship. This right extends to areas of research, freedom of expression, and use of information. In other words, faculty and other researchers should be free to pursue their intellectual interests without interference, so long as they maintain excellence in scholarship, freedom of exchange of information, and civility. Therefore, derogatory opinion or unpopular results of research should be able to be expressed and discussed so long as these and negative results are based on excellent scholarship and are presented in a fair, unbiased way.

## Financing American Education

While all developed countries subsidize education, including higher education, or finance it outright through the central government, the U.S. system of financial support is not only extremely inefficient and wasteful but is also to a large extent even counterproductive. The system relies on large-scale delegation of financial responsibility to local government and private institutions and sources. Consider post–high school education, for example. Financial aid, largely in the form of student loans, encourages abuse by schools and universities, misuse by students, profitable distortion of the tuition lending process to students by financial institutions, and inefficient use of educational opportunities.

The administration of the systems of financial support at the federal and local levels is generally incompetent and largely lacking controls which results in waste and lack of focus. The quality of higher education has generally declined, notwithstanding the isolated stellar performance of some universities. Most high-quality institutions excel in graduate education, which is largely self-financing, while most of the government support goes toward undergraduate education, where both quality and focus have steadily diminished.

The vast majority of U.S. college students enroll and undertake a college program with no particular professional or intellectual objective. The most common reasons students give for attending college are:

1. it is expected of them,
2. it is supposed to give them a better life,
3. it allows them to delay career decisions,
4. it permits them to defer working for a living, and
5. it is fun.

As a result, most enroll in liberal arts schools or in programs that allow them to defer the difficult and binding career decisions for four years, thus delaying their training for a career by the same amount of time. Most U.S. college students graduate from college with no real career skills. Undergraduate education has, in fact, become simply preprofessional education, such as premedical, prelaw, preengineenng, premanagement, or prescience, and college also functions as a general layover period for people who do not know what to do with their lives. It does not appear to occur to them that they will know as little about what they want to do with their lives after four years of college as before.

Federal aid for tuition is provided at over 8,500 colleges and schools. These include institutions from renowned nonprofit research universities to small for-profit trade schools. The only criteria for federal aid are a state license and accreditation by a private accreditation organization, both of which often require nothing more than completing application forms and paying a fee.

As in the case of health care, the cost of both private and public college and trade school education has grown at more than twice the rate of inflation. The federal student aid system has become a bureaucratic and organizational morass. Students deal with as many as six private financial intermediaries, many of which are subject to their own internal regulations. Similarly, there are numerous conflicts of interest as well as counterincentives in the system, which have cost the Department of Education billions. As a result, money available for new loans and grants has been reduced severely.

Much of the blame for this lies with the complexity of the federal financial aid system. More than 40 percent (or about 2.4 million of about 6 million) of all post–high school students received federal grants, loans, or both in fiscal 1992, at a cost to the taxpayer of $11 billion. More than half a million, 22 percent, of these students did not start to repay their debt as of 1995.

Students apply for loans through commercial lenders that in 1993 loaned about $18 billion in federally guaranteed student loans. Because of the 100 percent federal backing, lenders have little incentive to review credit or pursue defaults. The profit margin of lenders is attractive and risk-free. To increase funds, lenders will often sell loans to secondary markets, which now hold 52 percent of the $57 billion outstanding. Loans are normally administered by loan-servicing companies that deal mostly with secondary lenders.

Lenders, secondary lenders, and loan-servicing companies are audited and controlled by forty-six so-called nonprofit policing institutions, which then report back to the government. These guarantee agencies have no responsibility and are reimbursed by the government for any shortfall in collection on their lenders' bad loans.

In other words, a huge bureaucracy of private, largely profit-making institutions constitutes the student grant and loan programs. There is no incentive to assure quality in lending. In fact, the more loans are made, including bad loans, the larger the profits of the direct and secondary lenders and the more jobs are generated for guarantee agencies. The whole system is counterincentive and largely out of control.

There is much fraud and abuse in the system: students without valid high school diplomas are admitted; there is often conflict of interest in accreditation based on membership fees and not on quality; there is inflation of school attendance, times, and charges; and courses not taken by students are added to transcripts, grades inflated, illegal middlemen involved, and commissions and charges falsified. There is fabrication by both lenders and guarantee agencies.

The taxpayer pays the bill and students too often end up with no improvements in skill and a large student loan debt on which they will default. In 1991 alone, the federal government paid $6.1 billion to financial institutions for defaulted student loans.

The highest default rate is seen in loans to students of for-profit vocational schools (41 percent) and least for students of four-year private and public colleges (7 percent). There appears to be a negative correlation between the usefulness of the education or training and the default rate.

Stricter control or radical change in the student grant and aid programs is urgently required not only to save taxpayers money but also to improve the training of young Americans sorely needed to serve the increasingly technical demands of workplaces in the American economy and thereby nourish America's economic growth. Programs should be approved or even accredited by companies offering jobs to prospective graduates; the current system should be replaced with one that involves only a government lending agency and the school or university, with potential employers certifying that the course of study truly leads to the type of job that the student is preparing for.

Financing of state and public institutions of higher or post–high school learning is determined by the annual education budget of each state, which is, in turn, affected by who is in power, political priorities, and the economic conditions of the state. State educational budgets do not usually receive the priority they reasonably deserve, and budgets for state university and other post–high school education suffer under the new onslaught by local authorities who are trying to transfer primary and secondary educational costs from the local to the state level.

This transfer of funds affects the amount of state funding available for higher education. In most states, funding has not kept pace with inflation and increased enrollments, and at this time of diminishing funding there is increased pressure for these institutions to develop new programs in areas such as environmental engineering and policy.

As a result, financing state institutions of higher learning will become even more difficult in the future. This may lead to increases in tuition and fees, particularly for out-of-state and foreign students. Private institutions of higher learning finance their cost by means of:

1. tuition income,
2. funded research and research overhead,
3. fees,
4. donations, contributions, or other sponsorship from private or corporate donors, and
5. income from investment.

With rapidly increasing costs and declining income, particularly federally funded research income, universities have in recent years begun to generate added income from sources such as:

1. licensing of technology,
2. executive and professional education,
3. technology consultation fees,
4. consortia-funded research,
5. industry-funded research, and
6. foreign government–and industry-funded research.

This new approach works for large universities with extensive laboratories and/or for renowned professional schools but is difficult for a small school to implement. As a result, many smaller, particularly private, liberal arts universities may find it difficult to manage financially and become increasingly dependent on tuition income, a dependency that may necessitate lowering their admission standards.

Primary and secondary education is funded mainly by local communities. As a result, per pupil budgets vary widely not only throughout the country but also in any given region. In some states or even counties, the school budget per pupil can differ by more than a factor of two and, as a result, the quality of education varies widely. Although differences in quality of education are not solely a function of the budget per pupil, funding obviously plays a major role. Other factors are local priorities, requirements, and the local sociopolitical environment.

## University Executives' Pay

According to a survey by the *Chronicle of Higher Education* (September 1994), in 1992/93 eight university CEOs were paid more than $400,000, ten between $300,000 and $400,000, sixty-seven between $200,000 and $300,000 and sixty-two between $175,000 and $200,000. The pay of the university CEO seems to be completely unrelated to the status or size of the university or to its performance in either financial or academic terms. For example, the president of Boston University received $737,963 in 1992/93, nearly three times the compensation for the president of Harvard ($227,544 plus $37,039 benefits). Similarly, the president of tiny Wellesley College was paid nearly twice as much as the president of Harvard University in 1993. Recently (*Boston Globe,* February 18, 1997), Adelphi University's new board of trustees fired its president for failing to meet his responsibilities, yet he was paid $837,000 in salary and benefits in 1995, notwithstanding falling enrollment and rising tuition.

The pay of senior executives of many American universities has increased to levels where at many the pay of vice presidents, provosts, and other executives is now a multiple of the average pay of a tenured full professor at the same institution. At the same time, the number of senior executives has increased at most American institutions of higher learning, as mentioned before. This means that not only has the cost of administration increased in relation to the cost of teaching and research, but the proportion of executive pay as a function of administrative costs has also at a time when most American universities are in financial trouble escalated—all this at a time when most American universities are in financial trouble and many actually show significant operating deficits.

Many universities are now increasing teaching loads, reducing teaching and research staff, and increasing administrative expenses. This approach is exactly the opposite of what business schools at the same institutions teach industry in their TQM, strategic management and productivity courses.

The trend is particularly disturbing, as it is an important factor contributing to the rise in tuition far in excess of the rate of inflation. These institutions are also tax-exempt and use tax-exempt contributions to make up for shortfalls in tuition and other receipts, as well as for facility expansion and other expenditures, at a large added cost to the economy.

## The Role of Universities in the Advancement of Technology and Knowledge

The major inventions that led to the Industrial Revolution were not introduced by university researchers but by people engaged in manufacturing. James Watt, George Stephenson, and J. Brunel were engineers and tinkerers whose primary interest was in solving a problem, not advancing knowledge or explaining phenomena.

Scientific discoveries achieved at universities often generate ideas or advance technology but are seldom oriented toward problem solving, and many such discoveries contribute nothing to new technologies.

Many see the role of universities only as one of engaging in intellectual discourse and academic endeavors, with no particular problem focus. The goal of knowledge, as seen by the university researcher, is to explain phenomena or intellectual concepts—to develop ideas, not to solve real or perceived problems. If a solution happens to emerge, the academic researcher typically defines it in abstract, intellectual terms and not in practical terms.

This Western perception of the role of the university has been partially adopted by Oriental cultures as well as by universities in developing countries. Yet there is a question as to whether this role serves the wider purpose of higher learning, particularly for developing countries but also in countries with an intellectual, social, and cultural heritage distinctly different from that of the West.

Countries abound where both religion and education play very different roles than in Western culture, where both are closely tied to ancient moral teachings, and societal objectives. In fact, there is a question if the role of the university is primarily that of a research institution charged with advancing knowledge, in an absence of social concern or responsibility for the ultimate use to which this knowledge may be put. The more traditional concept of the university is that of a center of learning—learning not only about the knowledge developed by mankind throughout history in all areas of human concern but also about ourselves as individuals and as members of groups.

The early centers of learning that later grew into universities as we now know them were placed where experienced, thoughtful, and learned people attempted to explain natural, physical, chemical, biological, and social phenomena so as to use or cope with these happenings. The ultimate objective of learning was more effective understanding and thereby use of the phenomena by enhancing or reducing/neutralizing its impact. Knowledge was used for such advances as improved navigation or growing more and better food. The attempt, particularly by early Chinese and Greek teachers, scientists, and philosophers, was to make *use* of the results, to teach skills and knowledge that could improve life and being.

It is only in recent years that the advance of scientific knowledge and the development of technology have become discrete endeavors, a Western phenomenon that applies to science, engineering, medicine, and even the social sciences. For various reasons, universities—and particularly research universities—have largely disassociated themselves from the practical or useful application of the advances that they themselves bring about. Reasons include the following mutually inclusive reasons:

- academic isolation,
- academic snobbishness,
- inbreeding in universities, and
- fear of liability.

Learning, creation of knowledge, use of knowledge for the solution of problems or development of new products and processes, and ultimately the use and perfection of these discoveries were the original continuous and integrated function of places of learning. We have gone far in our distortion of these original ideals and goals. It is important for American universities to regain their link with real-world problems and issues and to reestablish an ability to advance knowledge and learning in the interest of mankind and not just in the interest of narrowly defined knowledge, much of it developed for its own sake. This change will require not only a more open approach to scientific learning and research but also an interest in the needs, weaknesses, hopes, and desires of people. We all ultimately strive to improve the quality of life, not merely for shallow self-satisfaction. To accomplish this, we may also have to involve teachers, researchers, and faculty more in real day-to-day problems and not isolate them in ivory towers.

## Educational Direction

Education must keep pace with the need for knowledge. Human knowledge increases incrementally, making learned knowledge and the resulting expertise rapidly obsolete. As a result, education—to be relevant throughout a lifetime—must be a continuous process; learning and knowledge must be updated at least periodically. On-the-job training and learning by doing, while important, are no longer sufficient as science and technology advance.

Society is changing in pace with technology, and the world is becoming a truly global village in which intersocietal and interpersonal relationships play an increasingly important role. Insular behavior—isolationism—is no longer possible on either a local or national level, as we become socially interdependent and as our resources and space diminish in a constantly shrinking global environment.

In the future, education must equip people to communicate, to live effective, orderly, and healthy lives, and to attain social and professional skills and must also assume the responsibility of maintaining, upgrading, and renewing knowledge and influencing social behavior in line with the changing society.

In other words, although we as individuals may increasingly have to specialize in order to gain in-depth competence in our field, we must also address problems from a multidisciplinary point of view, assure that solutions are not isolated and narrow, and consider all the important issues that make our answers true solutions.

Life must become a constant learning experience, and opportunities will have to be provided for all people to continue their learning. New technology provides both the challenge and opportunity for this.

## Education Performance in Primary and Secondary Schools

Public schools in the United States must become more accountable. Their administration should be rewarded by a system of rewards based on success and not by high salaries and benefits unrelated to performance. Consider measures such as increased percentages of graduates admitted to quality post–high school institutions of learning or improved levels of SAT scores, as well as delayed benefits such as increased income of graduates five or ten years after graduation. Similar criteria should also be applied to salaries of teachers, as well as to the total teaching budget, which influences the number of teaching positions available in any particular school system.

IBM's chairman and CEO Louis V. Gerstner, Jr., recently published a book titled *Reinventing Education,* in which he suggests that public school educators think like entrepreneurs, with innovation as the principal method used to reclaim the U.S. system of public educational institutions. This concept could be carried further to encourage students to also think like knowledge entrepreneurs.

There are many ways in which schools can improve, but the first step is to raise the performance level of the poorest students. The question usually raised is: where will the money come from to finance such developments? The answer is to sacrifice special skill education (such as musical instruments, etc.), which benefit only a select few and usually gifted students who enjoy parental support. These skills can easily be acquired outside of the public school system.

Decision-making powers on issues that deal with teaching and curriculum must be returned to the teachers and to the classroom. Effective feedback from students should be used to test the impact of new approaches on teaching, directly in the classroom and not just by abstract studies or theories. Students should be involved in decisions on teaching. Teaching should convey knowledge, instill skills, inspire a love of learning, induce effective social and cooperative behavior, and develop interpersonal and communications skills, and most important, teaching should develop social responsibility and a desire to contribute to society.

Schools, particularly in America, are now called upon to perform responsibilities assumed previously by parents. To accomplish this, schools must be permitted the accompanying freedom to enforce discipline and demand greater parental cooperation and must be freed from unwarranted interference by politicians, parents, and legal practitioners. Teachers cannot be given responsibility without power. They cannot be asked to act on behalf of parents without being given the same rights to discipline or even punish children under their tutelage, without fear of legal or other reprisal. We are now asking teachers to perform an impossible task.

We must eliminate lawlessness and antisocial behavior from the classroom, with severe punishment for those who interfere with the orderly conduct of schooling and not just a slap on the wrist but effective disincentives such as mandatory dismissal or even dispatch to boot camp. Similarly, parents who do not assume their parental responsibilities should first be instructed on how to perform these. If this does not work and it becomes evident that the parent is only using a child for selfish purposes, parental rights or economic benefits, should be gradually withdrawn. Parenting cannot be rewarded by payoff for itself. The payoff must be part of a contract that includes long-term social responsibility. If a parent is unwilling to assume his or her social responsibility, the economic reward of parenting and the right of control over the child must reasonably be revoked.

Many now see our welfare support as a system to encourage procreation as a means of income. In other words, production of otherwise-unwanted children has come to be seen as a method of economic support by many poor women who look upon childbearing less as family-building than as income-producing. The child then simply becomes a necessary burden. Most of these women are unprepared for motherhood and are often unable and unwilling to assume the related responsibilities. Schools must then assume many of the duties of parenthood when parents—particularly young single parents—do not. For example, so-called latchkey children should be required to stay after school to do their homework under school supervision because they have no one at home to encourage them to do their homework and consequently they ignore their assignments. Otherwise, the academic performance of these students will be a reflection of their home environment and not of their ability. In turn, part of the child support payments should go to the school to underwrite this supervision.

In other words, parents who take no interest in their children's schooling should forfeit their right to influence their children's education. Parental involvement should be natural, but unfortunately many "economic" parents—parents who produce children for the economic benefit—have no interest in their children's education. Adult education in parenting and responsibility must go hand in hand with economic support. If such a single parent does not respond and/or refuses to actively support the child and his or her school, the role of such a parent must be legally ignored and the school given the right to act in the child's best interest, including keeping the child in school after hours to do homework.

In addition, the educational performance of our primary and secondary schools must be brought up to world standards. This will be possible only if

1. national educational standards are established and enforced;
2. students are not allowed to advance without proof of adequate performance;
3. school budgets are equalized by cross-subsidization;
4. teachers are given control of the classroom;
5. educationally and family-disadvantaged students are put under the "family" care of the school and required to do their homework at school or under supervision;
6. emphasis is put on basic education and development of social, communication, and interpersonal skills to assure well-roundedness on graduation, with opportunities provided to gifted students to advance in special fields such as mathematics, science, and language;
7. the school year is extended to contact hours or school days equal to the number proven optimal by the educationally most successful countries, which usually have 40 percent more school hours per year than we do in the United States;
8. effective incentives are provided to teachers, with promotion and rewards tied to successful student performance; and
9. effective incentives are provided to students, with rewards and scholarships tied to both academic performance and social behavior as well to proven responsibility.

Unless the management and financing of primary education in America becomes more performance-oriented, we will continue to spend more than any other country on what is a failing primary and secondary educational system and its consequences. Basic education has become the most important factor of economic growth, growth of personal income, and improvement in the standard of living.

In the past, we have tried to solve this problem simply by putting more money into it. This solution has proven as ineffective as it is expensive, and a complete reevaluation of our basic educational system is now urgent. Higher levels of technology require a better-educated workforce to make technology truly contribute to economic growth and social well-being. Without it, we cannot take advantage of what advanced technology has to offer.

## Continuing Education and Workforce Training

The rapid advances that we see taking place in process and service technology are aimed at reduced unit production costs, larger-scale operation and resulting economies of scale, production of new products, improved product quality and introduction of difficult, novel products and services.

In parallel, the management and structure of manufacturing and service organizations are being changed to improve the quality and responsiveness of decision making. Manufacturing and services now respond to changing real-time demand instead of producing output according to a projected schedule to meet a hypothetically forecasted demand. This has led to authority being delegated to the level at which the information for decision resides and a resulting flattening of organizational or decision-making structures. It has also meant the adoption of new management techniques, such as Just-In-Time (JIT) and TQM, which make the processes more continuous and eliminate buffer stocks of raw materials and supply inventories. At the same time, processes are being automated; for example, the number of robots being used in U.S. manufacturing is now doubling every three to four years.

These developments have had major impact on work content and skill requirements. Fewer jobs are physical now, and more require specialized skills. In other words, both manufacturing and service industries in the United States are rapidly changing from being primarily labor- or muscle-based to being knowledge-based. As a result, training, knowledge, and intellect are now the more important requirements in industry. Workers need new skills to participate in this revolution, and those who do not acquire new qualifications may either slide in their job or actually lose it and ultimately become obsolete and thus unemployable.

These new qualifications are more necessary as responsibilities at the workplace become more technical, and the necessity applies equally to the manufacturing machine operator and to the office worker. To maintain a competent workforce requires the development and ready availability of training programs that prepare workers in the use of new production and service technology as well as in new techniques for workplace management. These new techniques might include statistical methods for TQM and effective control and management of JIT production flow.

The average educational and knowledge base of the American worker in manufacturing and service workplace is low compared to that in Japan. Few receive updated training after joining the workforce. The training and retraining of workers must be a continuous process, because technology continues to change. Worker training must become part of company strategy and become an essential, continuing investment. Technology investment without investment in worker training has proven to be less than effective.

Unfortunately, for many American companies worker training, particularly retraining, remains a low priority, partially because of the assumption that training/retraining and commitment to long-term employment go hand-in-hand. However, most American companies, accustomed to short-term optimization, have difficulty accepting the concept of long-term commitment on either side. There is, however, no alternative. To remain competitive we must adopt new technology, which in turn requires the training and the retraining of workers. The Japanese have made worker training an integral part of their management strategy. Most workers receive training at least once a year to upgrade or augment their skills. This is in addition to a strong educational foundation. Company-sponsored training may be on or off the job. It not only advances worker skills but also improves communication and collaboration among workers. As a result, Japanese companies have become much better in introducing new technology, including American technology, in terms of both time to effective use and improvement achieved by its use.

In general, worker training and retraining are not well developed in the United States. Even among large corporations, few have effective in-house or on-the-job training programs, and public or commercial training or continuing education programs are often insufficiently designed to meet the needs of the workers.

In the past, workers advanced largely on the basis of experience regardless of their level of education or training. This is no longer the case. In recent years the average real wage for workers in lower skilled areas actually fell, independent of cm experience. Wages are increasingly tied to usable skills—not to experience or even education.

Although many states and even local governments run vocational schools and community colleges, the bulk of such training is provided by private, usually profit-making, trade schools, many of which are not effectively monitored and their admissions, curriculum, and certificate award standards not regulated. There is an urgent need to set uniform, I hope national, standards for vocational and skill training and to require government licensing of training institutions. Industry has become a major user of educational establishments, and the quality of the training offered significantly affects its success and that of our economy at large.

## The Education of American Doctors

Most medical schools are now oriented toward high-tech medicine and medical research, much of which addresses rare and complex diseases. Even the smaller medical schools and teaching hospitals emulate this trend. As a result, most medical students are encouraged or even driven to take up a specialized field of medicine. It goes without saying that economic incentives influence this decision, because medical specialists in general earn double what general practitioners do.

There appears to be indirect pressure on young doctors not to opt for primary care, despite the fact that primary care physicians provide the necessary link between patients and specialists. In the United States, primary care doctors number fewer than 20 percent of all licensed doctors, and their average age is significantly higher than the overall average. Fewer than 23 percent of graduates now choose primary care medicine, a percentage that is projected to fall by the end of this century and will equal only half the percentage of primary care physicians in countries such as Canada, Germany, or France and about one-third of that in Britain.

As practiced in the United States, medical education ignores or downplays the basic premise of the medical calling: patient care, considered by many practitioners to be a waste of medical education and unworthy of the time of a trained doctor. Yet, the caring for the patient and patient care are really what make the practice of medicine a profession and what justifies its public support. While defining new cures or developing medications for obscure or not-so-obscure ailments is important, we certainly do not need three-quarters of our physicians to practice specialized medicine or medical research, leaving the care of the population to the few remaining. Most illnesses require general care, not only for their physical or biological aspect, but also for their accompanying fears and concerns. In this age of AIDS and other contagious diseases, people must have the opportunity to consult with primary care doctors regularly and not just doctors in an emergency or when they are ill. However, most Americans do not have a personal physician, and doctors have become, to most patients, simply referrals.

Medical education in the United States is largely at fault for this situation, as it puts little emphasis on personalized patient care or the doctor's attitude. It concentrates on teaching medical science and medical technology, while ignoring medical practice and the role of the doctor. It requires medical students to memorize details that are easily and more effectively retrieved by a computerized system. At the same time, medical students spend less and less time on the diagnosis of common or "medically uninteresting" problems. While they learn the intricacies of heart or liver transplants, for which a few thousand patients qualify every year, few learn how to deal effectively with lower back or knee problems, from which tens of millions suffer. We are simply told to take Motrin because there is really no cure for back or knee pain. When I was told this by several American orthopedic surgeons, I consulted a Chinese doctor about acupuncture therapy, which was remarkably successful after just a few applications. Yet I was ridiculed by my physician when I reported my success to him.

The human anatomy is complex, and its workings are affected by its physical, mental, biological, and nervous systems. Today medical education has become too technical, dealing primarily with physical and biological issues while ignoring the patient's mental, nervous, nutritional, and social needs which affect his well-being as much as physical and biological factors affect them. Few doctors are either trained in or concerned with these issues.

We talk of a superior American medical system. As suggested before, the system is superior for those who have a rare disease or ailment, require a transplant or high-tech medical services and qualify for admission to an accredited facility, and are covered to receive treatment. For the 99 percent of basic medical problems that we all face daily, the lack of adequate primary care, home visits, and family doctors makes the average American worse off than patients in less technologically advanced countries, where most doctors are trained to treat patients as individuals.

An important issue in medical education is the vast difference in standards not only of medical schools and programs, but also of state licensing board examinations. Worst of all is the fact that in addition to the American Board of Medical Specialists (ABMS), there are now over 126 unofficial or self-designated certification boards that use no definable standards. This means that any doctor or professed medical professional can become a board-licensed specialist. Similarly, medical schools abound but vary widely in terms of quality. Great pressure is now being exerted to permit the use of and offer training in alternative medicine. But this is being resisted by the medical establishment.

## Engineering Education

As with medicine and law, engineering education in the United States has become highly focused or specialized and, in many cases, is better described as an "engineering science" education. More students are trained as engineering researchers than as engineering systems designers, problem solvers, and decision makers. In fact, few graduating engineers are actually capable of assuming engineering responsibilities. This opens up the question of what constitutes a professional engineer and what competence should be required of the engineers of the future.

The public perception of engineering is that of problem solving. As a result, it is now common to talk about engineering or reengineering of corporations, universities, plants, or other entities and of solving social, economic, operational, and managerial problems by reengineering. In other words, while society assumes that engineering can resolve broad problems and addresses not only technological but also social and economic problems, engineers perceive themselves as narrowly focused technical and scientific specialists who, given a defined problem, can address it analytically; the problem is that they often do not know how to identify a problem or apply their solution. It is because of this failure that few engineers in the United States attain positions of leadership in industry or government.

Engineering is about doing things better, cheaper, and more reliably. Yet few engineers are able to show that their solution achieves these goals. When engineers lack confidence, as a result leadership, technical, and technological decisions that are actually engineering decisions are made by those who lack the necessary knowledge and experience.

Engineers are usually not taught, nor do they acquire, basic characteristics of leadership, such as a sense of priority, conviction, and an ability to convince others. They often have difficulty convincing even themselves. Most important, current engineering curricula are narrowly focused, which does not offer students the opportunity to develop a broad vision, a prerequisite not only for focusing one's own direction but also for creating believers in the cause.

Engineers are trained to analyze and solve problems that have been set or identified by others. The blame for the present failure of engineering education probably lies in part with the heavy emphasis on science, which was introduced in the sixties as an effort to catch up with *Sputnik* and which remains as an artifact. The space race is no longer our problem. Today's challenges, however mundane, are still exciting. They deal with applying technological and scientific discoveries to real-world problems and with productivity, quality, environmental impact, and social benefit. Although technological and scientific advances remain our major goals, they must now be achieved within this new framework.

This means that engineering education must include practical and team engineering, as well as problem solving where the best solution is not just a good engineering solution but one that properly weighs benefits to quality, economics, usability, reliability, and the environment. There is a critical need to broaden engineering education by more than a perfunctory requirement for a few humanities courses, to develop a well-rounded engineer who can lead, make decisions, and identify and solve problems.

Engineers must be subjected to a thorough cross-disciplinary education, specifically including training in engineering management and leadership, with a service, product, and process orientation. The curriculum should include interdisciplinary networking, team building, and project management, training that will equip graduates to address real and relevant problems.

Case studies of real engineering design and application should be included. Any engineering education is not complete without practical experience, perhaps even as an intern or an apprentice, which is a serious requirement in legal and medical curricula.

This new perspective may require a change in the method and delivery of engineering education. Mathematics, for example, should be taught to engineers as applied to engineering, not just as dry mathematics looking for a problem.

Engineering faculty should be encouraged, if not mandated, to spend sabbaticals not by simply extending their current, narrowly focused teaching and research at another institution or simply taking a rest, but in engineering for industry, applied consulting, or in government, in the identification and solution of real-world engineering problems. Only then will they be able to educate engineers, instead of just training new research assistants in a narrowly focused field.

Some argue that such an approach would impede engineering or technological advancement. What it may do is reduce technological advances that do not address real problems and will never be used. Too many real problems remain unaddressed to devote the present inordinate efforts to solving problems that do not exist in the real world.

Engineering education now suffers under a real credibility gap, with engineers not being trained to perform what society expects. In part this is due to a lack of feedback from employers, to unresponsiveness to students, and—bluntly put—simply to academic arrogance. Universities behave as if they know what students and society, need, but this "knowledge" is often a priori, faulty, or obsolete.

Society responds by devaluing engineers and engineering. Engineers are often blamed, directly or indirectly, for our environmental, economic, communications, health care, and other problems.

Another important gap in engineering education is the lack of a global perspective. Few engineering schools offer an effective program in project management, team engineering, or multinational engineering, notwithstanding the fact that the field increasingly involves global product, process, or infrastructure development. Few important engineering projects are restricted to a single country. Engineers must become more international if they are to be effective in the new marketplace, not just in engineering consulting and services but also in industrial product and process design. Also, the licensing of engineers is a rather curious process. In most states engineers can obtain professional licenses without attending engineering schools, by just passing an examination and proving experience.

## Educating Lawyers

Legal education is probably the most diverse. Law schools abound and vary from elite Ivy League law schools, such as Harvard, Yale, Chicago, and so forth, to small public and private schools, as well as license mills, which prepare students for bar examinations. Similarly, bar examinations not only vary widely but often do not require proof of attendance at a law school.

While most licensed lawyers attended accredited law school and often also served a clerkship to gain experience under the supervision of an experienced judge or lawyer, there are many who practice law with little formal education. There is an urgent need to set statewide and possibly national standards for legal education, experience, and licensing to protect the public.

## Performance of U.S. Higher Education

American higher education is offered by an array of public and private colleges and universities, community colleges, vocational and trade schools, and numerous organizations that offer professional courses or programs.

Universities and colleges vary, from public and private world-class research universities to for-profit colleges whose standards for admission and graduation are sometimes dubious. The same applies to two-year community colleges and vocational schools, some of which have very high standards while others are essentially a sham. As a result, it is practically impossible to judge or evaluate the performance of U.S. higher education, because it presents such a wide spectrum.

Although most U.S. private universities are nonprofit, many actually function as a corporation with a board of trustees or directors, which are usually appointed by the school's administration. As a result, university administrations leave themselves open to accusations of being inbred, self-serving, and self-perpetuating.

Many have also become inefficient and wasteful, with costs escalating at a rate of more than twice that of inflation. In fact, tuition and fees for four-years of college have risen from less than $17,000, $33,000 and $42,000 at public, private, and Ivy League colleges in 1975 to $53,300, $104,600, and $131,000 in 1996. They are expected to reach $176,800, $348,600, and $438,000 by year 2014. By and large, higher education is not market-driven and few efforts are made to match academic and societal needs to assure relevance of the education offered. This lack is magnified by the existing reward structure and by peer pressures that encourage research over teaching and publishing over real problem solving, even if the article or paper is only read by a few, if any, and has no relevance to society or even knowledge creation.

American research universities have been slow to recognize that the theoretical research markets are shrinking while the demand for practical solutions is rapidly growing as we face up to a myriad of new problems. At the same time, research or courses that address real-world problems are not respected but discouraged.

In general, U.S. education and the method of grading, particularly at the graduate level discourage teamwork except in case studies. On the contrary, they encourage competition. However, in the real world effective teamwork is essential, particularly in management, engineering, and medicine. There are indications that a major reason for the relative decline in U.S. competitiveness has been lack of teamworking skills on the part of American graduates who are neither encouraged nor taught such skills in our educational programs.

Similarly, most college courses are not aimed at developing professional skills, practical applications, or real-world problem solving, largely because most college teachers have never experienced the outside world and would not recognize a real-world problem if it hit them between the eyes. The percentage of college teachers who have advanced from graduate study to a faculty position without ever holding a nonacademic job is much larger in the United States than in most countries. This type of inbreeding may be attractive inasmuch as it provides a continuous progression, but it assures an increasing lack of understanding of real-world problems and needs. It further results in a decline of appreciation of the role of education in providing new competent cadres of intellectuals and professionals who can advance the interests of the American society, the nation, its economy, and the world.

Increasingly the value of a college education for anyone but professional doctors, lawyers, engineers, and accountants is being challenged. Furthermore, the way we educate professionals is being more and more scrutinized. In particular, the value of narrow specialization in the professions and the decline of depth in general professional education have resulted in fewer professionals who are able to serve the general needs of society. We have fewer and fewer general practitioners in medicine and engineering and, as a result, are less able to meet the basic professional needs of society in health care, legal services, and engineering.

Our university educational system has degenerated to a point of providing highly specialized professional education at one end of the spectrum and impractical general studies at the other. In general, we train neither well-educated people in the classical sense nor effective professionals who can serve the needs of the broader society.

Liberal arts and related education often lack depth and devote more attention to making students feel good about themselves than to intellectual challenges. On the professional education side, narrow specialization is encouraged because it satisfies faculty interest, but also because it offers potentially greater economic reward.

In this process, though, society is required to pay, directly or indirectly, for years of dilettantism or professional/economic ambitions, neither of which addresses the real needs of American society.

The cost of providing a college education to over 60 percent of our high school graduates is enormous, yet most will never become professionals in the true sense. The true economic cost of this must include loss of work output during those years. In reality, instead of entering the labor market after one or two years of skill training, these people squander tens of billions of dollars of public and private money, largely to defer career decisions and delay entering the real job market. Considering the chaos that is the job search process of liberal arts graduates, it is questionable that four years of college education prepares these graduates to better cope with reality or to get on with lives.

At the other extreme, we find the focused professional graduates who attend two to five years of graduate school and then specialize. As a result, we produce too few general medical practitioners, general legal counselors, engineers, financial experts, and managers and too many medical specialists, corporate lawyers, and others practicing in narrow but highly lucrative fields.

The result is that the needs of the public are not met by professionals. It is clear that our society cannot afford a state in which professional services are available to serve only specialized needs and where we squander valuable time and money on pampering students who want to remain in school, unwilling to face the world.

In many other industrialized nations, professional education starts immediately on entering college for both basic and advanced professional skills such as law, medicine, and engineering and is not delayed to graduate study. If we are to regain our competitiveness, we may have to advance our educational process and reduce or eliminate the two-to-four-year delay.

Many American universities, like our hospitals, invest in prestigious equipment and facilities, the need for which is seldom proven. Few universities, even when located in close proximity, share major equipment and facilities or, for that matter, faculty and services, even when each cannot justify such by themselves.

Universities urgently need to increase their focus on the needs of the professions. While a purely theoretic approach may be fine for an education in philosophy or literature, areas concerned with the direct needs of society, such as law, medicine, engineering, social science, and architecture, often require a more problem-oriented approach.

There is a regrettable lack of prestige and status of nondegree professional qualifications such as those offered by vocational schools and two-year colleges, as well as of various professional programs. People vaguely assume that a college degree is the door to success, even though facts often prove otherwise.

We must reestablish the value and status of nondegree professional qualifications and thereby provide the incentives to high school graduates, people who are not qualified for or interested in higher education and professional or science callings, to guide them to concentrate on gaining job skills without wasting four years with general pampering that improves neither their employment opportunities nor job effectiveness and does not necessarily add to their education or maturity.

I do not advocate large-scale elimination of liberal arts colleges but a refocusing by these schools toward skill-enhancing and fundamental educational programs. Too much time and effort is spent on making students "feel good," with self-esteem enhancement and similar subjects, instead of practical educational and professional skill courses.

Increasingly employers, dissatisfied with the results of college education, are hiring students right out of college to train them themselves. This has long been a practice in countries such as Japan and Germany. Our educational institutions must get closer to society, the workplace, and the economy to assure that they provide the needed education and skills to prepare for the challenges of the twenty-first century.

# 5

# American Criminal Justice and the Business of Law

The U.S. system of law is one of the most extensive in the world and certainly the largest system of law enforcement. There are more lawyers in the United States alone than in the rest of the world combined. We have one lawyer for every 318 people or for every 138 households, yet relatively few Americans turn to lawyers or courts for their legal needs. In fact, a recent Temple University study performed for the American Bar Association reports that 71 percent of low-income and 61 percent of moderate-income households choose not to deal with lawyers or courts for their legal problems. The common belief was that it would cost too much and would not help.

In other words, in a country that produces one lawyer for every 138 households and more than the rest of the world, much of the population never makes use of lawyers and, for that matter, the legal system. This is a serious indictment of our legal system, a segment of our economy that consumes over 15 percent of our GDP and costs over three times that of legal systems in any other industrialized country on a per capita basis. One issue may be the perception instilled by the very naming of the legal system as the "criminal justice system," emphasizing justice for the criminal and ignoring the victim and society at large.

Law enforcement in the United States is generally lax, with fewer criminals apprehended and even fewer convicted on a percentage basis than in any other developed country. In addition, nowhere is punishment more lenient, with many criminals ever serving their full term.

## Politics and the U.S. Legal System

The U.S. judicial system remains an enigma to many among the American public and an acute embarrassment to others. Many state legislatures are dominated by lawyers, as is also the national legislature in Washington. As voters usually lack the power to introduce change, the judicial system in many parts of the country remains highly politicized as well as self-serving, and judgments can be influenced by political connections or contributions instead of on the merit of the case. For example, a *Wall Street Journal* editorial (October 1,1993) called the Texas judicial system a "profit-making political playpen." Texas has no monopoly in this manner of dispensing justice as conflicts of interest permeate the system throughout the nation. Partisan elections and selection of judges with political motivations and overtones reduce public confidence in our system of justice and make it less effective than it should be. Even in states that pride themselves on maintaining a high level of judicial procedure and practice, political considerations or influence often taint the process.

## All the Guns Money Can Buy

It is interesting that as long as gun control is a local issue and involves murder, a child shot by accident, or a citizen maimed, it does not become a national headline. It requires the murder of foreign tourists in Florida with a potential loss of billions of dollars in foreign exchange and hundreds of thousands of jobs in the tourist industry for murder by handguns to become a national issue. Money is apparently the issue, and until someone or some group—for example, the tourist industry—outspends gun lobbies, little will happen.

Obviously, outlawing gun ownership will not by itself erase lawlessness. Our criminal justice system will have to be revamped into a *victims'* justice system, which gives priority to correcting for and punishing crimes and serves as a real deterrent. As it stands, many criminals are coddled. Those who are caught and convicted get a free ride in prison and are often released after serving just a fraction of their sentence. More than 60 percent of violent crimes in the United States are committed by repeat offenders, most of whom were on probation or were released long before the end of their term.

Criminals should serve their full sentence and should pay the full cost of incarceration by earnings from work. Able-bodied prisoners should work for their food and lodging as well as for the "protection" provided to them by prison guards who "shield them from the wrath of society"—an approach being taken by more and more developed nations.

Only if sentences become meaningful and prison punishment and work in prison a requirement will our victims' justice system provide meaningful deterrents and assure a reduction in criminal conduct. Together with gun control, a victims' justice system will work where all other approaches have failed to cope with the epidemic of crime in the United States.

While ready access to guns in the United States is an obvious contributor to lawlessness, particularly to violent crimes, the cost to the economy of lack of effective gun control has never been adequately studied. Cursory investigations, however, show these costs to be staggering. The following major elements must be considered in order to understand how our lack of gun control is affecting us:

1. health care costs of people injured as a result of gun attack;
2. lost work or output costs of people injured by gun attack;
3. increased police and security costs;
4. costs of incarceration and rehabilitation of violent criminals who would be deterred by effective gun control measures;
5. added costs of court and legal system;
6. added costs to the U.S. public education system;
7. material and emotional loss resulting from the desertion of neighborhoods, including existing public facilities, and the resulting decline in the condition of publicly owned infrastructure such as roads, parks, recreational areas, parking areas, and more;
8. added costs of juvenile crime and delinquency and consequent rehabilitation or corrective costs;
9. societal costs of reduction of freedom of movement and its detrimental effects on lifestyle; and
10. the enormous emotional and material burden of drug crime and rehabilitation costs, dramatically increased by easy access to guns.

These are just some of the major costs of our present lack of gun control.

While these costs cannot be computed accurately, reliable estimates can be made by evaluating direct or comparative annual costs.

Added annual health care costs are conservatively estimated at $80 billion, on the basis of the number of people injured by guns and the average cost of hospitalization and surgery for people with gunshot wounds.

Similarly, the cost of lost output is readily estimated by computing the number of people injured by guns and the average number of days these people take before returning to gainful employment, if ever. These costs add another $40 billion.

Added police and law enforcement costs are conservatively estimated to be $30 billion nationwide. Added costs of incarceration and rehabilitation are estimated by taking the number of prisoners convicted of gun-related crimes and assuming that about half of these would have expressed violence without guns, but with less destructive results. With effective gun control, the U.S. prison population would decline by an estimated 25 to 40 percent, saving the government about $80 billion annually.

Gun control could reduce court and legal system costs by about $5 billion. Added school system, infrastructure damage, and loss of use costs and added juvenile criminal and rehabilitation costs are on the order of $10 to $20 billion.

Finally, there are societal costs such as reduction in the freedom of movement and other quality-of-life threatening costs, sacrifices that bear heavily on society, as does the added cost of drug distribution enhanced by the availability of guns.

Overall, the economic cost of the lack of gun control in America probably exceeds $250 billion annually—or nearly 5 percent of our GNP. This is, incidentally, about twice the estimated street value of illegal drugs sold in the United States. As most of these costs are borne by public agencies, strict gun control and drug control have the combined potential of eliminating much of our budget deficit and of contributing significantly to reducing or eliminating our foreign exchange imbalance, as most drugs are imported, and to an effective improvement in U.S. productivity as well as in the quality of life in America.

The annual murder rate in the United States now stands at 23,250, or 9.3 per 100,000. Approximately 78,000 crimes committed in 1992 resulted in death or serious bodily injury, or 31.2 per 100,000, excluding rape that did not involve other physical injury to the victim. If we exclude political violence and war action, violence against individuals in the United States exceeded, by a factor of 5, that of all other industrialized nations combined on a per capita basis by a factor of 8, a serious indictment of our system.

The U.S. state prison population has more than doubled in the past ten years and now exceeds 700,000. Of these, 120,000 are imprisoned for drug offenses and 82,000 for violent crimes, nearly 30 percent of whom were convicted for murder and another 30 percent for attempted murder or similar violent crime and related weapons charges.

Guns are easily obtained by anyone in the United States, even in states that theoretically control guns. For example, nearly 250,000 Americans hold gun dealer licenses (Type 1 FFL) under which they can ship and receive firearms and ammunition in interstate commerce, via common carrier, and can purchase any kind of weapon wholesale. This commerce is conducted largely free of local and state regulation, which normally applies only to retail purchases. These gun dealer licenses are issued by the United States federal government for a fee of thirty dollars (for a three-year license) to anyone over age twenty-one with only a superficial background check. This means that even in states in which strict gun controls are imposed, criminals can legally set up gun dealerships.

A criminal can obtain a gun dealer's license from the Bureau of Alcohol, Tobacco, and Firearms (ATF) by having another person register for him. As a result, it is easier in most states to become a licensed gun dealer than to purchase a gun legally. According to Josh Sugarman, 74 percent of FFL license holders conduct business from their home and only 18 percent actually operate a gun store. Fewer than 6 percent of active FFL licenses are inspected annually.[1]

The number of guns in circulation in the United States is estimated to be well in excess of 300 million, including millions of high-powered assault weapons. Hunting and sports guns constitute a small fraction of the total in circulation, the vast majority now being handguns, semiautomatics, and other easily concealed weapons.

The United States is the only developed country with no federal or universal gun control. Most developing nations also impose gun control. Illegal possession of a gun is punished severely in most countries, sometimes by death—not by a slap on the wrist, which is the usual punishment in the United States.

The lack of gun control in this country has led to low standards of social behavior. We have now surrendered our inner cities and are in the process of surrendering our highways and byways as well as our towns and suburbs. Our major cities have given up their streets, with police and firefighters backing away from violent confrontation. School administrators often back away from rather than confront violence, lawlessness, or even bullying among students. They even go so far as to excuse such behavior on the grounds of social inequity for which society at large is responsible. Few high schools are gun-free, and weapons are not unknown even in primary schools. Guns are no longer just a means of self-protection; they are carried by students for status. In fact, inner city schools have become training grounds for drug dealing and other criminal activities, and little, if anything, is done to correct these conditions.

The sacrifices we make for lack of gun control therefore go well beyond the direct costs discussed previously. They include human tolls and touch the lives of every citizen. They include a significant portion our potentially productive youth who are lost to a life of crime, addiction, and nonproductivity; the loss of skill of young people who are condemned to a low level of education and social standards; the cost of remedial and other programs designed to help these young people to live a productive life; and the human costs of teenage crime, on families and on society.

It is obvious that if gun control is not introduced and enforced nationwide, the moral standards and quality of life in America will continue to decline, and the economic costs of the lack of gun control will mushroom to intolerable levels.

According to the press, violent crimes committed with handguns in the United States increased in 1992 by nearly 50 percent over the annual average of the five preceding years. Handguns were used in 931,000 crimes, 13,200 of which resulted in homicide. These handgun attacks constituted 55.6 percent of all murders in 1992 according to U.S. Department of Justice figures.

Murder by handguns was up 24 percent in 1992 from the previous five-year average. The argument that free access to guns is necessary to allow the public to protect itself was again contradicted by the fact that only 1 percent of victims of violent crime used firearms defensively. Similarly, of those who did defend themselves with a firearm, one out of five themselves suffered an injury in the incident. Firearms, particularly handguns, were the weapon of choice in most crimes, and firearms were stolen in 340,000 crimes in 1993. It is obvious that the access to firearms does not protect potential victims but does significantly increase the number of violent crimes committed in America.

The murder rate in major U.S. cities doubled between 1975 and 1990 (figure 9), escalating at about 4.3 percent per year. It has since turned

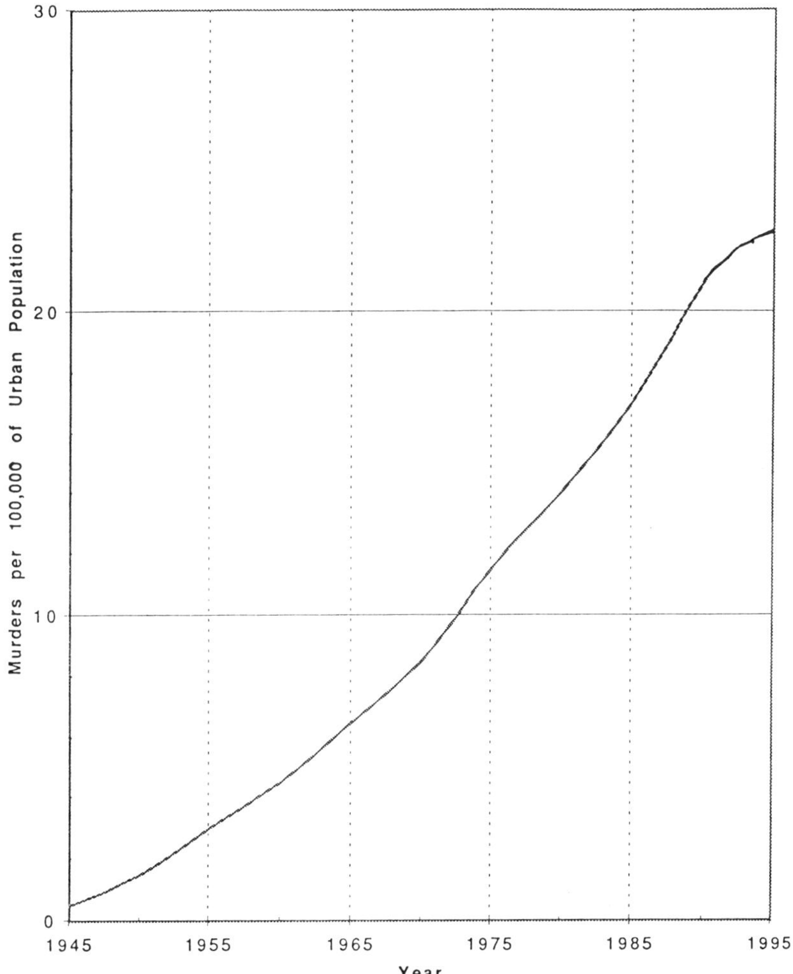


FIGURE 9 Murder Rates in Major U.S. Cities (Population 250,000 plus)

Source: U.S. Department of Justice

around and is growing at a much lower rate. It is too early to say if this is a temporary or permanent change in the trend. Over of 80 percent of murders are committed using handguns, and for each murder committed in a major city an additional thirty crimes are committed by criminals armed with guns. In fact, guns are used in the majority of crimes, including crimes against property that were previously committed by unarmed burglars.

There has been an improvement in violent crimes in cities such as New York in the last year or two as a result of greater police presence and more effective crime control. But nationwide the problem persists and will require drastic changes of policy to be resolved.

## Dangerous Youth

An alarming and wasteful number of American youth are dangerous, poorly educated, unmotivated, and often without any moral or ethical beliefs. The ready availability of guns and drugs combined with the breakdown of the family, the inadequacy of the educational system, the lack of societal standards, and ineffective law enforcement are all part of the antisocial, often criminal, behavior of an increasing segment of our youth.

The randomness of criminal acts committed by our youth, their don't-care attitude, the lack of fear of retribution, and even coldbloodedness and lack of remorse make this fastest-growing segment of American criminals a frightening and tragic phenomenon. At a time when children as young as ten years of age sell and use addictive drugs, use firearms, and steal cars, our approach to juvenile crime must be reevaluated. So long as our youth and their parents stand unaccountable and enjoy the fruits of crime with no fear of punishment, they will continue to commit horrible crimes for little or no reason. The direct cost imposed on U.S. society is tremendous, and this lack of culpability results in a growing segment of the population that has no respect for law, concern for society, or appreciation of the fundamental rights of others.

## Law Enforcement

The fundamental approach of U.S. law enforcement is one of command and control in which laws are enforced independently of their cost, effectiveness, and environmental conditions.

Laws now often impose short- and long-term strategic compliance requirements that have become very costly indeed, often outweighing the benefits, while at the same time the quality of compliance suffers. U.S. law enforcement by and large is neither preventing nor even reducing criminal activity. In fact, the more we enforce laws, the less effective they seem to become. This may be due to the fact that many laws have been enacted not on the basis of economic or social equity, nor to enhance personal safety and freedom, but to satisfy the special concerns of some special interest group. Our laws appear to favor the public less than individuals and special interest groups. In fact, the rights and interests of individuals are habitually given preference over the rights and interests of society. For example, the individual who disturbs people in a confined bus by blaring his radio is protected by his rights as an individual to do as he pleases in a public place, independent of the disturbance caused to others. The rights of the individual increasingly supersede the rights and interests of society. This interpretation has now reached a level where criminals receive more attention and greater protection than their victims.

## Prevention versus Enforcement and Rehabilitation

The American approach to public safety and maintenance of the law has, since World War II, gravitated toward enforcement and rehabilitation. Offenders were to be apprehended and, if convicted, were incarcerated. Prisons and other pre- and postdetention systems were designed to rehabilitate offenders, be they repeat murderers, child and sex abusers, burglars, or simply white-collar criminals.

As we have noted, the U.S. prison population is bulging at the seams, and over 70 percent of maximum security prisoners are repeat offenders. It is evident from these figures that incarceration is not an effective deterrent and, more important, rehabilitation does not work, regardless of the idealistic theories of social workers, psychiatrists, civil libertarians, and even some religious leaders. This is not to advocate strict adherence to the spirit of the Ten Commandments, that punishment should fit the crime in the strict sense, but it is evident that a murderer with no upbringing and a past reflecting only violence will not be easily converted by weekly rehabilitation sessions while functioning in an even more violent environment and ultimately released back into his or her original surroundings. Considering that over of all violent crimes in the United States are committed by repeat criminals who are often released after having served as little as one-third of their sentence, a reevaluation of our criminal justice system is obviously in order.

The public must no longer be asked to foot the bill for the ineffective "rehabilitation" of people who, statistics tell us, while on release still act as criminals and are highly likely to repeatedly attack members of the public. With 28,641 murders committed in 1992 alone (about equal to the number of suicides in the United States, violent death has become a common occurrence, and there are few of us whose lives have not been touched, either directly or indirectly, by vicious attack.

Murder rates soar despite enormous public expenditure. Homicides, from 1980 to 1992 grew from 35 to 75 per 100,000 in Washington, D.C., and 23 to 28 in New York City, with other major U.S. cities showing similar increases. Our urban housing developments have long been unsafe places to live, thus propagating their own corruption. A particularly disturbing aspect of this escalation is that we now see large-scale murder in smaller communities, even in rural or farming communities. The wide open spaces, forests, mountain trails, and beaches have become dangerous—not just late at night and not just for individuals, primarily females, but also for groups and in some places even for police and other law enforcement agencies.

Attacks are not just committed for economic reasons such as theft or robbery, for psychological reasons such as rape, or for racial/social reasons, but simply for the excitement, the challenge, and the senselessness of attack and murder, which the criminals themselves cannot begin to understand.

Senselessness by itself has become an incentive, and young criminals in particular find a perverted satisfaction and peer status in seemingly unmotivated criminal acts. This new development is something our criminal justice and rehabilitation systems are not prepared for, particularly as criminals are now often as young as fourteen years of age and regrettably, often younger still.

In the United States today more children aged ten to nineteen are killed by firearms than by all other causes combined. While a small percentage are killed in accidents, most are a result of intentional shootings, often without an apparent cause. Sadly, many young murder victims are killed by young criminals who often escape punishment solely because of their age.

The United States has become a violent society, and life in U.S. cities today is sometimes claimed to be more hazardous than life in foreign cities under siege. I personally felt safer walking the streets of Khan Kalili, the narrow alleys of the *shouk* of Cairo after the recent attacks on foreigners by fundamentalists, than walking the streets of downtown Boston. Our law enforcement and criminal rehabilitation system has failed miserably to prevent an increase in crime, particularly crime against individuals.

## Access to Institutional Services

We have argued for half a century about methods to assure equal access to a quality education, and with all the problems now facing U.S. education, equal access is, fortunately, not one of them. We have created a system with equal access, but often to a low-quality education. There are obvious differences in access to higher education, but these are not usually in terms of open-door or equity financing, but in terms of preparation to meet the demanding admission standards of colleges. This situation is often partially due to a lack of standards in primary schools, which are sometimes constrained by the limited financial resources of their surrounding communities. Inequality is often caused by cultural and social problems of the family that children inherit and that do not emphasize, support, or encourage learning as a worthwhile activity. In fact, access to quality education, particularly higher education, is sometimes easier for the disadvantaged than for the middle class.

Some are now advocating the introduction of a national health care system that would provide universal access to basic health care, even for those who are uninsured or who are not covered by Medicaid because they are on Social Security, out of work, or too poor to afford health care.

Nearly all people have pro forma access to education and health care, as hospitals and similar institutions cannot legally turn away anyone in need therefore are forced to simply increase their charges to paying or insured patients in order to cover the shortfall from those who cannot afford to or will not pay for treatment. This cross-subsidizing, though unfair, has existed for decades.

No such arrangements exist to provide access to lawyers. True, indigents are assigned court-appointed lawyers in trial cases, and in larger cities public legal aid services are available to the poor and elderly. Yet the majority of working middle-class Americans are denied access to legal assistance, as they cannot begin to afford legal fees of $150 to $300 per hour. Neither do they understand what legal services are required and, resultingly, the amount of time involved and how much they may cost. Few would even know how to obtain or qualify for affordable legal services. Few lawyers make precise proposals or explain in detail what procedures or services are required. In fact, few ordinary citizens understand what legal recourse or remedies are available.

Legal firms have no "outpatient" departments nor do courts or government offices provide for fee assistance in preparing even simple legal documents. All processes require the use of a lawyer, and the whole system is designed as a self-serving, back-scratching merry-go-round that assures lawyers are involved in the greatest possible number of steps and issues, even preparation of boilerplate documents that require little, if any, legal knowledge and are routinely prepared by clerks, secretaries, or paralegals. In fact, many are now generated by simple computer programs.

Lawyers often argue that contingency fee arrangements provide the poor and middle class with effective access to legal services. However, contingency fee services are offered only if:

1. the chance for success in the case is reasonably high,
2. the problem entails monetary damages, and
3. the defendant is either rich or insured.

Such services are generally not offered to trial defendants nor in commercial or other disputes from which one does not anticipate large awards.

Contingency fee arrangements have had devastating effects on the economy, as they usually result in inflated awards that require medical and other service providers to ensure against malpractice claims, the costs of which are passed on to the clients. Claimants receive only a fraction of the award, usually insufficient to make good the damage claimed. As a result, many services (medical, accounting, engineering, etc.) are now practiced defensively, in addition to requiring very high insurance coverage. It is estimated that these factors alone add an additional 10 to 15 percent to the cost of such services.[2]

## Legal Morality

At a bar examination on February 27, 1993, in Pasadena, California, one candidate suffered a severe seizure. Two other candidates who came to his aid were told that they would not be given compensatory time to finish the examination. They had spent a significant amount of time helping their colleague, an action that seriously affected their ability to complete their own examination in the time allotted. The examination proctors were rigid in their view that candidates were not to leave the examination for whatever reason. Only after a public outcry did the United States bar association relent and allow the three candidates to repeat the examination. Incidentally, it is astounding that only two candidates out of hundreds (many seated much closer to the victim) volunteered help.

This is just one example of the state of morality among aspiring or practicing lawyers in the United States who are increasingly concerned with their competitive position and their economic benefits more than with upholding legal principles or the role of law in advancing the good of society. The legal profession jealously guards its right to self-policing but has done an indifferent job of reprimanding its members, even in cases of gross misconduct such as overbilling or criminal acts such as theft of client funds.

## The Legal Profession

Public esteem for lawyers in the United States is generally low. They are generally perceived as greedy, selfish, insensitive, largely self-serving, and unresponsive to public needs. A largely self-policing body of professionals, they control both sides of the legal system and are thought of as highly unfair. They are viewed as forcing their services on the public. Unlike other professionals, such as doctors, whose services are elective (a sick person can choose to use or not to use a licensed doctor), a lawyer must be hired even if the client may be perfectly competent to draw up his or her own legal papers or to represent or someone else in a legal process. It is generally agreed that we have far too many lawyers (fully half of the entire world's total) and that lawyers are busy inventing new requirements for the use of their services.

Lawyers have infiltrated all branches and positions in the legislatures and administration of government—federal, state, and local. They make up the vast majority of legislators as well as senior administrators at all levels of government. As a result, government has become a legal self-serving process where legislators advance laws and regulations that require lawyers to interpret, implement, and challenge. Similarly, lawyers have gained increasing influence in health care education, and management by challenging the performance of other professions, while excluding themselves from similar challenge. When, for example, was a lawyer or law firm last threatened by a malpractice suit? Few, if any, lawyers carry malpractice insurance, for which doctors pay dearly.

Although in theory pro-se or self-advocacy litigants have a legal right to represent or defend themselves, judges hold a bias against this practice and do everything to discourage it. Recent examples show that this is not because nonlawyers are not well prepared or knowledgeable about the law, but because of a general disdain for self-advocacy by judges who feel a need to protect the turf of lawyers. In many cases litigants or preparers of legal documents, such as contracts, choose a pro-se or self-advocacy approach, not to save money so much as to assure quality. They have too often experienced shabby legal work, usually done by some anonymous, inexperienced clerk and not by the high-priced lawyer the client thought he or she had hired and paid for. Furthermore, lawyers seldom understand the technical and economic issues involved and may propose an approach or a contract that is ineffective from a business point of view.

## Lawyers' Ethics

There is an old joke about a lawyer who dies and tries to enter heaven. When he signs in and states his age as 74, the gatekeeper turns him away, saying that according to their records, based on the lawyer's own time sheets and bills to clients, he must be at least 300 years old, an age that disqualifies him from entering heaven.

Lawyers' billing practices have recently hit the limelight. Hillary Clinton's law partner, Hubbel, has been accused by his partners at the Rose

Law Firm in Little Rock of overcharging his clients. The billing practices in connection with the Armand D'Amato fraud conviction appeal are another example. The rosters are full of claims of improper billing by lawyers. Bar associations, among whose self-assigned responsibilities is the maintenance of the reputation or status of the legal profession and protection of its clients, have taken the position that to accommodate the needs of clients, lawyers are free to lie about facts as they relate to the services provided to a client. In the most basic case, this means hiding the precise type of services rendered and billing simply for "professional services."

This freedom obviously opens the door to many abuses. While lawyers may claim that this is done only in the interest of the client, the approach can easily be used to hide overbilling. By and large, lawyers neither claim nor exhibit any knowledge of basic financial management. It is curious, for example, that while most professionals include in their basic fees incidental expenses such as parking, copying, and postal charges, lawyers invariably charge these as an addition. Considering that a typical legal fee is $300/hour ($5/minute), if a lawyer spends two minutes to record three dollars' worth of incidental expenses, he automatically triples these expenses by padding them with his charge for the time spent on recording.

When lawyers are interrupted by a clients phone call, they often continue to let both time clocks run. Charging clients well in excess of the actual hours spent on legal work has become a pastime, particularly among lawyers who have inadequate demand for their services. In fact, many law firms force associates and partners to maximize their chargeable hours and to compete on that basis for promotion and pay.

There may be nothing illegal about these practices, but they certainly are highly unethical. In addition, they make legal service more expensive and therefore inaccessible to the average citizen.

The legal profession should not only interpret the law but represent it with themselves as guardians and should ensure that there is no sign of impropriety that affects their reputation. In recent years, this profession, which ostensibly represents the moral pinnacle of society has been reduced to an image akin to that of the proverbial used car salesman.

## The Cost of Corruption

While the costs of corruption and political payoffs have been in the limelight and governments (such as that of Italy) have recently experienced major reversals as a result of public disgust with corruption, we somehow assume that our laws and methods of law enforcement guard against corruption. There is increasing evidence to suggest that we are not immune to inflated project costs, contract irregularities, political payoffs, corruptive favors, inflated pricing, unnecessary procurements, and more, yet there is little done to expose and correct these practices.

A major factor in the lack of quality and poor safety standards in building construction and also in product manufacture is that inspectors can be bribed to overlook improprieties. Even law enforcement agencies are often caught up in bribery.

Corruption practices also can be found in various professional activities, in business, health care, and education. Cheating has become common: it no longer imposes a stigma on the perpetrator, as society becomes immune to infractions, and simply charges individuals with guarding themselves against these practices.

## Legal Image and Legal Monopoly

American lawyers appear to recognize the need for improvement in their public image. The American Bar Association (ABA), their central organization is reported to have hired a $170,000-*per-year* media expert for this purpose and provides him with a staff and budget to mend the perceived serious failure of the role and contribution of lawyers and the legal profession. According to ABA president J. Michael McWilliams, the public's views are the result of a "lack of understanding of the U.S. justice system," which, once improved, will remedy the negative perception people have of lawyers. At the same time, the ABA and state bar associations continue to defend a system that protects lawyers' monopoly and through its monopolistic, ineffective, self-policing system denies the general public access to the justice system.

These same organizations use the justice and law enforcement systems to their full extent to stop or discourage anyone—even experienced paralegals—from performing the most basic legal or pseudo-legal services. These are services that are performed by the same clerks or paralegals in the offices and firms of a lawyer. As we have seen, lawyers often make no contribution at all to the preparation of these documents, with the notable exception of adding a hefty fee to their cost, which triples or quadruples their cost to the client.

Lawyers have become so possessive in guarding their market that they now challenge even private citizens who attempt to write their own wills or trust documents, often using lawyer-designed software or reference works.

This monopoly extends from drafting the simplest contractual documents and procedures to justice and law enforcement of most things that affect the public. Traditionally, disciplinary processes against malpracticing lawyers or lawyers engaged in incompetent, fraudulent, or even criminal acts are performed by their peers and are closed to the public, even the complaining client. They are clearly concerned more with maintaining the coherence of the legal fraternity than with achieving justice and restitution for the aggrieved or victimized client. Even informal and ineffective admonitions resulting from these procedures are usually never made public. This self-serving procedure is ineffective and often results in rulings that are neither enforced nor effective as deterrents.

## Personal Safety and Crime in America

Crime has become an ever-present element of American life, assuming a social importance of its own. Crime is considered a social ill, the responsibility of society and not of the perpetrator. On the one hand, we consider individual rights supreme while, on the other, we assign to society the responsibility for individual crime. Criminals are often excused and society blamed for their acts on the grounds that they are socially or economically disadvantaged, educationally behind, or forced into drug use by their surroundings or other rationalizations. Yet, at the same time, society is prevented from correcting many of its ills because this would imply interference in the rights of the individual. Truly a "catch-22" situation!

We blame other countries for allowing or not preventing the export of drugs to the United States but are unwilling to crack down on drug users and dealers in the United States. We criticize violence elsewhere, particularly in foreign countries, but allow the free purchase, sale, possession, and use of firearms and other deadly weapons, so as not to offend a small minority of organized and highly vocal Americans, including the American Rifle Association. In Japan, *thirty-seven people*—all sportsmen—among

*112 million* are licensed and own guns, versus approximately 30 million out of 256 million in the United States. Astonishingly, the number of privately owned firearms in the United States far outnumbers the number of people in the United States. Gun ownership was justified historically by the need for self-protection. Today these reasons are moot, as gun ownership is hardly a protection against violent crime any longer. The data are clear: societies with strict gun control, which includes essentially all other developed countries, record a significantly lower crime rate, particularly murder, than the United States.

Since 1975 the murder rate in the United States has remained obstinately between eight or ten murders per 100,000 population (as shown in figure 10), an unacceptable rate that is twice that of any other developed country.

The United States had always been one of the world's most crime-ridden countries. Considering homicide, between 1950 and 1965 the United States averaged 5.1 murders and attempted murders per 100,000 population, nearly double the number of any other developed country. By 1985 that number had grown to 7.9 per 100,000 for murders alone, still well ahead of all other developed nations, though some countries, such as Sweden, have changed radically and have experienced homicides of over double their 1965 statistics. In terms of larceny, the United States has fallen behind some other developed nations.

The United States is the only developed country with no national law requiring a license for gun ownership. Licenses are required for driving a car, fishing, dog ownership, and in some states even for the riding of bicycles. We put a lot of emphasis on child safety and the safety of our physical environment, yet the most lethal of personal weapons is available to virtually anyone.

## Crime Pays in America

U.S. criminal justice is a "fraud perpetrated on the public," according to Florida state attorney general Katherine Fernandez Rundle, where ten-year sentences routinely mean eighteen months in jail, if that. Similarly, an increasing number of criminals are let free on technicalities. The U.S. legal system has been distorted by liberal ideas designed to protect the young, and particularly the disadvantaged, as to somehow atone for the failure of

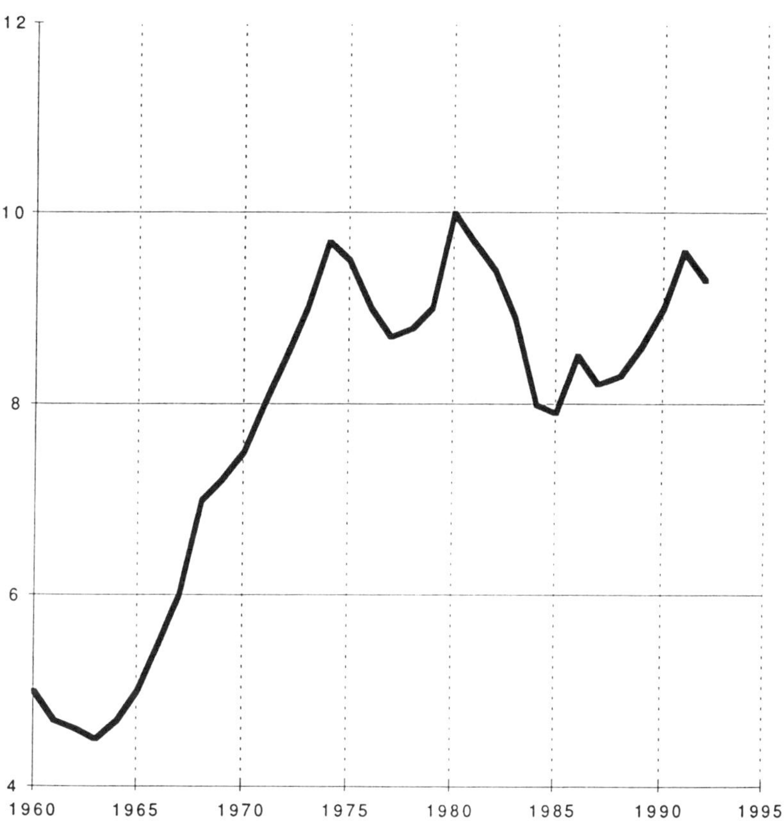


FIGURE 10 - The Murder Toll

The rate of homicides and manslaughter in the U.S. per 100,000 population

Source: Uniform Crime Reports, FBI

society in their fate, lack of education, and lack of family structure. Nearly half of all violent crimes are now perpetrated by the young (under twenty-one years of age), and half of these are by juveniles under eighteen years of age. These violent young criminals usually escape serious punishment and are often barely reprimanded. For many of them violence is a means to property or money as well as an outlet for their violent feelings. They often totally lack compassion and live with the knowledge that their crimes will go unpunished because they are underage. Crime in many neighborhoods has even become a status symbol! Most crimes by juvenile offenders are senseless terrorist and destruction-driven acts, yet these young criminals are not seen as criminals, but as victims. While there may be some truth to the general concept of societal guilt, our system punishes neither the young criminals nor their parents or others who led them, encouraged them or even supported them in these acts. Most important, parents are seldom held accountable for the acts of even twelve to fourteen-year-old criminals. If they are punished at all, the punishment is usually a symbolic slap on the wrist.

Today many crimes, particularly violent crimes, are committed by repeat criminals, people who consider themselves beyond or immune to the law, just as do young offenders. This is where our efforts must be directed. We now use the so-called "three strikes and you're out" rule, which implies that a criminal can be permanently incarcerated only on the third offense. In my opinion, this is only an encouragement for repeat offenders, who can easily interpret this ruling to mean that they have two free strikes before they are "out."

## Freeloading Criminals and Criminal Rights

Prisoners in the United States obtain free board and lodging, by and large, and do not have to work for their keep. While this condition may be acceptable for older or infirm prisoners presumed incapable of performing physical or other work, there is little, if any, justification for society paying for the upkeep of able-bodied criminals who are imprisoned because they have hurt or damaged that society. While I agree with a basic moral philosophy that outlaws the death penalty, it is not so clear that society has an obligation to pay for the maintenance of prisoners for short incarcerations or for those sentenced to life imprisonment who in many countries would have been punished by death.

An increasing number of countries provide only bare cells for able-bodied prisoners who must work and then pay for everything from furnishings to food, entertainment, use of sports equipment, and medical care. In the United States the public pays for their upkeep, including recreation, food, entertainment, vocational services, and more. Money earned by the prisoners, some of whom engage in personally lucrative and even illegal or criminal activities while in prison, is kept by the prisoner. It is unfair for society to pick up the hefty bill for these costs, and the practice is counter-incentive in terms of crime prevention. It is illogical and wasteful for society to support a prisoner while he or she banks the profits.

The United States has the highest rate of incarceration of any nation except Russia. Our 1.3 million prisoners in federal, state, and local jails at the end of 1993 translate into an incarceration rate of 519 per 100,000 population, an increase of 22 percent since 1989, according to a private study by the group the Sentencing Project, which advocates alternatives to imprisonment. Nearly half of all Americans incarcerated (583,000) are black. The system clearly is not working, as evidenced by the fact that incarceration as practiced does little to deter crime or to rehabilitate prisoners. In fact, the number of prisoners continues to increase by nearly 4 percent per year and may hit 600 per 100,000 population by 1997.

## Murder on the Cheap

The American criminal justice system has become a criminal pampering system that more often victimizes the victim than it punishes the criminal. Punishment or the potential for punishment is hardly a deterrent and, as a result, an increasing number of crimes, particularly violent crimes, are senseless, committed without a second thought.

Only one in ten homicides in the United States results in a conviction for murder, and the average conviction for murder results in a prison sentence of six years, with actual time served as little as seven months. In other words, there is no effective punishment in America, even for the crime of murder.

Although some states enforce the death penalty under some conditions, nationwide fewer than half of all convicted murderers are sentenced to death, and nearly 70 percent of such death sentences are either delayed indefinitely or reversed. Of the remaining 30 percent, appeals delay the execution process for an average of ten years, an imposed suffering widely recognized as infinitely far more costly in economic and human terms than is the execution itself. The probability of a convicted murderer being put to death is only 3.5 percent. Even mass murderers, where guilt is undeniable, are not sentenced to death, and the public is asked to pay the bill for life-long upkeep, in addition to the tragic social costs these heinous acts have already imposed on society.

## The Impending Demise of the U.S. Legal System

To the extent that the U.S. legal system is fair and democratic for criminals, it certainly is anything but efficient or effective. It purveys judgment at a snail's pace, often long after the judgments have ceased to be relevant or to serve their intended purpose. The system is based on the concept of community law enforcement, by peers, and an appeals system that assures continuation of cases long after irrefutable evidence has led to a correct judgment. The world's most expensive judicial system is often unjust, is economically and socially overpriced, lacks meaningful impact, and is largely obsolete and ineffective. It does not serve as a deterrent nor as a system of justice.

While in criminal cases, where lives can depend on the judgment and where issues are the life situations of ordinary citizens, juries certainly play an important role. However, in civil cases, there appears to be little justification for maintaining the jury system. Many of these cases require understanding of complex legal issues beyond the capability of a typical jury. Juries in such situations tend to be ruled by emotion, unrealistic economic assumptions, or other erroneous influences.

We already have some specialized legal systems, such as bankruptcy courts, which have proven efficient in terms of time and cost, as well as of the expertise of judges in complex bankruptcy issues. What we require are additional specialized expert adjudicating courts or systems that can efficiently and fairly resolve noncriminal issues.

## Maintaining the Letter and Losing the Spirit

An agreement is usually defined by the letter of a contract or understanding and the spirit under which the agreement is entered. Over the years, and under legal pressure, agreements by U.S. industrial firms are often maintained exclusively on the basis of the letter of the agreement, which has given lawyers, and not society, a monopoly on the interpretation and adjudication of agreements. This has made many agreements meaningless, as words or letters are twisted, reinterpreted, and used out of context, ignoring for the most part the spirit in which the original agreement was entered. This myopic approach to agreements adds dramatically to legal costs as agreements are narrowly interpreted, reinterpreted, and challenged. The approach also assumes that agreements are static and must be implemented by the letter as interpreted, no matter what happens. If conditions or other changes require a different approach then this again is simply an opportunity for new charges.

Agreements-to be useful—must define both narrow one-time as well as future requirements. This holds true in our personal as well as in business relations. Somehow we have become used to solving short-term problems while ignoring their long-term implications.

In other words, compliance with an agreement is often distorted to meet wording that may no longer apply when implemented, rather than to solve the problem as implied by the agreement, independent of the original wording.

This approach is directly opposed to that taken in the Orient and also quite different from the basic European approach. While much of the problem can be blamed on our legal system, most is the result of aggressive, adversarial relationships fostered by our business schools and lawyers. Managers and lawyers forever look for opportunities to profit from differences rather than for cooperation toward mutually beneficial solutions. In the United States we always appear to need winners and losers, instead of attempting to make everyone a winner. The result is not only lack of effective progress, but also disruptive interpersonal and interorganizational relationships that affect future developments.

We talk a lot about the importance of win-win relationships, while at the same time continuing to encourage adversarial conduct. In fact, we train our managers and lawyers in the art of establishing and using adversarial advantage, independent of fairness or even of the moral and ethical implications involved. Winning is all. This situation will not change until we see a shift in values and a restructuring of our legal system to maintain justice and assure public safety, morality and freedom.

## Legal Economics

I have always been puzzled by the economics of "lawyering." Despite the obscene rates lawyers often charge for their services, their annual income represents only about one-fourth of the total cost of the U.S. legal system. The legal system—courts, law enforcement, lawyers, and other advocates—is burdened with a huge overhead, due largely to the inefficiency of the administration of law and public security.

Lawyers generally use a rate-skewed approach to economics. I have on numerous occasions watched a lawyer spend ten minutes or more than fifty dollars' worth of billable time to record five to ten dollars' worth of copying expenses. The absurdity of this exercise appears to escape the legal mind.

Law firms are among the few professional organizations that charge clients for trivial charges. Most professions absorb these expenses as part of their overhead. The fact that the cost of recording and billing vastly exceeds these charges eludes them, or could it be that they simply use this as a way to add to billable hours?

Similarly, legal processes themselves often ignore economic absurdities. An example is a case involving about $1 million claimed damages, where both parties spent twice this amount in legal fees and expert witnesses to make their case. Similarly, class action cases, brought usually by lawyers, mainly reward lawyers and usually little, if any, benefit to the participants who are often forced to spend millions of hours in collecting information to support the claim. In a typical class action case, the plaintiffs regain pennies on each dollar lost, after investing untold hours to back up the claim. From personal experience, in a case where I lost several thousand dollars I spent thirty-five hours researching and substantiating the claim, won the case, and was awarded $27.80. I now discard any request for participation in a class action, which, experience tells me, profits only the lawyers bringing the case. The losers are not only the plaintiffs but the taxpayers who must shoulder many of the expenses associated with these cases.

Lawyers in general are unaware or, more important, unconcerned with the economics or economic implications of their actions and procedures, so long as their costs are covered. Quite often the costs of legal procedures now exceed the value of the action, with the public picking up the difference.

It is important to insist that lawyers, like other professionals operating a business, justify the economic benefits, costs, and economic viability of their procedures before being allowed to proceed. Legal procedures, with the exception of criminal and family cases, are much like other professional projects, which must be economically justified before being allowed to proceed. If this idea of economic justification were enforced, a substantial number of cases, particularly the frivolous cases that clog our courts, would be eliminated, our court system greatly relieved, and the public guarded from enormous tax burdens.

A huge percentage of cases brought before courts today are frivolous and are entered largely to test the system. The defendant must settle in order to get rid of the nuisance and often bears the legal expense and adverse publicity, however ill-founded the charge. Many lawyers make it a practice to try frivolous cases just to collect their share of the proceeds, which, in many cases, is the bulk of the settlement.

Counterincentives must be introduced to prevent this absurd waste of court time and public expenditure. These could include a requirement for an escrowed deposit or bond of a value equal to the claim that is forfeited if the claim is disproven and the charges are dismissed.

At this time underemployed lawyers are encouraged to file idle charges or claims, be they ambulance-chasing, automobile accident, sexual harassment, or securities (class action) claims. These lawyers have nothing to lose but their underused time, but the public and the falsely accused sacrifice enormous amounts of time, expenses, and court congestion.

Lawyers who repeatedly bring unsubstantiatable or knowingly false claims should be censored or disbarred, very much as an engineer who designs a foundation on the basis of insufficient survey data or a researcher who fakes test results has his or her licenses withdrawn or is otherwise prevented from continuing practices that are against the public interest.

As we have seen, the legal profession has continually maintained self-regulation and self-censoring and usually protects their own against liability for misconduct or misuse of public resources. Lawyers must be accountable and subject to public involvement and exposure. We cannot afford to allow the guardians of our law to be above the law themselves.

## The Forgotten Victim and Society

The American legal system is designed to ensure justice for all, but these rights are largely extended to the criminals, with victims of crime or society at large often ignored. We have, in truth, a criminal justice or justice for the criminal system, not a system that protects lawful individuals and their rights. We are the only country in the world with vocal criminal rights advocates and organizations; yet there are few effective victim rights lobbies. Criminals' demands are news and are in the limelight daily. Victims are usually forgotten and often make little or no news. Prisoners run businesses, distribute drugs, sue, and even run gangs, all from within their prisons.

Not only are we a violence-ridden society, but we are more concerned with and interested in the criminal and how he or she is treated than with what happens to the victims of crime. They rarely make the news. From a moral point of view this is sickening, and it has become a contributing factor to crime in America. In a real sense we glorify the criminal to the level of hero or antihero, while the victim is forgotten. Who can recall the name or fate of any victim of the James brothers, the Daltons, Billy the Kid, Dillinger, Butch Cassidy, Pretty Boy Floyd, Babyface Nelson, Bonnie and Clyde, Son of Sam, "The Ponzi Scheme," Willie Sutton, or the Brinks gang? These criminals are presented as quick, courageous, unique, imaginative, successful, and sometimes standing alone against a corrupt establishment. This distortion to legend, as much as anything, has set the stage for perpetuation of crime in America.

## The Performance of the U.S. Legal System

The U.S. legal and law enforcement system stands broken and unable to fulfill its promise. The recently enacted crime bill, which put an additional 100,000 cops on the street, outlaws certain types of assault weapons, and finances various crime prevention programs, has at least had some impact on crime in the United States. The problem is not lack of cops or lack of prevention programs, but a lack of will to enforce. Crime without punishment is more prevalent in the United States than in most countries, not only because criminals are not apprehended but because of the skewed perspective of our criminal justice system. Only 10 percent of burglars are arrested and fewer than 1.2 percent are actually imprisoned. Fewer than half of murderers are arrested, and on average they are back on the street in less than six years. These are volatile issues that reach beyond percentages, into the daily lives of every one of us.

With 544,000 cops (0.214 percent of the population), plus over 1.5 million private security guards, we employ three to four times as many police and security guards per capita as any other developed country. Even so, we spend nearly five times more for lawyers than we do for police protection.

Our basic law enforcement policies are both based on and hampered by our respect for individual rights. These rights are often exaggerated and are applied at a cost to society. As a result, a smaller percentage of criminals in the United States are caught and convicted than in any other industrialized country, with a much shorter sentence being served.

Notwithstanding the expenditure of over 15 percent of our GNP, our legal and law enforcement system does not work. Crime is a principal concern of the American public, second only to health care. We have been robbed of our freedom and quality of life, but it is not too late to correct the situation. Additional cops, prisons, and crime prevention programs are just Band-Aids and are not the new paradigm required to correct the fundamental ills of our system. Much more radical measures will have to be taken if we are to regain control of our streets and our way of life.

This will not be easy, particularly if we are not willing to compromise some of our traditional ideals in the light of changing reality. An example is our continued laxity in containing juvenile crime, now growing at twice the rate of overall violent crime. Troubling projections place the increase on juveniles fifteen to nineteen years of age at 21 percent in the next ten years; violent juvenile crime arrests, which reached 150,000 in 1993, may well double by 2005.

Wider availability of guns, a lax legal system, and ineffective social and educational systems are largely to blame. The problem is that juvenile criminals become adult criminals, which means that after 2005 the growth rate of violent crime in the United States will accelerate to twice the current rate. Our law enforcement system has proven totally incapable of dealing with this problem. We need not only more police and prisons but a radical change in our social system and in the way societal rewards and punishments are given.

We are simultaneously the most crime-ridden and the most liberal and permissive society. Liberal values, permissiveness, nondiscriminating social systems, and support of individual rights independent of their effect on the community at large are fine, idealistic concepts that may work in a society that arrests fifty thousand juvenile offenders annually, in a well-educated and community-spirited society. It does not and cannot work in a society that is increasingly uneducated, values neither family nor community, and primarily rewards selfish interests.

We must stop throwing money at this problem, which has not helped in the past. What we need is a change in our liberal philosophy, the courage to face the reality that people are not all inherently good, and a determination that individual rights and society's good are invariably linked and interdependent. There are successful approaches. In San Francisco, some criminals are given the chance to rehabilitate themselves by working in regular jobs under a strict code of behavior of no violence, no drugs, and no foul language in the Delancey House, a self-supporting institution that has successfully returned over 9,000 prisoners to useful citizenship without public expenditure, saving millions of dollars in costs of incarceration.

We need more of these approaches and must severely punish incorrigible criminals while giving others a real change for rehabilitation. Just locking people up and releasing them after a short time makes things worse.

# 6
# Rethinking American Institutions

American institutions are at the heart of our nation's potential. They are the critical economic and strategic contributors to our position as the world's leader: they provide the legal, intellectual, social, and scientific foundation for our success and the moral and ethical basis for our sustained faith and leadership. Our institutions are for and by the people. People make institutions. They are not ruled but served by them. Once institutions serve themselves more and people less, they forfeit their right to popular support.

After two centuries of success, we as a nation have now allowed our institutions to degenerate to a degree that the effectiveness of our health, education, and criminal justice systems is seriously questioned, and in some quarters disparaged, in terms of their social contribution and moral values. We have permitted many unscrupulous people to assume their management. The superb professional capability of many of our medical, educational, and legal institutions is still there. We still produce many leading physicians, legal minds, and academic/research scholars, as well as committed and well-trained teachers, nurses, and law enforcement professionals and judges. What is wrong is the institutional structure and management, often ineffective, decadent, and misused, sometimes even encouraging direct and indirect corruption. Many of our institutions have become largely inefficient enterprises run by self-serving administrators.

The many competent and well-meaning professionals that serve these institutions have long attempted to restore their original purpose, objective, and mission, with little success. This lack of success is due to the strong control of the institutional structure by institutional administrators and their supporters. Not only are educational, health care, and legal institutions largely run by ineffective managers, but their organizational structure has become a morass of disfunctionalism. For example, when advanced labor-saving office, information, and communications technology is introduced, the administration nevertheless grows as technically competent people are hired to use the new technology, while the old staff remains, adding instead of saving labor. While in manufacturing investments in technology normally result in a more than proportional reduction in labor, our institutions have by and large achieved the opposite. Today our law enforcement, health care, and educational institutions by and large employ proportionally more staff in accounting and bookkeeping than they did when these functions were all performed manually.

These are not isolated cases. First-class mail takes on average twice as long to reach its destination now as fifty years ago, before the advent of post office automation, zip code readers, computerized sorting, and airmail. In fact, letters within the greater Boston area were delivered in less time by horse and buggy in the last century than they are today.

Institutions will regain their traditional function, competence, and role only by reinvention, which must be implemented from the bottom up and in a manner that assures retention of all their professional capabilities. This can be done only from within the institutions, lest their inherent capabilities be lost. We must radically change our institutions if we are to maintain our leadership and regain our economic prowess.

Michael Hammer and James Champy defined "reengineenng" as the fundamental rethinking and radical redesign of business processes to achieve dramatic improvements in contemporary measures of performance such as cost, quality, service, and speed.[1] What is needed to improve the performance of our vital institutions goes beyond rethinking and redesign and must include radical reinvention and restructuring.

The redefining of American institutions as organizations that truly serve the public interest may appear to be impossible. In fact, you may think me a dreamer in the conviction that we can reinvent America's institutions. We can reinstall the meaning of our timeless Constitution and bring it and its benefits back to the people. We can make our institutions serve the people and not largely themselves; we can restructure them to perform efficiently.

Institutions must change with people's needs, with the needs of the economy and society, the availability of technology, and the demands of the social environment. Having allowed our institutions to become self-serving and usurp the public purse, we must now regain them in the public interest.

Institutions control too much of our political establishment and systems and consume too much of our national product. We have made major progress in improving the efficiency of our agriculture and manufacturing and are becoming increasingly competitive in terms of world-class excellence and quality. To some extent this is also true in many of our service sectors. However when it comes to institutional sectors, such as health care, education, and legal or law enforcement, we move in the opposite direction and increase costs while allowing service quality and accessibility to decline.

It is sad to note recent statistics on job creation in the United States. Productive sectors, particularly manufacturing and agriculture, have declining employment, while most service sectors are barely holding their own or offer only a sprinkling of new or replacement jobs. The largest increase in job offerings and, by recent count, over half of all new and replacement job openings are in the institutional sectors.

Government at the local level is expanding. These jobs consume public resources, but they do not create wealth or in most cases even value. Many create nothing of public use or benefit. In many cases where government or public institutional employment has shrunk, it is the result of outsourcing or privatization, not improved efficiency.

Institutional costs are now spiraling upward and may constitute an even larger percentage of GDP, unless this trend is halted, costs are contained, and their rate of growth is reversed. Otherwise we may move toward national insolvency, a state that would convert us from a leader into a server nation to the rest of the world, which would then own much of our assets and whatever value we had created in the past.

## Loss of Institutional Values

A major cause of the decline in institutional responsiveness is the loss of basic values and the direction taken by our law, health, and educational institutions. This country was built on faith and a belief in human goodness, courage, honesty, commitment, and fairness—a willingness to join in the common good. The law was originally designed to assure effective relationships among citizens and the protection of the individual in the interests of a well-conceived society.

Health care was designed to protect citizens from ills and to provide them with access to healing services. Education was introduced to advance the competence to self-govern and to enhance the quality of life of the citizenry. Many of our institutions have now lost sight of these basic values.

They have degenerated into businesses that operate under the guise of institutional services.

To be effective, institutions must not only perform their function, but they must also reflect the social, moral, and cultural needs of the society they serve. American institutions have moved away from their constituents and now reflect less and less their original soul (if you will) and values. In fact, U.S. legal, educational, and health care systems are now remote for many Americans and often function not as part of society but as independent entities with their own objectives and values, which, in many cases, do not reflect those of the society they are here to serve.

The agendas of these institutions emphasize their own economic and sometimes even political goals. Above all, they are focused on maintaining as well as enhancing their own base and power. This is done even when there is no longer a need for their functioning or purpose.

The United States is unique in the way its institutions try to influence public opinion and government support. In few other countries do legal, health, and educational institutions use advertising, the media, and expensive political lobbying as well as influence peddling to control the public and political environment. Instead of responding to the changing requirements of society in an effective and efficient manner, institutions quite often try to influence public and political opinion to justify their own interests.

## Need for Institutional Self-Criticism

In recent years American institutions have become so enamored with their importance and their role to society that most have forgotten the need for self-evaluation or reevaluation and self-criticism. In fact, many have developed an internal paradigm that interprets any type of criticism, however productive and meaningful, whether from inside or outside the institution, an act of treason. Essentially, institutions have lost their capacity for self-criticism, often exemplified by a loss in capacity for change. They also try to set standards for education, health care, and law enforcement, and tell the public what it needs or will get.

Leaders of American institutions somehow feel anointed to judge the good of society, although they usually represent only their own institution and are often appointed by a board carefully selected by the institution's own senior administrators. These same institutional leaders are often incapable of effectively managing or leading even their own institutions. Many institutions are no longer focused on service and their customers but have become self-justifying organizations whose role cannot be questioned. There is an urgent need to reestablish internal and external checks and balances that encourage and protect internal and external criticism, particularly when advanced for the benefit and interest of the institution at large and its role in society.

Unless institutions learn the importance of continuous reevaluation and self-criticism, they will truly degenerate into crumbling, obsolete ivory towers. Many appear to be adrift in their own perception of society's needs and their own importance. They encourage little feedback. To serve society they must clearly increase the participation of the people affected in developing their programs and services. They similarly must become more open and more accountable to the public, which foots their bills.

Our institutions were developed to serve the essential needs of society, education, health care, and personal protection. These used to be the responsibilities of families or local communities and emerged as larger regional or even national functions only in recent times. In many countries they were transferred to government, but in the United States we continue today to have an unclear system in which institutions are established to perform these functions yet are without uniform standards or controls. In education and health care not only do we have public private institutions, but their standards, funding, functions, and even responsibilities vary widely throughout the country. Law enforcement similarly is divided into local, state, and federal, often with unclear jurisdictions. The role or responsibility of the family or the public versus that of these diverse institutions is quite murky, and many of our problems are the result of the lack of understanding or clarity of responsibility.

The future of America as a world leader and thriving, competitive economy largely depends on its ability and willingness to reform its institutions. We have discussed how America's major institutions have grown out of control and now consume an inordinate percentage of the national wealth and output, and we have seen how they have become increasingly self-serving and ineffective. They also have contributed to a national feeling of impotence in dealing with our societal and moral problems. These developments affect our national morale, economic prowess, social fiber, and international standing.

Recent proposals designed to improve the institutional service sectors such as health care, criminal justice, and education mainly addressed the demand side of these institutions. They are designed to improve accessibility, with little effort devoted to pinpointing the supply side, such as costs, quality, delivery, and effectiveness or performance. In fact, few proposals suggest tampering with the institutions themselves.

We talk of universal health care, resource-blind admission to higher education, and uniform provision of criminal justice to more equitably satisfy demand, but the real problems are the supply side of these institutional services. Our public institutions are not universally accessible or are otherwise discriminating because they are inefficient or simply incompetent. We lack accessible, affordable health care because it costs too much and is often ineffective and not because of discrimination against some sectors of society. Health care is expensive primarily because it is inefficiently run, sometimes corrupt, and encourages people and institutions to maximize their own benefits and profits by not providing the best service at minimum cost. We need radical reform of our institutional and service sectors and must reestablish more effective objectives and incentives to institutional providers. This will assure that they provide the quality, accessibility, and performance in the supply of their services. We must reorganize our institutions to respond to the needs of the public. We must make them customer-oriented and quality-conscious.

Health care, education, and criminal justice increasingly focus on extreme needs and less on meeting the general needs of American society. We have the finest health care for underweight premature babies and the terminally ill. We spend a disproportionate amount of money on saving the one-pound babies, knowing perfectly well that the chances of success are small and that even if we succeed the result will probably require lifelong radical medical intervention and care. We keep tens of thousands of terminally ill patients alive by artificial means and with a quality of life that is often not worth much. We spend fortunes on high-tech procedures and interventions when the chances of success are dim and the outcome at best extends life for a short time and at a low level of quality of life.

At the same time, common medical problems that affect the vast majority of people, such as the common cold, backaches, arthritis, digestive problems and so on, receive little attention and sufferers receive little treatment. Even if they do, treatment is often perfunctory or superficial and usually requires a visit to an emergency room where the patient with a high temperature or in severe pain then waits for long hours as "real" emergency cases are being treated.

Furthermore emergency-duty doctors are quite often interns, with little experience. In other words, the American medical system concentrates on taking care of the very old and infirm and the very young as well as those with very complex medical problems that require or offer the opportunity for high-tech intervention. This approach favors the wealthy and indigent, who can either afford the expense or the time for high-tech or emergency treatment of run-of-the-mill problems or are covered by government health care programs. The majority of working Americans do not obtain the quality of medical services that meets their needs.

Emergency rooms are full of people with minor cuts, bruises, colds, or sprains who take advantage of the fact that emergency facilities must treat everyone. At the same time, working people who cannot afford the time for emergency room treatment or have no primary care physician (which is, unfortunately, the case with the majority of middle-class Americans) or who get appointments in the distant future when the problem should have disappeared basically receive no medical support. Effective preventative medicine is not given either the attention or resources required to prevent the occurrence of most common ailments.

Considering education, we face a similar problem. Our current system of education focuses on the learning-impaired, educationally disadvantaged, and special educational needs on one hand and the gifted on the other. We have excellent programs for special needs students and for the gifted. We generate more Nobel laureates per capita than any other nation. However, the average math or science scores of an American student are among the lowest in developed nations. Similarly, the percentage of functionally illiterate adult Americans is higher than that of any other developed nation and, for that matter, some developing nations.

We spend enormous sums and efforts to satisfy special needs while letting the standards of education for the average student slip to levels where most will not really be functional in modern society. We produce a very small percentage of highly educated people and let the majority graduate with no effective education or usable skills. We also make comparatively little effort to prevent or remedy our educational shortcomings with greater parental involvement or continuing education or training.

Criminal justice similarly concentrates on serving focused problems of the poor and the rich. It gives more attention to assuring justice to criminals than to victims. In fact, it often considers or redefines criminals as the victims of *their* victims. In other words, the criminal justice system mainly serves the contraveners of the laws and not the law-abiding citizens. Its clients are the criminals, and the public is just an interfering nuisance.

To reform our three principal institutions, the objectives of these institutions must be redefined and their priorities and goals reestablished. They must reorganize and concentrate on the needs of society at large and not the focused fringes they now mainly serve. Emphasis must again be on assuring a healthy, well-educated, and well-protected society where each citizen feels a part of institutions and considers them his or hers. This requires radical reform and a return to basics and the fundamental functions they were set up to serve.

This may be painful because it may require taking the power from the politicians and institutional managers and restoring it to the health providers, educators, and law enforcers. It may require reestablishing program and institutional objectives to meet the needs of society at large and not mainly those of special interest groups. To achieve this, we will have to evaluate our institutional structures and reestablish institutional goals. We have done this in other areas. We have reengineered large and small corporations. We are reorganizing government. Now the reformation of our institutions is our most urgent problem. If this is not done, our institutions will become increasingly heavy, ineffective stones around our necks, which will ultimately destroy America, not only as a world leader and economy, but also as a society.

## Reconnection of American Institutions

American institutions have become disconnected from society at large. They once *were* the society and were an integral part of each community but are now distinct and sovereign entities. Few Americans feel that they are part of law enforcement, education, or health care systems or that these institutions are there to serve them. Few Americans have their own lawyer or even doctor. Many of us, if not most, grope for legal, health, or educational assistance only when needed and often find such services virtually impossible to obtain. We somehow view these institutions as self-centered and not really part of society.

If they are to be effective, our institutions will have to reconnect and become an integral part of society and of each community. They must become society's institutions and not primarily business-oriented, narrowly focused organizations that provide services on their own terms and with their own objectives in mind.

Reconnection will require a radical change in the way institutions are run and perceive themselves, as well as the ways in which they relate to their community and to society at large. Reconnection implies being service-oriented and aiming to first satisfy the needs of the public.

It is necessary to link the needs of the public and society and institutional goals to assure effective connection. Without it, institutions will not only become more and more isolated, but they will lose their direction. For institutions to perform well, they must continuously adjust to the global needs of society and serve the bulk of society and not just focused extremes. They are there to support society at large and to help it advance in terms of education, health care, and public safety to improve the quality of life for the public. Their function is not to concentrate their efforts and resources on fringe problems.

## Emphasis on Institutional Prevention versus Care

In recent years, American legal, health care, and educational institutions have concentrated on curing the ills of American society, such as crime, deteriorating health, and educational failures. Most of these efforts have been ineffective because they address the effects and not the causes or symptoms of these ills. Precautionary measures and preventative approaches could be much more effective and significantly cheaper than the reactive methods now employed. Many societies have found that crime prevention is more effective than crime fighting, prevention of illness more effective than treating diseases, and prevention of apathetic illiteracy more effective than remedial education, training, and economic support of the uneducated.

However, overwhelming evidence to the contrary, American institutions and the lawmakers who regulate them and provide their budgets continue to concentrate on a cure even if it is impossible or has proven to be completely ineffective. Prevention is cheaper and more effective than a cure, and it involves and educates the public and reduces our dependency on institutions. Apparently, therein lies the problem. A public more knowledgeable about health, education, and law and one that prevents problems in these areas would significantly reduce both the influence of the institutions and its dependence on them. In turn, this would greatly diminish their role in society and influence on or control over society, something many leaders of our institutions and their supporters abhor. However, there is no alternative if we are to maintain American leadership.

Prevention will make us a more effective, healthier, more educated, more knowledgeable, and safer society, one where interpersonal relations are based mainly on social and not financial or career objectives, where people are cooperative and friendly and not basically assertive and confrontational, and where helping others is a social grace and a natural way of behavior and is not considered merely an act of naïveté.

Unfortunately, this change will not be introduced by our political or institutional leadership. They have too large a vested interest in the status quo. It must be introduced from the bottom up by the public and be based increasingly on approaches that prevent ills from occurring and call less and less on institutional help. This change will be resisted by our institutions that often have the support of our politicians. Their deep pockets also provide them with the power to convert the media to their viewpoint. But change we must! Prevention of societal ills and not their treatment must become the principal national objective.

## Alternatives to Crime

Alternatives to crime for young and old offenders can improve safety and reduce the burden on the criminal justice system. Preventing crime should be the principal objective of the justice system, and a "cure" by punishment is only a method for the removal of embedded ills. Young offenders must not be simply incarcerated but should be enrolled in a good habit- and skill- forming program similar to a well-designed boot camp. They should be removed from their family environment when it is evident that the family is detrimental or that the home environment contributes to their lawlessness.

Stern boot-camp-type programs can detoxify their habits, instill self-esteem and skills, and, above all, enforce discipline. They should work for their keep as a lesson in the value of work. They must learn teamwork, cooperation, and respect, along with an appreciation for their own potential. They should not be released until they prove capable of assuming a responsible role as a member of society, a willingness and ability to work for a living, and an attitude that is not asocial. Their release should be based on their progress toward responsible citizenship and not a set date.

As mentioned before, America is among only a few countries where most convicted criminals are given a free ride. They are given comfortable prison quarters, TV, sport facilities, food, and clothing. In fact, prisoners and their advocates maintain this as a right and have successfully sued and won major awards when prisoners were not provided with private washing or toilet or other facilities they felt were necessary. They demand that society pay for all this while the criminal is not liable for his or her upkeep nor for restitution to his or her victims. From a purely logical or even theological point of view, this is clearly wrong. Prison incarceration is not only designed to remove an offender from opportunities for further criminal destruction but also to reeducate the criminal and to obtain some restitution for the victims or society. This absurdity is magnified when prisoners continue to receive welfare and similar support payments even while in prison.

In many other civilized societies, prisoners must work to pay for their keep as well as to make restitution to their victims and to society before being released. This not only educates offenders but also trains them toward becoming self-supporting members of society much more effectively than does our pampering and forgiving penal system, which is concerned primarily with criminals' rights and not victims' justice.

The percentage of repeat offenders in violent and nonviolent crimes in the United States is two to three times that of any other developed country, a clear sign of the lack of effectiveness of our approach. More than 60 percent of all murders in the United States are committed by released murderers—a tragic statistic. The recently introduced "three strikes and you're out" concept, under which a prisoner is not imprisoned permanently until after conviction for three capital offenses, is not only a farce but a clear violation of the rights of society at large. It is amazing that even now, when America holds the title for the most crime-ridden of developed nations, our politicians do not tackle the crime problem head-on.

The alternatives to crime that our justice system could employ for both young and old offenders require a change of attitude and a will to tackle the problem. They require a restructuring of priorities and a concern for the rights of society over the rights of those convicted of attacking it.

Our crime-fighting ability is curiously constrained by old-style liberals concerned with the importance of freedom and the rights of the individual, including the rights of criminals no matter what the cost to society.

These liberals are joined by right-wing nationalists and opponents to gun control, both of whom have their own agenda. We appear to be lost between liberals, who believe that criminal behavior is the fault of society and firearm advocates who would justify the universal arming of American society.

## Institutional Downsizing for Productivity and Quality Improvement

The objective of institutional downsizing is not service or output curtailment. It is productivity and quality enhancement and the cost savings realized by the cutting of unnecessary levels in institutional management hierarchy, by delegating authority to the lowest competent level, eliminating unnecessary functions and people, and reassessing the priorities of the organization.

This new approach requires a reassessment of the need for assistants, associates, and deputies at the department- or division-head level, as well as the reevaluation of the level at which decisions are made in an organization. In recent years decision-making powers in U.S. institutions have moved up instead of down, notwithstanding the fact that relevant information is often more readily available at the lower levels. This trend appears to be a response of management to the ready accessibility of information by restricting its effective use at lower levels. Instead of removing layers of unnecessary upper-middle management, such institutions have added to them, resulting in further isolating top management. University provosts are now supported by deputy, associate, and assistant provosts, all with their own staff, a trend that is replicated at the dean and department-head levels. The same is evident in hospitals, government agencies, and inefficient companies. As a result, institutional management is further removed from the real issues and concerns of the institutions.

The proper functions of top management are strategic, yet in recent years institutional management has often taken over the operational decision functions, reducing authority at the departmental level without a full knowledge of what needs to be done. This upward decision-making movement is contrary to recent successful experiences in downsizing and downward delegation of decision making in industry in an attempt to improve productivity and quality by eliminating some middle management and making top management responsible for strategic issues only. The response has been universally positive, and companies, such as Chrysler, Motorola, and Boeing that adopted this approach have regained their competitive edge. Improvement is based on the recognition that people in general will do their best if entrusted with responsibility, particularly for decisions that affect themselves and their own work. The process is also working well in efficiently run public agencies and institutions that have been downsizing from the top down and not from the bottom up.

However, many American universities and hospitals appear to be moving in the opposite direction, with their productive units, the faculty, and health care professionals entrusted with fewer and fewer decision-making powers. It seems that university and hospital management believe that their professional staff cannot be trusted with any but academic decisions. Had Chrysler or IBM taken this approach, they would now be bankrupt. But universities and hospitals do not go bankrupt; they simply raise more money or reduce their services.

According to *Business Week* (December 20,1993), in the new organizational model you manage across a flat organizational structure, with the productive factors assuming most of the operational decisions—not from up to down. This is a concept most forward-looking corporations have grasped by now, but universities, hospitals, and similar institutions appear to resist it, apparently not because they do not recognize the need for such a change, but because they do not want to give up power at the top.

Institutions must become nimbler competitors by eliminating unnecessary administrative layers and becoming true horizontal organizations. If corporations can organize workers into self-managing teams, delegating responsibilities to the productive or worker level, surely American universities and hospitals can delegate more responsibility to their productive levels—the faculty and health care professionals who are the only real output-producers at these institutions. Obviously, this will require that they take more responsibility for wider issues, a thing administrators abhor and with which some professionals may no longer be comfortable. But regaining academic productivity and fiscal soundness requires that faculty and health care providers reclaim their traditional responsibilities.

The hierarchical management system used is often defended as being essential to prevent abuses, but in reality it delays decisions and results in costly errors, without reducing abuses. It also discourages motivation and eliminates incentive for novel contributions by faculty and health care providers, beyond their narrowly focused professional interests. In other words, this system discourages faculty cooperation and thereby the ability of the university to address the relevant large-scale interdisciplinary problems that dominate today.

## Redirecting American Health Care

There is no doubt that American medical technology is second to none and that our medical specialists are superbly trained and competent. Our problem is one of skewed numbers of specialists and primary care physicians, however, not of the quality of doctors and medical care. The problem is that there are too many specialists and too few general practitioners, too many sophisticated hospitals and too few emergency as well as basic clinics. There are also too many high-tech diagnostic centers and too few basic medical test facilities and laboratories. The United States is the best place in the world for an organ transplant or other sophisticated medical procedure and one of the worst places to come down with a severe cold, disabling backache, sprained ankle, or other ordinary impairment. There are no home visits, and hospital emergency rooms are overcrowded, largely with nonemergency cases who have no place else to go. They are not really equipped to handle such nonemergency cases efficiently. Most Americans turn to the hospital emergency room for treatment, as few have a personal physician, and even for those who are so fortunate, the physician is often not available for non-critical cases without a long wait. Also, if a patient is too ill to drive or walk to a treatment center, he or she cannot take a taxi but must use an ambulance at twenty times the cost, as most public and private insurers do not pay for use of a taxi or private car but will pay in such cases for ambulance transport. The system now operates to force up costs and reduce accessibility.

## Institutional Management

Over the last thirty years the management of institutions, particularly in education and health care, has undergone a radical change from management by peers of peers to management by professional (and often not so professional) managers. Most American universities, hospitals, and research institutions were originally headed by renowned scientists, educators, or doctors, often elected by their own peers. No more! Today most institutional administrators are neither renowned professionals nor freely elected by their professional or academic peers.

The change was apparently inspired by the idea that these institutions required "professional" management. The experiences, however, indicate that many institutional managers were more interested in solidifying their controls than in assuring improvement in institutional, professional, and financial performance. Most important, though, is the increasing lack of leadership in many of these institutions with management more and more out of touch with faculty and medical staff.

We must reestablish the coherence of our health care and educational institutions, and to some extent also that of our legal system, by empowering the professionals with the strategic management of their respective institutions and by reestablishing leadership by peers of peers, replacing the present imposed hierarchy of self-styled institutional managers.

We must reestablish leadership by the faculty and medical profession and internal bonds of trust if we are to regain control of the institutions that made this country great. We must release these institutions from management that does not lead and follows its own agenda. Our institutions must once again act as public resources that function in the public interest. This requires a reassertion of the primacy of the faculty and medical professionals in their respective institutions. It requires a return to the basic principles of institutional democracy.

## Use of Institutional Expenditures of Institutional Function

It is interesting to note what percentages of our health care, educational, and criminal justice system expenditures are spent on providing required health care, education, and criminal justice or law enforcement. We have fairly reliable numbers on how much we spend on doctors and nurses, teachers and instructors, and police, jailers, prosecutors, and judges. These professionals obviously require a significant support staff, facilities, equipment, supplies, and services to perform their basic functions. The question is: how much? Even if we assume that all the doctors, nurses, teachers, police officers, judges, and so on, are actually needed, we soon find that their total cost, including benefits and other costs, such as costs of support staff, facilities, and equipment, consume but a small fraction of total institutional system expenditures. If we add all direct and indirect costs, including that of all support staff such as secretaries, janitors, and security personnel, we find that even then only about half of the expenditures for these institutions can be accounted for.

For example, even though we have more doctors and nurses per capita than any other country, their total costs, including support and facility/equipment costs, are under one-third of our total health care expenditures. Similar ratios are found to exist in education, where costs for teachers are even lower as a percentage of total educational system costs. Criminal justice is somewhat different because law enforcement has many more components than just police and court–related expenditures.

The question is: on what is the rest of the money spent? Universities spend an increasing amount of money on marketing, public relations, and fund-raising, as do health care institutions. In addition, both of these types of institution spend more and more on infrastructure, prestigious diagnostic equipment, computers and communications systems, lobbying, outside consultants, lawyers, and insurance.

The percentage of costs directly or indirectly associated with health care and education is now less than 50 percent of the total spent on these institutions and is becoming ever smaller—this at a time of public outcry at both the cost and performance of health care and educational service providers. The costs of criminal justice have similarly gone astray, with the direct costs of law enforcement, public safety, judicial services, and correction now consuming less than half of the total and also declining. These institutions appear to have lost touch with the society they are supposed to serve. Society wants effective no-frills education, preventative treatment and health care, and effective law enforcement and public safety. It does not want a highly politicized and largely self-serving set of institutions that impose their perceptions of health care, education, and criminal justice on society.

## The Disconnectedness of Society

American society appears to be more disconnected today than at any other time in history. While racial separation has been practiced for nearly 200 years and is slow to be dismantled, other equally harmful forms of separation and disconnection are emerging in its place. This is the result of greater income differentials between the rich and the poor and is also due to a decimation of the traditional middle class, the backbone of American society for at least the last century, with most people falling toward the poverty level and only a few advancing toward affluence. American society is becoming more and more bipolar. Class consciousness and antagonism, which once barely existed, are now coming to the forefront. This is due not only to increasing economic differences but also differences in lifestyle, cultural preferences, and disparity of opportunity.

The traditional concept of America as the land of equal opportunity is rapidly being replaced by the belief that opportunities are for the culturally, socially, and economically advantaged and that others can find opportunity only in crime and asocial behavior.

America is becoming more class-conscious, with a mounting lack of connectedness among the classes and groups within society. Mobility and opportunity have declined, and an outlook of economic and social stagnation, probably more than anything, causes America's discontent and hopelessness, which in return cause lawlessness and antagonism.

American institutions are largely responsible for this condition. The way we deal with crime, welfare, health care, and education affects attitudes and the connectedness of society. The land of equal opportunity, of effective cultural and social integration, appears less so now.

Our educational system caters to the lowest achievers, graduating people who barely attain basic literacy, along with our high achievers. We discriminate against the hardworking, competent students by holding them back so that we do not disturb the egos of those who do not care to be educated.

Sixty-five percent of U.S. high school students enter higher education, compared to 50 percent in Japan, 40 percent in France and Germany, and 30 percent in the United Kingdom, Austria, and Switzerland. At the same time, the level of attainment in mathematics and science of U.S. high school students is well below that not only of developed countries but also of most East Asian countries such as China, Korea, and Taiwan. For many in America, higher education is largely remedial high school education.

While U.S. high schools and colleges generally dispense a rather mediocre education, some produce excellence beyond that achieved by institutions in the rest of the world. This tremendous imbalance in the quality of American high school and even more higher education is the principal reason for the tremendous waste in people's time and money on education. It means that even the most mediocre student from an ineffective high school can find a university that will accept him and allow him to spend four years there. Even though most private universities—which means the vast majority of American universities—are supposedly nonprofit institutions, they are generally businesses with the overriding objective of maximizing revenues. While most students in foreign universities are there to learn a profession, the majority of U.S. undergraduates are just spending time, with little, if any, professional orientation.

## Relevance of College Education

American universities have always maintained that college education is the key to success and to a better life. By and large, Americans have bought this promise. However, a very large percentage of successful Americans never went to college. As reported in *Forbes* (September 1995), only 46 percent of highly successful entrepreneurs finished college and 29 percent never even started college. These numbers are just one indication of an increasing concern with the relevance of an American college education. Similarly, a majority of college graduates do not make effective, if any, use of their college education in their working life.

The decline of middle management, the traditional stepping-stone for college graduates, is just one of the reasons why fewer big companies search campuses for new recruits. While many jobs require advanced education and training, these are often not offered in American colleges. In fact, most American universities have little perception of the needs of today's job market and their faculty and administration are often ignorant of the changing requirements. They somehow think that they know best what industrial or other employers need. This is not surprising, as few of them have ever set foot outside academia.

As a result, many now rebel at the high cost of a college education, because the direct link between investment in a college education and its contribution to life earnings or career potentials has become quite murky. Many colleges find that not only are applications for admission way down, but many more applicants demand financial aid or special deals. While at this time only the smaller and less prestigious colleges are hit by this phenomena, it appears that the trend will soon encompass American colleges in general as applicants and their supporters demand proof of the relevance of a college education as a key to success.

In the last twenty years the cost of a college education has nearly doubled in relation to average family income. It has grown from under 1.6 to over 3 times the average family income in the United States, and many question its value, particularly if lost income during college years is added to the costs. In other words, a college graduate today must make up not only the cost of college education or about $50,000 to $100,000 but also an equal or larger amount of income foregone by going to college.

It is increasingly difficult to show that a four-year college education adds $100,000 to $200,000 to life-earning potentials. Graduate school attendance, while very costly, may improve the situation, but only if it is narrowly job-focused. Graduate schools are usually focused on narrow professional areas. Their costs are justifiable by the increase in earnings such degrees may assure. Though this is not true of all graduate degrees, graduate education in law, medicine, or business is usually worth the additional expenditure of $70,000 to $150,000 and loss of two or three years' income, at least for now.

Lifetime earnings of professionals with such degrees are often ten times or more the added expenditure for graduate education. In most countries of the world, professional education in medicine, law, business, engineering, science, etc., commences with the freshman year and the professional focus is immediately maintained. Although many undergraduate programs provide a basis for professional education, particularly in engineering and science, the lack of such professional focus during undergraduate education adds an average of two or three years to the attainment of professional competence and credentials in the United States. For example, in England or Germany lawyers can complete their college requirements for a law degree in five years, versus four plus three, or seven years in the United States. The same applies to the medical and other fields.

The question is really: what is the worth of a nonfocused undergraduate college education? Many claim that it develops the educated person. However, in a large number of cases it really largely serves to remedy deficiencies in high school education and to permit a delay in making hard career decisions for young people. After teaching college for over thirty-five years, I have come to the conclusion that delaying such decisions does not make them easier or better.

In the meantime, we waste precious potentially rewarding years of our young people at a great cost to them, their parents, and the taxpayer. There is neither a need nor justification for the majority of our high school graduates to go to college when the number of jobs requiring a college education is much less than half the average number of people graduating. The savings in direct costs would be of the order of $100 billion per year and the added productive output generated by four years of additional work by students forgoing a meaningless college experience would probably be even larger.

The emphasis of a college education should not be on the learning of facts but on problem discovery, definition, and solution. For a college education to be worth its cost in time and money, students should learn skills.

A recent government report claims that employers in general have essentially given up on relying on colleges to properly prepare students for required work skills. This is a serious indictment of our universities and must be corrected if academic institutions are to fulfill their responsibility and promise to the public.

## Academic Values

Overcharging both students and research sponsors by some universities has reduced public confidence. In addition, American universities are increasingly being criticized for a decreasing quality of teaching as well as the relevance of their educational programs, particularly at the undergraduate level.

A basic college education is now quite often a sham. Undergraduate courses are rarely taught by professors, and with an increasing number of foreigners crowding graduate schools, many graduate teaching assistants who teach undergraduates are barely capable of speaking English. This obviously affects the quality of undergraduate teaching.

Yet universities continue to sell themselves on the basis of their renowned faculty and convey the impression that students will actually be taught by these respected teachers. This continues in graduate study, where faculty are more involved but often use students to further their narrow research interests, which are often inconsistent with the professional objectives of the students.

There is also an interesting development in the internal value system of colleges. Faculty status, promotion, and rewards used to be valued on the basis of the quality of and contribution to teaching and research and were measured by student responses, class sizes, publications, peer evaluations, and professional status. Most of these are increasingly given only superficial consideration, with other factors gaining in importance. These include loyalty to the "institution," fund-raising, research support, and public as well as internal relations.

Universities now expect the blind loyalty of a distinguished group of professionals hired as faculty but treated as fungible workers whose principal loyalty is expected to be toward the "institution" and not their professional, research, education and, obviously, truth.

We have a system of universities that exemplifies the best and probably the worst in the world. Many American universities are a mockery as academic institutions, and their accreditation should have been revoked long ago. But we allow them to go on to give everyone a chance for a college education. What college education? Some of our colleges would not pass as competent high schools in many countries or, for that matter, in many demanding American communities. In turn, this contributes to the lack of connectedness in our society. Worthless college diplomas increase the societal gap, as disenchanted youths often find themselves without marketable skills at age twenty-two or even twenty-four, this after having studied for four years, spending their parents' or borrowed money, for an experience largely designed to simply defer difficult career decisions and entering of the workforce. America was once a country with a wide middle class, comprised of skilled blue-collar workers, semiprofessionals, professionals, businesspeople, artists, and more. The decline in blue-collar and other types of skill training and the loss of prestige of blue-collar work is a major reason for the decimation of the middle class in America.

Other institutions, such as criminal justice, similarly contributed to this development by making effective legal services available or affordable only to the poor and the rich. While health care is somewhat more egalitarian, it also provides major advantages to the poor and rich respectively, with the middle class either not effectively covered or paying an unfair share.

The result, as we have seen, is increased disconnection. Society was once dominated by a vast middle class open to all, which comprised the bulk of Americans, all proud to be part of it. The middle class is now gradually shrinking and losing influence. Government policies and decisions are now influenced by the needs of the poor or the demands of the rich, with the invisible middle class now left out of the process.

Our institutions have a major responsibility for this development, as it is they who foster the trend of training people with either highly marketable or nonmarketable skills. The income gap between professionals and the semiskilled or even skilled workers is growing, as is the income gap between nurses and doctors, accountants and financial planners, and legal aides and lawyers.

The economic equality that developed in the United States following World War II, which elevated skilled workers to the level of professionals, resulted in a dominant middle class. This made postwar America unique. We had basically no so-called working class, a small poor class, and an equally small rich class. Everyone was or aspired to be middle-class. Real wages increased for practically everyone in the middle class, and living standards continuously rose. Yet in the last five to ten years things have changed dramatically, with increasingly wide disparities in middle-class incomes. In turn, this is decimating the middle class, with many falling back into the working poor and only a few rising into the rich or wealthy class.

## Management of American Education

American education must be reformed if we are to reverse the decline in educational standards, moral values, and economic performance. There are many problems with the system. Some of these are structural while others are the result of a lack of control or standards.

The United States spends more per student at any level of education than any country in the world. In fact, we spend nearly twice as much per student on primary and high school education than the European Union average. Yet we have seen that the average level of competence of an American high school graduate is far below that of his or her European or East Asian counterpart.

There is basically no American educational quality control, no national standards, and few state or locally enforced standards. with over half of high school graduates going on to attend a university, higher education is chosen by many not so much to obtain professional knowledge and skills but for the following more negative reasons:

1. to correct an ineffective high school education;
2. to delay the choice of a career and starting of a job, and
3. to continue free-wheeling.

This situation results in tremendous waste, not only of our national wealth and tax dollars, but also in lost output as entry to the job market is delayed by many who do not benefit from higher education.

Universities have not delivered on the promise that investment in higher education will result in economic growth. By and large they continue to deliver a relatively small number of superbly trained professionals from the so-called elite professional schools, and a huge, dominant percentage of college graduates with no marketable skills. In addition, few of the latter group can claim even to have advanced their education.

The recently passed education bill provides federal resources to make financing of college education more accessible. While this may be laudable in cases where it helps competent, deserving students, it is the wrong approach when it simply adds to the accessibility of college education.

While our higher education system fails, we can also see on-the-job, vocational, and continuing education or training woefully lacking, in both quality and in support. According to A. Carneval, chief economist of the American Society for Training and Development, U.S. employers spend only $30 billion (or 1 percent of payroll) on training, retraining, and education (of which 90 percent is spent by fewer than half of all U.S. firms). By comparison, German firms spend 2 percent and Japanese 2 to 4 percent. Similarly, government expenditures of these countries for such training is more than twice that spent by American government agencies whose primary thrust is in training the unemployed.

One reason advanced for the low level of commitment by American firms to continuing education and training is the perceived mobility of American workers. Yet this instability could be corrected by offering more effective job incentives and by more effective tax incentives by government to firms.

One area often quoted as an American success is executive education, for which firms spend large amounts of money. While many executive training programs are effective, most have no measurable standards and simply offer the latest fad in executive techniques. Many concentrate more on teaching methodology than on the understanding of the basics and applications.

There is a general perception that U.S. education is costly and ineffective, that it is largely designed to make students feel good, and that it somehow attempts to make education pleasurable and entertaining. Many in industry also contend that American universities are not very good at disseminating knowledge in this information age, as academics now often lag behind in their own understanding and use of technology and, even more important, in applications development, as emphasis is often given to pure and basic knowledge, even if it does not help solve problems or advance understanding. As a result, many U.S. firms choose proven consultants and private training organizations over universities to provide executive and technical training. In fact, only a small portion of the $30 billion spent by U.S firms on continuing education was actually spent on academic courses or programs offered by universities.

Since 1984, educational costs, particularly the cost of higher education, have risen at nearly twice the rate of inflation (with university tuition increasing at more than 8.2 percent, or 4 percent per year, in real terms). Yet teaching and academic salaries have barely kept pace with inflation. The sharp rise in educational costs can be largely attributed to increases in bureaucracy, high administrative salaries, and often ineffective management.

Although many American universities now offer programs in quality and productivity management, few, if any, have successfully applied the methods they teach and often even preach. TQM requires hard decisions, the elimination of unnecessary staff and services, restructuring of programs to meet the needs of the customer, JIT development, and offering of courses, subjects, and research projects and, most important, continuous self-criticism. It requires an organization that reevaluates itself, its structure, and its performance in a detached way. The organization must be able to look at itself as others see it and as a reflection of its real performance, not its perceived status or past accomplishments.

Many American universities live on dreams of past glory and accomplishment. These dreams are often emphasized by growing numbers of academic public relations and marketing specialists who themselves are often out of touch with the real state of accomplishment and capability of the institutions they represent and are unable to evaluate or even understand academic issues. The problem is amplified by the increasing lack of contact among academic administrators, faculty, and researchers. As a result, academic administrators often perceive themselves to be the university and see or consider the faculty as adjunct employees who are able to make whatever contribution only because of the institution and its environment, as established and maintained by the administration.

The late Indira Gandhi, former prime minister of India, once observed that there are two kinds of people—those who do the work and those who take the credit. American universities have apparently proved this concept, allowing the latter to "administer" the former. The faculty, who established the reputation of the university, have somehow been convinced that their contribution is made possible only by the institution, its environment, and the opportunity or freedom it provides, which, in turn, are all credited to the administration. Thus by a skewed argument the credit for the achievements of the institutions "rightly" go to the administration and other insiders who make it all possible. As a result, credit by association has become a major method of rewarding loyalty. In many cases, this has caused major discontent and even discord among faculty and between faculty and administration of universities when the faculty feels left out.

The top executives of major American universities were once eminent scholars in science, engineering, management, medicine, law, or other important disciplines. They were selected and elected by their peers. In recent years this tradition has changed. Now many of our greatest institutions of higher education are led by people with no such credentials.

It appears that the selection is often a compromise. Fewer top-notch scholars are now willing to become academic executives, not only because it involves onerous administration and fund-raising but also, more important, because it removes them from the academic environment and their peers. In other words, it involves increased administration, public relations, fund-raising, politics, and marketing, and decreased—if any—academic and scholarly leadership.

University presidents now function as salespeople and fund-raisers, at the sacrifice of contact with the faculty and with the academic institution itself. Officers of some institutions of higher learning are essentially merely business executives of the institution. Elementary and high schools are run in very much the same way, with management increasingly preoccupied with politics, administration, and fiscal issues and decreasingly with educational leadership.

This may be a proper way to run academic and educational institutions *if* such emphasis on fiscal and operational management were superior under such focused administration. However, the facts contradict this assumption. In virtually every case, the assumption of management of academic and educational institutions by nonscholars/educators or administrators has resulted in an uncontrolled growth of the institutional bureaucracy, a downgrading of scholarly achievement, and incompetent fiscal management as well as economic and educational waste. In other words, the changing emphasis of educational management has caused the decline in scholarly and educational standards as well as in fiscal performance. In light of these developments it is clearly desirable to attract and return noted scholars and educators to the leadership of our educational institutions.

## Reforming American Primary Education

There have been numerous attempts at improving American primary education at its various levels. The results have usually been short-lived. We regularly introduced new methods of education, often under the guise of psychological and pedagogical legitimacy. We have introduced sociological treatment and programs designed to make students "feel good about themselves" even if they did not learn anything. We made teachers pass and complete numerous tests that evaluated and reevaluated their competence and approach to teaching. Nevertheless, the competence and performance of teachers continue to decline, as do student test scores in many parts of America. At the same time, the status of teachers has declined.

It is now time to discontinue experiments with novel methods, reduce educational bureaucracy, concentrate on the basics of education, raise the standards of achievement in all school subjects, and reward good teachers and students and punish the nonperformers thus providing meaningful incentives and disincentives for students and teachers alike. Classes should be small enough to provide meaningful student-teacher interaction.

Students who fail a subject should be required to repeat it and if they fail a majority of subjects must be required to repeat the entire grade's work. School days should be lengthened to at least seven contact hours in high school and six contact hours in junior high. The school year should similarly consist of at least 200 school days as it is in many countries now.

Public high schools are not challenging enough according to 1,300 teenagers polled by the nonprofit group Public Agenda, as reported in *U.S. News and World Report* on February 24, 1997. "Teach us more, assure greater order and structure, and take use more seriously" is the major request of these students. "You expect too little from us, and we live *down* to your expectations" is another complaint. Students want us to do more for them so that they can do more. Our expectations are too low. As reported in the same issue, while eighth-graders in the United States barely master arithmetic, fractions, and elementary algebra, those in Germany and Japan, for example, are doing advanced algebra and geometry. In fact, by the time U.S. students graduate from a high school, they are usually two years behind those in countries such as Japan, Singapore, Korea, Germany, and more.

Today schools are expected to assume many parental responsibilities, a policy that encourages parents to take less interest in their children's education, social behavior, and health care. Instead of helping the children, these school activities have resulted in an overall decline of parental interest and care, with parents simply handing these responsibilities over to the school.

Education is the key to success in American life, and it is the key to advancement for the so-called disadvantaged. Parents and children must be taught that morality, culture, and education together are necessary ingredients for success. Parents must resume responsibility for their child's behavior as well as for their preparation for school and must be involved in and be held responsible for their children's performance by meaningful incentives. Unless parenting is returned to the home, leaving the teachers free to concentrate on education and training, American education will continue the present decline. Obviously much of the fault lies with our current social and social welfare systems, which reward lack of parental responsibility. Some welfare families automatically register every one of their offspring as being "slightly retarded" in an effort to collect annual benefits of sometimes over $5,000 per year. Under such circumstances, many capable students learn to act as if they are slightly retarded and, like their family, become wards of the state for life. The welfare system is thus propagated in the same families for generations.

Welfare and education are closely linked, with the first dragging down the second. In other words, they feed upon each other and perpetuate the joint system of economic dependence and educational demise. The chances of a child of parents on welfare receiving an education that will allow him or her to contribute effectively and earn a reasonable living in our society are very small indeed, not because the child is less capable but because the system forces him or her to perform below capability. Instead of challenging children, it offers numerous disincentives to the acquisition of an education.

American primary education will have to provide effective incentives and disincentives to fulfill its educational promise and bring its cost down. Among suggestions for improvement are the following:

1. Parents must be made to assume greater responsibility for and interest in the education of their children. Parents who decline any interest in and responsibility for their children's education may have to have some of their parental rights removed. For example, such parents may have their child allowance withheld and also the money used to feed and supervise the child outside the home for the afternoons. In addition or in its place, such parents would have to participate in parental training that provides them with the skills and motivation to act as responsible parents who understand and accept family values before qualifying for a restoration of child support funds to their control.
2. Schools, and parents for that matter, must demand and enforce greater discipline of their children. Children must not be asked to make choices but be given the opportunities to experience various alternatives. Discipline should be taught and children properly rewarded for good behavior. Schools must develop positive peer pressure against any child who misbehaves or is otherwise undisciplined and enforce a system of punishment deemed fair and accepted by children's peers. Making children their own judges teaches them both discipline and values.
3. The school year should be extended and school days made longer and more consistent with ordinary workdays. In a society where an increasing number of families have a single parent or two working parents, it is unreasonable for schools to expect parents to be able to take care of their children for the better part of the afternoon. Afternoons should be spent on homework, quiet study, time out, and recreation, including visits to sights and museums. Not only would this clear valuable class time for fundamental education, but it would also provide students lacking an effective substitute family or home environment with effective, supervised homework performance and would equalize opportunities among students. Lengthening the school year would also reduce the differences in learning opportunities between advantaged and disadvantaged children. Advantaged children often spend their vacations in focused summer camps or other activities that provide valuable learning experiences, while disadvantaged children are

usually left to fend for themselves and often spend their vacation time learning about crime.

4. The number of primary school staff with direct teaching and supervisory (contact) duties should be increased and the number of noncontact administrative and teacher or program supervisory personnel reduced. Today the percentage of administrative and housekeeping staff at our schools has increased out of all proportion to a level where much fewer than half the staff of our schools are actually involved in education and supervision. The ratio of directly involved staff to other staff has declined continuously since 1970 and appears to be a major reason for the decline in educational performance of students, student discipline, and the relations between teachers, students, and parents. In other words, there is no shortage of staff to perform these duties. It simply requires moving paper shufflers into productive contact jobs. In 1994/95 there were 2.505 million teachers in U.S. public primary and secondary schools, with an average salary of $35,819. In other words, $89 million was spent on teachers' salaries. This is only 33 percent of the total revenue of public elementary and secondary schools in the United States, which received that year $19.59 billion from the federal government, $123.090 billion from state, and $125.08 billion from local government, for a total of $267.76 billion (source: National Education Association). Even after adding the cost of benefits, total direct cost of teaching remains at less than 44 percent of total revenue. Similarly, expenditures per student increased from $375, $816, $2,272, and $4,962 between 1959/60, 1969/70, 1979/80, and 1989/90 (source: U.S. Department of Education). By the end of this decade, the expenditures are expected to be above $10,000 per student.
5. The status of teachers must be improved so that students and parents consider teachers role models and examples of success. While pay is important, position, responsibility, and prestige are equally if not more important. Teachers must control schools and principals or superintendents should be peers among peers and not a separate class of professional school administrators.

Primary and high school education in America must be taken more seriously by parents, teachers and the children themselves. Its purpose is not to entertain or take care of children but to educate children, train them in basic skills, and establish effective social behavior and a sense of responsibility. Primary schools are not supposed to be just fun places, nor are they places that should assume parental responsibilities and tasks. Parents cannot transfer disciplining responsibilities to teachers. Only when parents and schools are working together and parents exert their authority on discipline can schools perform well. Schools must have the parents' full support, and parents should neither transfer their responsibilities to schools nor undermine the teachers' authority and function. In many cases, this may require parental education. This is difficult with single working or nonworking, teenage, and uneducated or unmotivated parents, but unless primary education involves parents it cannot and will not succeed.

One possibility is to have Saturday morning sessions for parents and children in the school environment. Children could show their parents what they have learned, and parents would be instructed how to help educate their children while their children play. Such mandatory parental involvement of parents in primary education has proven an attractive and effective approach that pays many dividends by educating both parents and children and results in getting them closer and more respectful of each other.

## Reforming High Schools and Precollege Education

While there are some high schools that provide effective higher education, most have become adolescent holding tanks or institutions in which education or learning is provided as one of many, often unrelated, activities. Many times sports and social programs assume much greater importance than learning and education. One problem is obviously the lack of both inter- and intraschool educational standards. Similarly, the unjust concern with the psychological impact of making students repeat subjects or complete class years has pulled down general standards and become very discouraging to well-performing, talented, and hardworking students. In other words, students advance and ultimately graduate no matter how they perform.

The high schools of America bear a significant responsibility for the high unemployment and low earning or job potential of many minority and other students. High schools are expected, and indeed attempt, to do many things that are not their function and as a result fail in their principal goals of educating and training adolescents in America to become educated, socially competent, and responsible as well as self-sufficient members of society ready to embark on the challenging adventure of life—to both contribute and to enjoy.

Instead, many of our high schools graduate angry, uneducated, irresponsible, asocial individuals with little will or competence to face life. While not all of this is the fault of high school education, much of it is. Many of our high schools have their priorities wrong and cater mainly to outside pressures instead of the needs of their students.

Political, fiscal, and social pressures more than educational and behavioral objectives dictate the programs and performance of many of our high schools. As a result, fewer and fewer high school graduates are capable of assuming interesting and rewarding career opportunities. Then they either opt for the holding opportunity of a meaningless college education or one of flipping burgers or performing similar jobs unless they are among the few really motivated and focused high school graduates for whom college is a challenge and a real professional education.

There are many who claim that young people need the opportunity to play, to gain experience, and to grow. This is true. But even that must be based on a well-conceived approach that has focus, develops knowledge and social skills, and provides a well-rounded educational experience. We require our high school students to study foreign languages, literature, and history, but few ever achieve the ability to use a foreign language, understand literature, or interpret history anywhere near the level of, for example, high school graduates in Europe. The reason appears to be that most of these subjects are taught in a perfunctory manner with a singular American outlook and a presumption that these things do not really matter. In other words, we go through the motions of basic education without imparting real understanding and excitement in the achievement of such knowledge.

Education should not only convey knowledge but also teach problem solving. Stale knowledge without an ability to use it is of little value. Schools should teach thinking and not facts that are soon forgotten, outdated, or irrelevant. We must reform our schools if we are to succeed as a democratic society.

## The Changing Role of University Administration

The recent announcement that the president of Harvard had to take an indefinite leave from his post because of exhaustion stunned many inside and outside the academic establishment. It also caused an evaluation of the changing role of university administrators, who are now primarily fund-raisers. Unlike other fund-raising organizations, with both a focused giver market and purpose or use plans, university fund-raising is usually diffused on both counts. Previously it was primarily directed toward alumni, who were, if successful, informed that their success was to a large extent the result of the education they received and then induced to contribute to the source of their success, their alma mater. A large number of special alumni-giving tools were devised varying from straight defined and undefined contributions to donations of buildings, programs, or named professorships.

Until recently alumni-giving constituted the major source of funds raised by American universities. It was a well-organized activity and included large numbers of events designed to tie alumni to the institution, such as reunions, alumni travel, alumni clubs, alumni seminars, and more. In recent years though, fund-raising, particularly at major universities, has expanded radically beyond alumni and other forms of closed circle giving. It has become a national and even worldwide competitive effort at raising funds from corporations, governments, institutions, rich individuals, estates, and more, many of whom had no previous relation with or benefited from a particular university.

Universities and similarly hospitals have become insatiably dependent on fund-raising to meet their ever-growing budgets, notwithstanding often large endowments and low faculty and health care provider salaries.

Fund-raising has become the principal concern and in most cases the responsibility of university' and hospital presidents and other executives. As a result, fewer and fewer university presidents and executives are selected for their academic or scholarly credentials rather than their financial acumen and fund-raising contacts and abilities.

In many cases, fund-raising has become an end to itself. As it gains in importance, an increasing percentage of the funds raised are spent on fund-raising. In the past, fund-raising was done by academics as an integral part of academic public relations. Today these institutions employ hordes of well-paid, full-time professional fund-raisers. A major objective of institutional fund-raising is to generate adequate funds for raising additional funds. Fund-raising has become a principal function of the senior management of institutions that in turn surround themselves with many layers of fund-raising support staff who in turn require new space and support services.

Before long institutional fund-raising is expected to become an end in itself, much like charitable fund-raising, where often as little as 10 to 40 percent of the funds raised go to pay for the activities for which the funds are raised. In medical and educational fund-raising we are rapidly moving toward these norms. At some universities the president's and provost's offices have been expanded to include many vice presidents, associate/assistant provosts, and their staff.

In some instances, senior management has grown by 1,000 percent over a few years, with most of the new positions aimed at fund-raising. Not only does this significantly increase the cost of fund-raising, but the internal competition and positioning of fund-raisers often confuse, or even discourage potential donors or sponsors.

The efficiency of fund-raising—or the percentage of funds used to raise funds has grown from 8 to 12 percent to well over 40 percent in some institutions, with 60 percent or less of funds raised actually used to help pay for educational and research programs or university investments. Even that percentage may be high, as some indirect fund-raising costs are often buried in the institution's overhead.

The role of American universities has changed from that of purveyors of knowledge and isolated centers of scholarship and research to that of institutions that increasingly assume a much broader and sometimes a more influential role. Today universities and the academic community they represent assist in the formulation of technical, scientific, economic, and social policy. In some instances, they even affect defense and international policy. They affect policy by not only their teaching and research, but also by their direct or indirect involvement in the policy- or decision- making processes.

At the same time, it is interesting to note that with the increasing democratization of the public view and the evolution of liberal values among the academic community, private American universities are run more and more like commercial corporations instead of communities of scholars. Over seventy years ago William Graham Summer made the remark that "industry may be republican; it can never be democratic." The university, as an industrial corporation, has become less and less democratic, and power, as noted before, has gradually slipped from a shared base of faculty and administration to the sole prerogative of the administration.

Like professional, nonowning corporate management in traditional industrial corporations, this new elite of professional managers of academic institutions is a government body unto themselves, with little, if any, consideration for or responsibility to their constituents among faculty, staff, and students. Their accountability is basically only to the board of trustees, whose membership is usually selected, appointed, and controlled by this same administration.

Faculty, who for as long as universities have existed as independent institutions of learning have guided the running of the university and taken responsible roles in its administration, are today hardly involved. Where faculty involvement exists, it is often more imaginary than real. Like other "political" systems, universities have used their own means for legitimizing the basic changes that were previously collectively practiced for hundreds of years. The trimmings of collective administration still exist, though, and universities, like corporations, go through the motions of a collectively administered institution with farcical solemnity. It is this solemnity that throws the faculty off and misleads the public. As in "corporate shareholders" meetings, business is conducted with slick efficiency. Elections of top management and reviews of budgets and plans are, in some cases, still performed with at least the participation of the faculty. However, these sessions are nothing but political subterfuge, farcical shows where decisions are preempted and submerged under layers and layers of formality and rigmarole.

## Faculty Perception of Benefits

Another concern or perception is the difference in the remuneration, fringe benefits, and quality of the working environment between faculty and administration in supposedly equivalent positions This includes salaries, office size and location, furnishings, secretarial services, parking, and other direct and indirect benefits. Similarly, faculty offices, classrooms, and other primary educational facilities appear to have a very low priority in budgetary and other resource allocations.

These differences often extend beyond material issues and include social or status differentials as well. For example, lower-level administrative staff may be entrusted with expense accounts, while a senior faculty member may not qualify for such a privilege independent of his or her need to entertain visitors or sponsors. Universities have traditionally maintained that low faculty salaries are justified by the large number of direct and indirect fringe benefits offered to faculty. In recent years, though, practically all "faculty-particular" fringe benefits have been extended to include university administrators. This includes tuition assistance, use of subsidized faculty dining, parking, children's tuition assistance, medical services, etc.

## Treatment of Former Faculty

Another interesting issue is the relation of the university to former, and particularly retired, faculty. Foreign universities still hold to the tradition of granting former faculty members special honors and privileges. They recognize that keeping the channels open and permitting junior faculty and students to tap the enormous accumulation of knowledge, experience, and judgment of senior faculty is not only a priceless asset but assures the continuity so essential to the furthering of the growth of knowledge.

The industrial university maintains the tradition of giving former faculty the "Emeritus" title, but this has really become another meaningless formality. Should the professor emeritus elect to continue to teach or do research—albeit at little or no cost to the university—he or she will more often than not be delegated to a dingy alcove, provided with no secretarial or other services and be ignored or conveniently "forgotten" in all social or formal functions. It is as if the university fears that the past eminence of retired faculty may serve as a discouragement to junior faculty. A more plausible explanation, though, is probably that the administration, as represented by department heads, who are not usually selected for their scholarly contributions or reputation, feels distinctly uncomfortable with active "emeriti" around.

However, there are a few exceptions to this rule among some of the professional schools. With the elimination of compulsory retirement at sixty-five, many universities are now groping for subtle and often not so subtle ways to "encourage" senior faculty to depart after a lifetime of service. This approach by American universities is particularly curious as they alone among American corporations employ a majority of professionals who spend their whole career at one institution.

Faculty are usually highly immobile and, once tenured at an average

age of thirty-six, remain at the same university until retirement. The university is therefore not one of many places of work, but the one place to which the faculty member devoted his or her life, work, energies, and ideas. Yet after retirement, faculty are usually all but ignored. Many retired faculty are unable to cope with such a change in environment, never having experienced anything but a vital, active, intellectually stimulating life as a member of the academic community.

### Peer Relationships

Universities are generally perceived as genteel institutions in which interpersonal relationships are devoid of envy and ambition and where scholarship and learning are the primary concerns of peers. Yet unscrupulous drive, jealousy, and maliciousness are probably as widespread among junior and senior faculty or faculty and administration as is in the most ambitious and driving commercial firms. The genteel behavior is nothing but a facade.

The general principles of "professionalism" adopted by the legal, medical, and other professions, under which colleagues and their work are not adversely criticized except in private, apparently are deemed not to apply to academics. The need for openness of discussions of scholarship and research as well as criticism of professional and personal issues is used as justification for undermining peers. As a result, academic institutions by and large are not fair, genteel environments but places where backstabbing is most common.

### Liberalism in the University

Liberalism and democracy are preached but hardly practiced in our universities. Tolerance applies only to the like-minded, and differences of opinion are disdained in practice instead of encouraged. Many universities have serious labor problems, and most of the universities confronted with the specter of faculty unionization have fought such a development tooth and nail instead of encouraging or at least discussing the underlying issues. Most committees and usually all committee chairmen are "appointed," and many committees are padded by the appointment of members of the administration. Together with the "appointed" chairperson, they then often form a "majority" of the committee. Liberalism and democratic principles are widely preached, and universities, without fail, will support liberal and democratic issues as long as they do not affect their internal workings.

## Operational Efficiency

Average U.S. university costs and tuition have risen at a rate nearly twice that of faculty salaries, and the question is therefore: where does this money go?

Administrative costs and management inefficiency seem to be the primary cause. Although they use tax-exempt and often free, donated facilities, university-supplied meals and services usually cost significantly more than equivalent meals and services supplied by private, tax paying, and profit-making restaurants, copying centers, and other purveyors of services. They are able to do this because they have a captive market. University-administered pension funds have generally performed well below privately administered funds. Yet universities are the cradles of American management education. Few university administrators could qualify to manage anything but a university.

## Leadership Role

Universities have provided leaders throughout recent history. The rise and fall of civilization and economies have closely paralleled developments in the academic institutions of many nations. The rise of Japanese economic power, the fall of the Shah of Iran, and many recent happenings originated in their respective country's universities.

The American economy has grown in recent years, our technical and economic leadership continuous, yet our morale and self-confidence are eroding. At the same time, our universities fail to assume their historic role and seem to be preoccupied with explaining and apologizing for our failures and justifying the continued status quo of their methods, roles, and structures. A Japanese student when asked why he studied management at a U.S. university when Japan's management appeared to be so much more successful replied that he came to learn how not to manage, something American universities seem to teach well.

## Impact on Educational Functions

While the new industrial university continues to convey knowledge and method to its students, there is a question whether it is able to teach values and judgment. Students have become increasingly skeptical of many of the approaches used by the university. The primary concern is with the lack of consistency and a certain amount of hypocrisy. Similarly, the increasing alienation of faculty and administration often affects the commitment of the faculty, with a resulting impact on the educational process.

As university costs and particularly university overhead or administrative costs continue their phenomenal rise, faculty are more and more pressed to generate funding from outside sources, with a resulting growth of faculty time spent on proposal writing, lobbying, or research. The victims are obviously the students, who are given a decreasing amount of faculty time.

## Teaching or Research?

Good teaching is not only not rewarded but actually disdained at some universities where it is considered a waste and a distraction from research and fund-raising. While there are many good reasons for incorporating research in education and the American research universities have become the leaders not just among American institutions of higher learning but worldwide, the relative importance and recognition given to teaching must be reestablished.

Obviously, the principal reason for these developments is money. Research is where, at least in the past, the money was. Immense federal and other research grants were available and funded the growth of research universities. But times are changing and universities will have to kick some of the outside-funded research addiction and learn to make research and teaching one.

Improving America's educational system is one of its greatest challenges. Education must emphasize real learning—not cramming and not just passing. Learning must not only be an experience but become a habit, something that serves throughout life and assures continuous improvement.

Each person learns differently and needs different stimuli to experience real learning. To learn effectively, students must learn to think and to acquire as well as use knowledge. Education, particularly in American universities, must be restructured from the bottom up and not, as traditionally done, from the top down. Top-downers are usually people who have little experience in teaching or have not taught for years. Therefore, the resistance to educational reform usually comes from administrators, with little, if any, feedback from the customers—the university students and their parents.

### Reengineering the University

Many universities are now reengineering themselves. This often means a downsizing of their productive activities, such as teaching, and an increase in fund-raising and administrative functions designed to improve the bottom line. This trend is a counterincentive and will lead to a further decline of higher education. it reduces the efficiency and quality of education and research and moves decision-making functions even further from the classroom.

## Job Training

Everyone in the workplace from chief executive to the lowly production worker, requires continuous job training and skill enhancements. It is no longer good enough to enter the workplace with effective skills. Skills must be continuously updated, honed, and improved. This is because not only does work content, environment, and demand change all the time, but technologies and tools available for the work also change over time.

To stay effective today, job retraining must be nearly continuous, or at least, very periodic. Many manufacturing firms, such as Motorola, recognize this need and have established job training schemes throughout their organization. Even top management periodically attends job training sessions, and worker job training is an integral part of corporate strategy.

American educational institutions have not yet hopped on this bandwagon. In fact, job training or midcareer education part-time or full-time, in short or extensive programs, is not given the emphasis it deserves by most educational institutions, particularly our major universities—this at a time of rapidly advancing technology and radical changes in the job market. Our educational institutions seem to fail to recognize the needs of society and try to carry on business as usual in a rapidly changing world.

## Managing Criminal Justice

The U.S. criminal justice system needs a complete overhaul if it is to reverse the trend toward increased lawlessness, insecurity, and moral decline. The cost of lawlessness in the United States, which includes the cost of the criminal justice system, the cost of insurance against crime, and the cost of uninsured damage caused by crime, now tops $1 trillion, or 16.8 percent of the 1993 GNP.

The system is no longer able to keep up. Our prisons are overcrowded, with more than one million prisoners. Our courts are overloaded and often take years to hear a case. Only 3 percent of felons arrested ever go to trial now. Plea bargains and dismissals account for 97 percent. Only 23 percent of murder and manslaughter arrests result in trials, with 5 percent of stolen property and 11 percent of rape arrests ever adjudicated. Therefore, toughening sentencing laws will have little effect, as so few criminals go to trial. For their own reasons, including self-interest, prosecutors and judges assist and encourage dangerous criminals to plea-bargain. The reasons include political interests, popularity, and, most important, only cases with a high probability of conviction being tried.

Our criminal justice system does not work and has largely lost the confidence of the public, independent of the amount of money spent on it. People feel insecure, unprotected, and with little recourse. As in education and health care, society views criminal justice in America as a system that serves criminals and the extremes of society in social and economic terms but not society at large. It no longer is a system that serves the average American, the large middle class, and the law-abiding citizen.

It is a system that has lost much of its accountability and accessibility. It is no longer a system of law for or by the people, but a politicized and self-serving system with a huge bureaucracy that is more concerned with attaining political objectives than law enforcement. It makes victims out of criminals and blames society for their crimes. It has lost sight of its basic objectives of the law and the rights of society at large to a safe, honest, and free environment in which to pursue life. Criminal justice in America must reestablish its fundamental functions as a service of and to society, a safeguard of basic rights for every law-abiding citizen. As it stands, not only is it ineffective in preventing or controlling crime, but it provides, above all, protection for the criminals. It does not emphasize prevention but crime solving, something at which it is not very good.

It considers criminals victims of society and reimposes unrepentant criminals on society over and over again after they serve fractions of their sentences. It does not reeducate criminals but releases them and makes society responsible for their reeducation. Americans have become paranoid about crime not only because crime stalks society everywhere, but because they feel impotent in an environment where criminals are considered victims and released over and over again to repeat their crimes. A simple evaluation of the data between 1980 and 1990 shows that over 60 percent of violent crimes and an even larger percentage of rapes alone were committed by repeat criminals, most of whom were discharged after serving only a fraction of their sentences.

As shown table 7, over 45 percent of inmates had three or more prior sentences and a full 19 percent six or more prior sentences (1992). Similarly, over 55 percent of offenders imprisoned in 1991 for violent offenses had committed previous violent offenses. The average time served for murder was a paltry eight years and for rape, five years, a small fraction of the sentences imposed and served in most developed countries. Our prisons are really revolving doors for criminals. They certainly do not rehabilitate nor do they motivate criminals toward a lawful life. In other words, our penal system is a failure. It neither punishes nor rehabilitates effectively. Even more important, it does not provide an effective deterrent to crime, as the punishment, even if caught, is out of proportion to the crime. The risks are small and the rewards are usually large. More important, this low-risk system now encourages more and more senseless crime.

## Redefinition of Societal Values

Today we have only one-twentieth the number of law enforcement officers per criminals that we had thirty years ago. As a result, we now accept many criminal and unlawful acts without even an attempt at prevention or punishment. In fact, many acts considered crimes thirty years ago are no longer prosecuted, and society has become used to accepting certain types of traditional crimes as acceptable behavior.

In many cases, our reinterpretation of civil liberties has redefined moral and legal values to an extent where the boundaries between right and wrong have become extremely murky. The result is a general concern with acceptable behavior, as few now know what is right or wrong. Societal values are deeply rooted in moral and religious beliefs, and are now subject to not only continuous updating but, more important, challenge. Obviously, societal values must be changed, while changes in the human environment that have sustained civilized society throughout the ages must be removed or radically altered.

## Pampered Criminals

In the United States criminal justice is often interpreted as a system protecting the criminal's rights. There is more concern for the treatment and rights of criminals than justice for and rights of their victims. In fact, not only are victims' rights often forgotten, but the issue is interpreted by many to be politically incorrect. *Rehabilitation* is the march word even when statistics and experience show the ineffectiveness of such approaches, certainly for hardened capital crime offenders.

In many cases, we now make an illness out of crime. Crimes are excusable if the criminal could not help himself or herself while committing the crime. We make illnesses now of every type of crime and often substitute chemical or medical treatment of criminals for punishment.

We are unique in this regard. While some child molesters may have mental disorders contributing to their behavior, it is much more difficult and convincing to show the relation between violent criminal behavior and medical conditions. Social factors may contribute, but these again cannot be interpreted as medical conditions. Too often we excuse criminal behavior based on social disadvantages and resulting medical conditions. The cases where the violent antisocial behavior is cured by medical treatment are rare indeed.

Criminals have become used to demanding and getting services few poor working people are able to afford—from recreational facilities, quality food, and skill training to extensive medical services. The average cost of maintaining a criminal in custody in the United States is appreciably

## TABLE 7 - U.S. PRISON STATISTICS (1994)

Source: Bureau of Justice Statistics, National Corrections Reporting Program, 1992.

| | | | Prisoners | Prisons |
|---|---|---|---|---|
| Population | State | | 919,142 | 1,291 |
| | Federal | | 93,708 | 70 |
| | | Total | 1,012,850 | 1,361 |
| | Black | | 1,432/100,000 black population | |
| | White | | 203/100,000 white population | |
| Admissions | Black | | 54.2% (1992) | |
| | White | | 44.9% (1992) | |
| | Men | | 950,979 - 93.9% (1992) | |
| | Women | | 61,872 - 6.1% (1992) | |
| State Court Commitments (1992) | New | | 188,211 | |
| | Parole Revocation | | 127,060 | |
| | Other | | 16,008 | |
| Returns | 3 or more prior sentences | 45% | | |
| | 6 or more prior sentences | 19% | | |
| | 11 or more prior sentences | 6.6% | | |

Source: Survey of State Prison Inmates, 1991.

| | | | Return Offenders | |
|---|---|---|---|---|
| | | First Prior | Violent | Non-Violent |
| Offenses (1991) | Violent | 65% | 55% | 35% |
| | Property | 10% | 22% | 32% |
| | Drug | 22% | 16% | 24% |
| | Public Order | 3% | 7% | 9% |
| Average Time Served (1991) | Murder | 8 years | | |
| | Rape | 5 years | | |
| | Robbery | 3.25 years | | |

| Inmate Population (1992) | | Male | Female |
|---|---|---|---|
| | 18-19 | 24,000 | 1,140 |
| | 20-24 | 141,500 | 7,300 |
| | 25-29 | 189,300 | 12,000 |
| | 30-34 | 170,825 | 11,160 |
| | 35-39 | 115,200 | 7,500 |
| | 40-44 | 73,600 | 3,900 |
| | 45 + | 80,000 | 3,500 |

| Prison Population (State and Federal) | | |
|---|---|---|
| | 1970 | 97/100,000 |
| | 1980 | 139/100,000 |
| | 1990 | 235/100,000 |
| | 1994 | 373/100,000 |

Source: U.S. Department of Justice - Bureau of Justice Statistics, Survey of Prison POpulation

higher than the income of a poor working family. In fact, the living standard of many incarcerated criminals is higher than that of many working poor.

On top of this, criminals are usually allowed to earn money, continue to obtain government aid under social and other programs and engage in all kinds of entrepreneurial activities. Yet little, if any, of these earnings goes to pay for the cost of maintenance, including costs for nonessentials such as recreation, training, entertainment, and more. We are the only country in the world that pampers its criminals in this manner.

This is combined with a justice system that allows even dangerous criminals to serve but a small fraction of their sentence before being released. No wonder our criminal justice system is no deterrent to crime. With the risk of being apprehended and charged only at 10 to 20 percent for violent crimes and a probability of less than 50 percent of having to serve more than 35 percent of the sentence, the chance of incarceration for more than five years as a result of a violent crime (murder, rape, etc.) is only 5 to 10 percent, small enough a probability to make the crime nearly risk-free.

## Justice Not Winning in Legal Disputes

Finding the truth and assuring justice is often not the objective in a trial. Winning is the most important objective of prosecutors and defense attorneys in criminal and other trials. Winning brings political and economic rewards. It also brings publicity and fame. Justice usually takes a secondary role in the objectives of prosecutors and lawyers alike. They are not really concerned with the interest of the public, the pain of the victims, the physical and economic harm, or that justice be achieved. They are often in it for the glory, the money, and the opportunities the trial offers.

These developments are a distortion of the way the legal system is supposed to work. It was designed to assure justice and to be a system of law enforcement by the people and for the people. It has now degenerated into a largely self-serving, often corrupt, and seldom just system of justice, one that caters mostly to the criminals and provides little protection for the general public. It is more concerned with blaming society for its lack of compassion for the criminals than with punishing them and helping the victims. Society is increasingly held responsible for the acts of lawless individuals who are assumed to have no duty toward the same society that is held responsible for them. This is a skewed, self-defeating approach that makes the victim responsible for the acts of the criminal, truly a recipe for the ultimate destruction of society as we know it and still try to maintain.

## Fitness for Execution

David Keefe, lawyer for serial killer John Wayne Gacy, tried and convicted in 1980 of the brutal murder of thirty-three men and boys, argued before his scheduled execution that Gacy might not be fit to be executed because his mental condition had seriously deteriorated since his trial. Keefe felt that this was a cause for appeal against the execution. The very idea that a convicted murderer's mental condition arising after conviction should be considered in appealing a sentence appears preposterous, to say the least. There was no question that his mental condition was an exonerating circumstance causing the crime, but here the absurd argument is that the sentence for the crime caused the criminal such mental anguish that he is no longer fit to be subjected to it. Instead his lawyer would like society to pay for maintaining his client in jail and, obviously, cover all related costs, including his legal costs.

I have no problem with people like Mr. Keefe. They are only doing their job within an absurdly distorted legal system. They serve legal institutions that have lost their focus on assuring protection and justice for society and not mainly those who flaunt society's interests and norms.

Our criminal system pampers convicted felons to a degree that has little to do with human values. Our parole system is a sham, with the majority of parolees back in jail within a short period of time. Reeducation of prisoners should concentrate on providing them with opportunities to do useful work that allows them to earn money to pay for their keep and compensate their victims, among other things, or to at least train them to perform useful tasks that contribute to their self-worth, self-esteem, and value to society. It should not concentrate largely on physical education and the building up of nonusable skills, at least in terms of value to service or earning potential.

## Frivolous Lawsuits and Medical Complaints

Major burdens and costs in our legal and health care system are caused by frivolous lawsuits and medical complaints. Thirty percent of all lawsuits in the United States are now brought by prisoners in jail and over 95 percent of these suits are dismissed because they are not substantiated, or lack substance or, as in most cases, are actually frivolous and were filed solely to congest or burden the legal system.

A similar number of lawsuits are damage, wrongful treatment, or similar suits that are filed not because the plaintiff has an actual grievance but because he or she and/or his or her lawyer simply believes that in the vast majority of cases defendants will settle instead of risking huge amounts of money and time defending against even the most trivial, frivolous, or even ridiculous and often wrong charge. Unfortunately, insurance companies encourage these frivolous suits by settling rather than fighting the claims because, they say, it is cheaper.

Our legal system has really gone astray and now no longer serves to maintain the law but is used mainly for plaintiffs and lawyers as a legal way to extract money. In other words, nearly 66 percent of all the lawsuits filed are really traps in which the legal system is used to rob innocent citizens and companies using the threat of the legal system and its costs.

Congress has tried to deal with this issue and according to recently filed tort reform bills a loser must pay court and related cost rules should be adopted. On the other hand, this may discourage poor plaintiffs from filling legitimate complaints. There are better ways to discourage and punish frivolous lawsuits, and real disincentives must be introduced that include punitive penalties and that include disbarment.

## The Protection of Lawyers

The American bar has constituted "consumer protection committees" that are supposedly designed to protect clients from unscrupulous or incompetent lawyers. In reality, according to a study by *Halt,* an organization reform trying to reform the legal system, 90 percent of all complaints against lawyers are dismissed with no action taken, and the rest often result in no more than a slap on the wrist, even when the damage to the client was substantial or even tragic.

Lawyers habitually overcharge even on contingency lawsuits. Of the

$40 billion spent by Americans in 1994 on damage lawsuits, more than 50 percent went to pay lawyer and court costs. Lawyers, just like doctors, insist that they require self-regulation because only they understand the requirements of their profession. Why not let engineers, shopkeepers, and banks also regulate themselves?

## Trial by Jury

The O. J. Simpson trial, probably more than any other recent example, shows the flaws of our jury system. Not only is it inefficient and slow, but there is a serious question as to whether juries can really determine guilt and dispense justice. It is not only that life has become very complicated and technology has introduced many complex issues and procedures, but it is very difficult now to establish fair, unbiased juries, at a time of near-real-time transmission of news and information. Therefore, few, if any, people in a community are immune to exposure to verbal and often even visual presentations of events they may later be called upon to adjudicate.

Society today is so diverse that it is nearly impossible to convene a jury of one's peers. With the exception of small communities in which most people live comparable lives, modern cities in America have such a diverse population that any random group of citizens selected for jury duty in such an environment does not really constitute a jury of peers.

Lifestyles and expectations are so diverse that few really understand life issues of others. Few, and particularly affluent, whites understand issues facing poor, disadvantaged blacks, and white-collar professionals often cannot imagine the problems of blue-collar workers.

Trial by jury in America rests on the Sixth and Seventh Amendments of the Constitution. It was designed to assure fairness and judgment by peers who understood the environment and circumstances under which the criminal act occurred and the value of losses incurred. The system now has expanded to a monstrous distortion of the original concept, with jurors dishing out judgments and awards that bear little relationship to the crime committed or to the cost of damage incurred.

In England which invented the jury system only 5 percent of criminal and 1 percent of civil suits are tried by jury. Also, only ten out of twelve jury votes are required for conviction in Britain. Similarly, incitement to litigation and contingency fees are illegal. In other words if we were to transplant the British system to America, a large number of lawyers would lose their livelihood.

Also in England the losing plaintiff pays a defendant's expenses. Juries are usually made up of people who do not understand the underlying issues of a case and as a result judge often on the basis of opinions, likes, dislikes, and peripheral factors.

In recent times, particularly as I write with the embarrassing Simpson trial congesting our communication channels, the American jury system of justice has come under increasing attack. Most civil law countries have eliminated jury trials by now, and the United States alone holds 90 percent of all jury trials in the world at this time. We somehow accept that juries must be composed of people who usually must render a unanimous verdict. Yet there is nothing in our Constitution to that effect, and all types of juries of peers could be constituted under the Constitution.

A jury could have fewer, maybe as few as six people, and the verdict may be imposed by a simple majority, and need not be unanimous. A jury could be made up of judges, experts, or professional jurors, or we could have a system without any jury. Such a system would be infinitely more efficient and probably also more effective. It would be less affected by group dynamics and the dominance of some jurors. It would similarly be much more knowledgeable without losing the experience of one's peers that is at the heart of the jury system. Today juries often act not so much as judges of the defendant as social judges who feel it is their right and/or duty to correct social ills rather than determine the degree of guilt and appropriate punishment.

## Tort Reform

The cost of unjustified or frivolous lawsuits in terms of both cost of litigation and higher insurance premiums is estimated to be about $130 billion per year, or more than $1,000 per year for every American family. These costs result in higher product and service costs to cover the costs of liability insurance.

A major part of the costs are introduced by contingency fees that not only inflate claims but also assure that a significant proportion of the settlement is not used for remedy but to pay inflated legal costs.

Also, billing practices by lawyers have come under severe attack not only by the public but more recently by lawyers' associations themselves. It is not only bill padding but also double-charging, surcharges on out-of-pocket expenses, and similar practices that give the legal profession a bad name.

## Disillusion with the Justice System

Judges who withhold evidence from juries victimize the victims. The reason given is usually that evidence of prior criminality, violence, or asocial behavior would prejudice a jury and cause them to judge a criminal not on the basis of his or her crime but on the basis of his or her history. In other words, the assumption is that each crime can only be judged on its own merits and that prior criminal behavior, even if it provides or contributes to a motive, should not play a role in a case. A justice system thus disavows positive and negative learning or the role of experience in human behavior. This goes against not only our basic understanding of human learning but also acquisition of trends of human or social behavior. You cannot judge only on the basis of one narrow case.

Human behavior is the result of history and experience, and few human acts are the result of irrational impulses. A good legal system will protect society and victims and not dispense retribution, as revenge has no social value. On the other hand, it will use learning and experience to continuously improve itself and its understanding of fairness and justice.

One issue is often the role of the lawyer who represents his or her client and not necessarily the truth. Defense lawyers and prosecutors seek to win and do not seek to assure justice. They serve their clients, not society or even the interests of society. A lawyer who knows that his or her client is a threat to society or others if released will still fight to have that client released. In a way, this is similar to a doctor who releases a patient with a highly infectious disease because the doctor needs the space or the patient wants out. We would consider this highly asocial, but we permit it in our justice system all the time.

Older civilizations and even some modern societies require that people who break the law pay for the damage caused to individuals and society. We, on the other hand, are primarily concerned with justice to the perpetrator, the criminal, and not the victim or society.

## Controlling the Costs of Legal Transactions

The only professional service whose costs are difficult to predict are legal transactions. Doctors, accountants, engineers, and architects are generally prepared to estimate or quote the cost of common transactions. Not so with lawyers. They often will not provide such quotes for even simple transactions such as drawing up a will or contract, a transaction more often than not performed by a legal assistant and not a lawyer anyway. There is an urgent need for greater accountability by lawyers to their clients.

Most legal services required by the general public are routine, such as the drawing up of wills, contracts, deeds, licenses, and even the bulk of uncontested divorces. There is little reason why price lists for these services cannot be published. At least a list of typical or maximum charges could be provided by bar associations, very much like lists now available for most common medical and other services. The reason this is not done is probably that the real charges would look so outlandish as to make the legal profession look absurdly foolish, greedy, or both.

Drawing up a will and prenuptial agreement typically costs $1,000 to $2,000 even if all the information is readily provided by the client, a clerk draws up the will and agreement in about an hour (using standard forms into which client-provided figures are entered), and the lawyer spends barely fifteen minutes with the clients to explain the documents. This happened to me recently and, as I found out later, is close to the norm.

## Affordable Legal Services

On the surface the legal system in the United States is supposed to be accessible to all and to treat all equally. That is how it was designed and supposed to work: a system in which all citizens are treated the same and are assumed to be innocent unless proven guilty and, in most cases of serious crimes, proven guilty by a jury of their peers. Reality is different. Legal fees usually start with retainers of thousands of dollars, which are demanded by lawyers before they even seriously consider a case or start legal work. Hourly fees of $150 to $400 are customary, and every little expense, such as copying, parking, filing, etc., is charged separately.

As a result, most middle-class Americans—which means most working Americans—have been priced out of the legal system and cannot really afford their day in court. The poor and the rich are well served by the legal system, but the average American really has no access to it. Even if they are able to afford legal help, they are often forced into settling or dropping their case, however well-founded, because they cannot afford the costs of extended legal procedures, or the legal system indirectly forces them to settle by dragging the case out to reduce the cost to the system.

The awards from winning in court are usually meaningless because legal costs absorb most, if not all, of them. In fact, it is curious that legal fees often bear a direct relationship to the award, which drives many to contract directly on a contingent fee basis. Only a few lawyers are willing to charge flat fees or use ceilings, a practice that is standard in most other services.

As noted before, legal services are monopolized and legal access by the average citizen may be a right under the Constitution but the law has been perverted into a monopolized service only available to the indigent and the rich. In other words, it is only available to those for whom the government pays the bill or those rich enough to afford it. Hundreds of billions of dollars of taxpayer money are spent to defend criminals using taxes paid mostly by middle-class Americans who themselves cannot afford legal services or access to the court system.

Legal services must be accessible and affordable to all. The obscene rates charged by lawyers and other legal professionals and for services must be controlled. Rates of hundreds of dollars per hour for legal services are unconscionable and unjustified. Lawyers should earn decent incomes, but these should be in line with those of other top professionals. There is nothing wrong with good lawyers making hundreds of thousands of dollars per year, but millions are not justified.

## Effectiveness of American Health Care

We are proud of our medical system and particularly our achievements in medical technology. We rightfully assume that our capability to deal with medical problems is second to none. Yet considering statistics such as infant deaths or other assumed preventable health hazards, we do not compare favorably with many other countries.

We basically treat illness but not the cause of illness. We spend a lot on curing but little on prevention. Yet it has been known for a long time that the mechanisms of disease are not the causes of disease. In other words, our approach to health care does not influence the incidence of disease; it only intervenes to help in curing it or, more often, reducing its ill effects.

By and large Americans live an unhealthy life. We eat the wrong food, breathe polluted air, and exercise occasionally on machines but generally not in our daily life. We do not walk or play and use our bodies. We spend most of our nonworking time in automobiles and other enclosed spaces. Outdoor cafés or long walks to work or shops are the exception and not the rule in America. We try to correct this by exercise and even diet binges. But these, again, are corrective approaches. They do not prevent obesity or disease.

Medical interventions are designed to cure ills, but they similarly add to ills. Thirty-six percent of all hospital patients are sick because of medical intervention, such as wrong diagnosis, treatment, or medication. Similarly, a significant number of patients are admitted because of drug reactions.

American health care costs are expected to exceed $1 trillion by 1996/97 and $1.2 trillion by the year 2000. As shown in the following table, its costs as a percentage of GNP will by then exceed 16.4 percent, with a per capita expenditure of $5,712. Medicare, Medicaid, and state/local government-funded costs will increase from 41 percent to 48 percent of total health care cost between 1980 and the year 2000.

Medicare alone will increase from $177 billion in 1994 to $350 billion in 2000 and to $439 billion in year 2004. The major reason for these cost increases, which outpace inflation and/or the cost of living by a factor of nearly 3, is not improvement in health care or the high cost of advanced medical technology, but the fact that consumers have no stake in the health care system per se.

**U.S. Health Care Costs**

| Year | 1980 | 1990 | 2000 |
|---|---|---|---|
| Total (trillion) | .2501 | 0.6662 | 1.6 |
| Percent GNP | 9.2 | 12.2 | 16.4 |
| Per capita | $1,063 | $2,566 | $5,712 |
| Private health insurance percentage | 29 | 33 | 30 |
| State/local government | 14 | 14 | 15 |
| Medicare | 16 | 17 | 18.5 |
| Medicaid | 11 | 11 | 15 |
| Out-of-pocket payments | 25 | 20 | 18 |
| Other private spending | 5 | 5 | 4 |
| Total | 100 percent | 100 percent | 100 percent |

Source: U.S. Government Congressional Budget Office.

Patients must become more cost-conscious particularly when covered by Medicare or other health insurance. While some medical procedures are subject to price controls, only the maximum price should be controlled, to permit price competition among providers. Patients should similarly be given incentives to search for the most cost effective quality medical provider.

The paperwork involved in the provision of medical services is inexcusable and must be reduced by eliminating much of the unnecessary bureaucracy that does little, if anything, to prevent misuse. Fraud has become a major issue, and both unscrupulous practitioners and patients are often involved in such practices, which often include billing for services not rendered and/or use of unnecessary or wasteful procedures.

One way to reduce Medicare costs is to make elderly consumers of Medicare services a party to cost containment. Newt Gingrich has suggested, for example, that Medicare patients who uncover fraudulent, erroneous, or excessive charges for Medicare services be given 10 percent of the money saved or recouped. This type of approach would not only put service providers on notice but would also make service consumers more concerned with charges. Obviously, such a system would have to be designed to discourage collusion between providers and service recipients.

## Health and Bedside Manners

Medicine has largely become a science, and medical education today is based on high-tech diagnostic and treatment methods. Few recently trained doctors really know how to deal with patients, interpret their feelings and reactions, and cope with not just the complex problems of physical ailments or diseases, but the social, psychological, and personal issues that underlie most medical problems.

Medicine has become a science in which the human is ignored. Doctors and other health care providers must learn not just the science but the art of health care—the needs of the AIDS patient, the elderly, the drug abuser, and the victim of violence. Health care professionals must learn to understand that physical diagnosis and treatment may only work if they understand the social, neurological, and psychological issues as well.

Health providers must learn not only to understand people but also how to make patients feel at ease and confide in them. Bedside manners, which have been lost in U.S. health care because of the scientific approach and the pressure of time or economics must be reinstituted if American health care is to reinvent itself and become responsive to the real medical needs of our society.

American health care has been dehumanized over the last thirty or forty years. Doctors' and nurses' smiles are largely plastic, and most contacts, even in complex cases, are routine. Time is strictly rationed and patients' personal needs and feelings are seldom considered. They are essentially numbers admitted for particular procedures.

Health care in America is a business, and doctors are businesspeople. As a result, the function of health care and that of doctors is generally not to keep people healthy but to treat and heal people, often using costly procedures. Doctors, like other businesspeople, consider time as money and thus try to economize on their time. This often results in ridiculously short doctors' visits, inadequate to properly diagnose a patient's symptoms. Similarly, doctors often prescribe many expensive tests or surgeries and other treatments not because they are necessary but because they are profitable for the doctor, save doctors' time, and/or reduce the risk of malpractice suits. Doctors in America are by and large conformists and try to prescribe accepted procedures and tests even if they know or are convinced that there will be few, if any, benefits for the patient.

It is evident that a broader approach to health care is required that does not concentrate only on cure, largely to the exclusion of preventative measures. This is particularly important now, when many people live under increased stress, which not only affects their lifestyle and increases their exposure to unhealthy eating and living but also affects their ability to take timely preventative measures or recognize their need for treatment or cure. It is not only that human aging accelerates under stress, but human ability to maintain a healthy lifestyle is impeded by stress.

It is important to more effectively integrate and coordinate the functions of mind and body and let the body's own intelligence define the need for lifestyle changes, preventative measures, and internal healing responses. Recent research indicates clearly that positive thinking, a pleasant supportive environment, interesting and exciting surroundings, and meaningful challenges are the best incentives for people and their bodies to heal themselves.

## Health Care Consulting

Mergers in the health care industry are designed to improve health care delivery and costs. The main beneficiaries of this trend now appear to be management consultancies, which are estimated to cash in 2 to 3 percent of the revenues generated by the health care industry now. This is worth $15 to $20 billion a year.

The consultancies serving as merger consultants are also active as deal makers and therefore often cash in twice. They similarly get involved in the design and management of treatments and procedures as well as patient record keeping and test or diagnostic control, which is assumed to assure that only necessary tests are performed and tests are not repeated unnecessarily.

While in theory this sounds reasonable, the problem is the inherent conflict of interest of consultants who are advisers, deal makers as managers of diagnostic and test procedures, and in record keeping or information management. They similarly are often parties to mergers and acquisitions that may involve activities in which they themselves have an interest.

## Doctors on Trial

There is increasing concern with the effects of the methods of training of American doctors on their behavior and performance. Internship is not, as in other professions, a method of providing opportunities for practical training and learning from experience but has become professional servitude and an around-the-clock boot camp. Working 30 or more hours in a row and 100 hours per week is quite common for medical interns in some of the "best" American hospitals.

Overwork does not contribute to learning or experience but does affect the ability to reflect on one's work and improve one's methods. There is little excuse for overworking interns except greed by hospitals and supervising doctors. Interns often man outpatient and emergency rooms, which cater largely to uninsured, underinsured, and indigents as well as Medicare or Medicaid patients; in other words, people who do not discriminate and are not able to judge or question the quality of care given to them.

When interns treat well-insured or well-to-do patients they often do this on behalf or in the name of a physician who then charges exorbitant rates even when he or she did not perform the procedures. In other words, interns are used to taking care of fully insured or affluent patients as well but not in their own name. This adds to their workload, which has already become untenable and irresponsible in many of our hospitals.

An increasing number of patients taken care of by interns are misdiagnosed and mistreated, often as a result of overwork or time pressures. Similarly, people with health insurance are often targets of costly and even dangerous procedures they do not need. It is sometimes claimed that doctors are only qualified to make corrective health decisions. They are trained to cure, not to prevent, illness, to use only toxic medicines and invasive techniques to affect a cure. As a result, more and more invasive treatments are used and preventative medicine is barely practiced.

## Combating the Scourge of Drug Addiction

Our approach to drug addiction has failed. It has not curbed drug imports and distribution or addiction. Drug addiction affects American society in many ways. It is responsible for about 15 percent of our medical costs and over 20 percent of our law enforcement and related costs. It similarly adds significantly to the costs of education. These costs have been growing every year for at least the last thirty years, and drug addiction now endangers the viability and effectiveness of these major institutions. The effects on society at large and our social systems are even more severe. Drug addiction divides our society and our families.

We spend tens of billions a year now to combat drug entry and distribution, particularly on interdicting drug invasion, yet drugs, including hard drugs, are easily obtainable anywhere. We are supposed to go after the major drug dealers but usually apprehend the small distributors, who now fill our jails to over capacity. We spend little on user education and nothing on the education of parents and others. We mix up our concern for civil liberty with the liberty of drug dealers and tax evaders to live and spend well beyond their legally reported income.

The burden of the drug addiction epidemic on our health care system is becoming intolerable. It is estimated that as much as 20 percent of our health care costs today are directly or indirectly related to drug use and that these expenditures are rising at a greater rate than health care costs in general.

## Public Access to Institutions

As noted, the three institutions discussed are supposed to serve society but, in reality, have become less and less accessible to the general public. Only the rich and poor among us really have access to our legal system. A significant proportion of our population is not covered by health care, and even educational opportunities are largely inaccessible, particularly to those most in need of educational upgrading.

An even larger proportion of the American middle class is losing access to these institutions at a time when they need these services more than ever before. Rapid social and technological change requires people to acquire advanced knowledge and skill levels or sink to the level of the poor and unemployed. Costs of medical care are rising at three times the rate of inflation and more than twice the rate of growth of income. This makes proper health care less and less affordable to lower-middle-class Americans.

The increasing complexity of our lives and invasion of legal processes into all phases of human activity exposes more and more law-abiding middle-class Americans to legal threats. Few have access to or can afford proper legal services, and therefore, more often than not they simply give in or pay up without challenge or legal defense. Our health care, educational, and legal institutions have become self-serving and in many cases isolated.

Our institutions must again become the people's institutions, not just a few ivory towers in a sea of substandard services. This is not a criticism of particular institutions but of a system that has allowed superbly designed institutions to decline into a selfish, inefficient morass. Let us pull up our sleeves and go to work at restructuring them and thereby regain not only America but also the moral, economic, and military leadership of the world.

To change our institutions, we will have to challenge them. Institutions are, by their very nature, conservative. They represent a myriad of vested interests. They must be shaken up even if this affects their very foundation. The challenge may lead to reinvention of these institutions, more in line with the new societal, economic, and technological environment.

Once institutions recognize their role in society and begin to work as an integral part of society, they will themselves thrive to succeed in their new role and obviously should take credit for their contribution. This is fine as long as they reorient themselves in the direction of societies' need and not their own narrow, selfish interests.

# 7

# Where Are We and Why Do We Not Do Better?

The most fundamental question is: do our institutions do what we need them to do? The answer is: definitely no. We pay several times as much as any other nation for institutional services in law, education, and health care on a per capita basis and get neither adequate nor comprehensive services. We remain a nation with one of every five adults functionally illiterate, a people afraid for their safety, and many unable to afford or obtain adequate health care.

Our health system takes care of the very old, the very poor, and the rich, but the working middle class is only partially covered. Even when covered, people are provided with high tech care, but the system does little for people who need help with run-of-the-mill ailments. Public safety is at an all-time low, and many of the streets of America are often ruled by criminals, at least at night. It is too late for marginal, politically correct improvements. It is also ineffective to just throw additional money at most of these problems. We have done this for over thirty years now without success. In fact, the more money we devote to these issues without radical changes in the system, the worse the situation seems to become. Adding to health care, law enforcement, or educational funding is not going to help. It is time to recognize that our institutions do not work effectively and are wasteful, largely mismanaged, and unable to improve from within. Thirty years of throwing dollar after dollar at these institutions has only made them more wasteful and ineffective.

Universities have raised tuition and other costs at twice the rate of inflation on average for many years and are still in deep financial trouble because their ineffectiveness grew at an even greater rate during the same period. Our health care and law enforcement costs have grown at nearly twice the combined rate of inflation and population growth, and the access to and quality of health care and law enforcement have actually declined. Institutions must show improvements in quality, productivity, and responsiveness. They should speak the language of progress. They cannot be stationary institutions that demand dues and respect from the public without moving with the times. They must serve society's needs, as determined by society and not by increasingly self-serving institutions. In other words, they must reinvent themselves and prove their value.

## Taking Back the Institution

It is only in the last forty or fifty years, and primarily in America, that institutional management has emerged as a professional specialty. We now have professional university, hospital, and legal institutional executives and managers. As noted, university presidents and senior executives are no longer chosen by the faculty as peers among peers but are usually appointed by a board of directors or trustees. The same applies to hospitals, HMOs, and legal or law enforcement institutions. As a result, we now have a cadre of professional institutional executives and managers who consider the faculty, medical, law enforcement, and legal professionals and staff of their respective institutions expendable production workers who have no role in management and policy making.

It appears that a major problem with our institutions, particularly in education and health care, is that they have been hijacked by increasingly more powerful groups of administrators who consider faculty, doctors, teachers, nurses, and researchers as hired hands and themselves as the institution.

The number of major universities and hospitals headed by respected scientists, engineers, scholars, or doctors is declining every year, with professional career institutional administrators filling their positions. True, some of these were once professionals, and opted to make institutional administration their career. It is often difficult to determine if this choice was made because they did not feel competent in advancing a respectable career in teaching, research, medicine or simply decided that administrators advance more rapidly and make more money without the hassles of academic or medical practice and peer review.

This trend is at the center of concern for the quality, condition, and service of our medical and educational institutions and, to a lesser extent, law enforcement institutions. Most of the issues that caused these institutions to deviate from their basic missions and functions can be traced to this transfer of power from institutional management by academic and medical peers to management by so-called specialized institutional professional administrators. They are also responsible for the huge cost escalations of health and educational services. Costs cannot be contained and quality maintained in a self-serving environment in which institutions are run by professional outsiders whose goals do not necessarily identify with the basic objectives of the educators or medical professionals in their organizations, nor with those of society these institutions are designed to serve.

Since renowned scholars were replaced by administrators as heads or senior executives of major universities, salaries of administrators have gone up astronomically. These salaries used to bear some relationship to faculty or medical professional salaries and university administrators, who in the past were elected by their faculty peers and usually returned to the ranks of the faculty after the period of service as administrators. This is no longer so. Nowadays university presidents commonly do not make one or two times but three to four times the salary of a full professor at their institution.

There could be some justification for this if such administrators really proved to be better managers, but in most cases this is not only not so, but their style also causes alienation of faculty and sometimes even students, resulting in a decline in the quality of educational services. They are neither good managers nor effective academic or medical leaders. They perceive their principal function to be that of raising money and serving as public relations and not academic leaders. Fund-raising has become an end unto itself and consumes not only an increasing amount of time of university administrators but also an increasing percentage of administrative costs, which in turn have escalated in response to the greater focus on fund-raising. This has become a vicious circle.

Previously funds were primarily raised by faculty who relied on the network of alumni and industry/government contacts. Today it is usually done by well-paid professional fund-raisers who use faculty to back them up but reserve all the credit for themselves. While this may have increased fund-raising revenues, it has probably increased the cost of fund-raising even more, leaving a smaller net total revenue after fund-raising expenses than previously achieved with less focused fund-raising. Universities have vastly increased the number of professional fund-raisers. In fact, the increase in fund-raisers exceeds the decrease in faculty supposedly forced by cost-cutting requirements. It is doubtful, though, that the added cost of fund-raising is justified by the new funding generated.

In fact the major emphasis today is on fund-raising and not on improving the intellectual content of education, improving teaching, nurturing learning, and transmitting and advancing knowledge, which contributes to the improvement in the quality of life and human well-being, but on fund-raising. The emphasis is on how we get more money, not how do we do things more effectively and economically and expand the range of our services in light of our basic function, as defined previously.

The emphasis of academic administrators has moved from the supply side to a very narrow demand side. It is increasingly evident that not only is there a decreasing focus on the principal missions of education and research, but there is too much concentration of political and economic power in the administration or bureaucracy of our educational and health care institutions. It affects managerial control, which is now primarily in the hands of the administration, with little say on working conditions, budgets, or politics by the providers or users of the services the institutions are designed to provide.

There is a real danger that we may lose our institutional services, because without proper focus and leadership their role may become immaterial. We must take our institutions back lest we end up with hollow shells of their past glory that spent most of their resources justifying themselves instead of providing educational, research, and medical services. This has already happened in some charitable, research, and so-called nonprofit health care organizations that sometime spent much of their revenues on themselves.

## Reinventing Institutions and Downsizing Their Organizations

Changing institutions and improving their performance are nowadays often tied to the downsizing of their organization, reducing organizational levels and the total number of staff, particularly in nonessential functions. Institutions have been particularly inept at controlling the mushrooming of middle and upper management. They have automated or computerized their accounting and bookkeeping systems by adding computer, database, information, and communications experts to these functions and not by retraining and downsizing the existing staff of these departments. They have by and large not yet learned the important advantages of outsourcing.

The economics of most of our institutions are in disarray. Costs seem to be out of control. The values and costs of many institutional services are unknown, and their quality appears to be declining. Instead of trying to rebuild our institutions from the bottom up, with the interests of their customers and users foremost in mind, most reorganize from the top down and only with input from within, with little consideration for the people that the institutions should serve.

It is time we recognize that American education, health care, and criminal justice do not work—at least do not work the way they were designed to work. They are no longer the institutions that serve the American public and solve its social and economic problems but to a large extent are responsible for perpetuating or even causing some of the problems they are supposed to solve. They focus primarily on solving problems only at the periphery, as noted before. They do not cater to the needs of society at large but concentrate largely on satisfying special needs and the self-interests of the institution themselves and their administrations.

There is an urgent need to reorganize American institutions, particularly in education and health care, from the bottom up and to eliminate a major part of unnecessary middle and upper middle management, to reestablish top management's strategic functions in educational and health care leadership, and to delegate decisions to the competent level of the faculty and health care professionals.

As an example, universities and hospitals used to have lean hierarchical management structures of five to eight levels, from secretarial and laboratory support staff to chairpeople, president, or administrator. While forward-looking industrial firms are reestablishing such responsive organizational structures, universities and hospitals are moving in the opposite direction by introducing more hierarchial management structures which often have as many as ten to fifteen levels, as shown in figure 11.

This not only causes lower efficiency but also increases isolation of the professional, productive part of the institutional organization such as faculty and medical staff. Instead of working as professional teams, they now quite often work as hierarchical groups with strict assignments of responsibility and authority. This impedes collegial relations, causes a less cooperative environment, and increases authoritarianism. In fact, both the organization and the system of rewards, including promotion, make it increasingly difficult to maintain meaningful collegial cooperation and

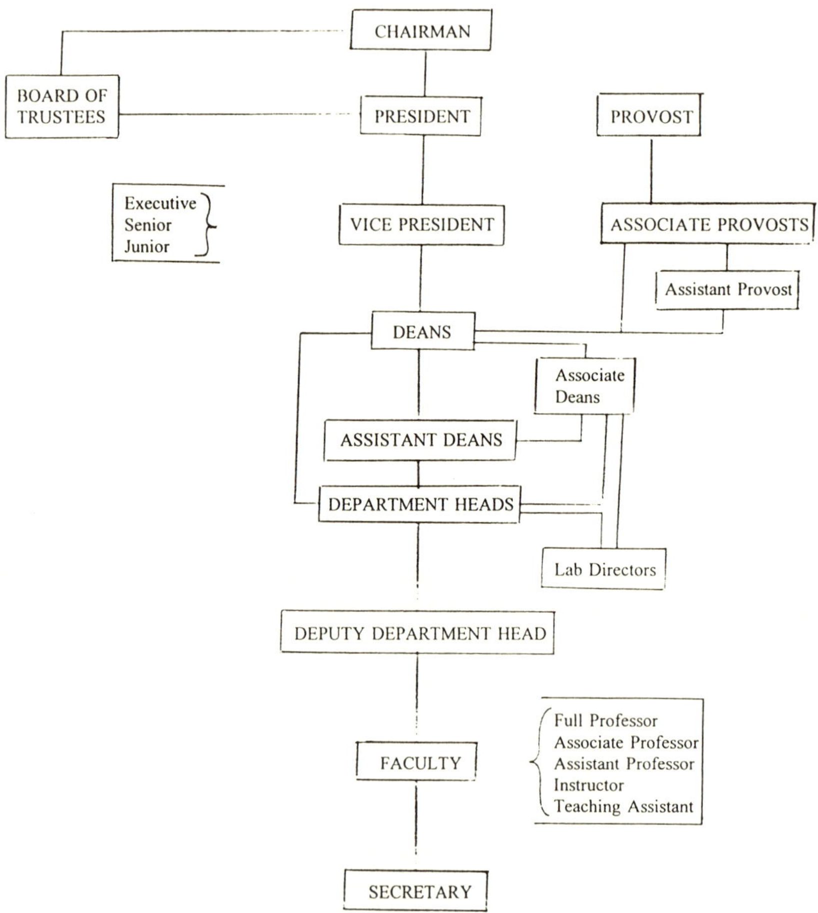


FIGURE 11 - TYPICAL UNIVERSITY HIERARCHY

teamwork. This not only affects the performance of these institutions but impedes their academic and professional quality. Academic freedom is now much more narrowly defined and focuses on theory alone. Content and delivery are increasingly determined by administrative fads.

In hospitals and health care facilities the situation is quite similar, although their legal liability adds another dimension to the control and administration of medical services. Rigid rules on procedures and tests are often imposed not for medical reasons but to improve revenue and reduce exposure to liability. The losers are the customers, the users of the institutions, who pay for added costs in time and money and increasingly assume the related risks.

In the past, faculty assumed many senior administrative positions for various periods and those elected department heads, deans, provosts, or other administrative posts invariably returned to their faculty positions after completing their tenure in such an administrative job. Their base remained the faculty, to which they continued to pledge their loyalty.

In the new industrial or corporate university, faculty elevated to administrative positions more and more infrequently return to teaching and research faculty positions. The faculty or peer group also has only a minor, if any, input to the selection of a faculty member from within or outside the university for such administrative positions. As a result, department heads no longer serve as department chairpeople and therefore as heads of a collegiate group of faculty in the running of an academic department but assume the role of department managers, whose loyalty and accountability are primarily to the administration. They are no longer peers among peers chosen by their peers but largely administratively selected and self-styled, nonrepresentative appointees. An increasing number of administrative positions that used to be offered to faculty are filled by outsiders—often professional administrators.

The budgetary process or fiscal power is increasingly used by university administrations as the primary method of administrative control. Fiscal management therefore, instead of emphasizing the needs and support of educational programs in the management of institutions of higher learning, has become the guideline by which the central administration controls an institution. In many universities today, the route from faculty to administration is one-way, and administrative positions are no longer filled on a rotating basis or on the recommendation of the concerned faculty. Administrative positions, such as department head or dean, are more like a career grade in an increasingly hierarchical university administration.

Not only the university itself but even units of the institution, such as departments and laboratories, are therefore governed by the administration and not the faculty. This has led to increasing alienation between faculty and administration, and faculty finds administration unresponsive to requests or suggestions from the faculty. One result is the decline of faculty participation in so-called faculty meetings, which are attended more regularly and in increasing numbers by administration than by faculty. The reason may be lack of interest, lack of time, or simply that the faculty considers faculty meetings farces and the results of such meetings largely predetermined. This, it is often felt, may be because faculty have little opportunity to formulate faculty meeting agendas or the fact that these meetings are generally called, organized, and chaired by the administration.

Similar conditions exist today in the health care industry and in law enforcement and in particular in hospitals and law enforcement facilities such as courts and prisons, where administration and control are now largely in the hands of professional managers. These not only administer but often direct the policies of these facilities.

## Institutional Performance

Institutions that outperform others do not necessarily have better educational, health or law professionals or more motivated people working for them. They are usually better organized, encourage teamwork, involve participatory management, and delegate decision-making authority to the lowest or most competent level while maintaining effective standards. They encourage pride and provide meaningful incentives and recognition.

Institutional performance has declined radically in recent years. The percentage of total expenditures spent on actual medical treatment, law enforcement, and crime prevention or, for that matter, on education and academic research today is a smaller fraction of the total spent by society on these essential institutions.

According to the U.S. Department of Education, American public schools cost American taxpayers over $295 billion in 1992, or about $5,920 per student or $118 per hour of instruction. This is twice the cost of public education in the next most expensive country, Switzerland. Similarly, we spent twice as much on medical services and significantly more on our justice and crime prevention system than the next most expensive country in the world. In other words, in these three major types of institutions the proportion of total expenditures for their direct functions, teaching and research, medical services and research, and law enforcement and criminal justice is becoming smaller and smaller.

Less than one-third of the total cost of education at all levels is spent for teachers, professors, researchers, and others directly involved in teaching or research. The percentage of cost of direct health care providers and others involved in patient care, tests, and procedures is even smaller. Similarly the percentage of law enforcement and related costs spent on police, courts, prisons, public prosecutors, and others directly involved in the legal and law enforcement system is less than one-third of the total spent.

Where does the rest go? Well, in education it goes to pay for inordinately large administrations, public officials, and all kinds of peripherals such as fund-raising. The same applies to health care, where insurance adds significantly to costs. In the legal system, lawyers, insurers, and regulators add the bulk of the financial burden.

There is no question that a significant percentage of the costs of these institutions could be saved with little effect on the quality and availability of education, health care, legal services, and justice the ways these institutions are structured and run were changed. There is an urgent need to return power to the teachers, health care providers, and law enforcement professionals.

It is interesting to note that overhead costs associated with these types of institutions are significantly lower in most other advanced industrialized countries with equal or higher levels of education, health care, and legal protection. A typical first-class hospital in Switzerland, Germany, or Israel only employs about one-third as many non–direct health care providers as a U.S. hospital of equal size (based on number of beds), types of services offered, and the technology or procedures used. The same applies to schools, universities, law courts, and more. Education and health care provider costs should be required to grow at a rate no larger than the increase in population or number of people served and the rate of inflation.

There is a substantial difference between the performance of our institutions as explained by public sector economists and their actual performance. Economic theory essentially assumes that institutions respond honestly and rationally to public demand and that they work in the public interest. However, institutions are made up of people, most of whom work in their personal interest. In other words, human selflessness, cooperation, and coordination are taken for granted by these theorists, who similarly assume costless transactions in the institutions.

But transaction costs today dominate the costs of institutional services. The value of institutions is in the utility of all the attributes they provide to the public. Yet the public has little information on the institutions, their costs, and the value as well as cost of the services they provide.

Most of our institutions pursue narrow goals. They often maximize their utility instead of that of those they are designed to serve. This may have harmful effects, as the institutional self-interests and those of their clients differ. Institutions guard themselves from external review, criticism, and regulation by various formal and informal constraints and often erect artificial administrative, professional, or academic barriers to prevent transparency.

## Social Irresponsibility

To correct our unaffordable institutional ills, we will have to cope with and reduce social irresponsibility. Few, if any, other societies deal with social problems as callously as we do. At the same time, we are the world's major critic of the human rights violations of others. True, we do not shoot or even imprison political opponents and any American can voice any opinion as long as he or she is willing to take the social, economic, political, and career consequences. Frankly, these can all be more costly than straight imprisonment, though obviously so much more subtle. They affect us over a long period of time—possibly even a lifetime. This is particularly so in our institutions, where you are expected to toe the line and to follow the establishment guidelines and policies. Lawyer, doctor, or educator who opposes some of the peer organizations, pronouncements, or rulings, particularly those dealing with self-policing, becomes an outcast. So much for freedom of speech and opinion!

It does not matter if you are a faculty member who questions a promotion, tenure, or even program decision, a doctor who questions a hospital procedure, or a lawyer who exposes inappropriate or even illegal practices or charges. Whistle-blowers or simple professionals concerned with the moral, ethical, or professional quality of their calling are not welcome in the institutionalized environments of American health care, education, and law enforcement. But these issues go much further and involve us as individuals and members of families, groups, or communities.

We do not really take care of our old, infirm or sick, young, homeless, or deserted. We solve these societal problems not by taking individual responsibility at least for those we should care and be responsible for but by institutionalizing the problem.

Old age homes, mental institutions, homeless shelters, foster homes, and other institutional solutions of our social problems are largely American inventions designed to make social problems not an individual's but collective responsibility. We institutionalize five times as many old, mentally disturbed, inform, poor, and homeless on a per capita basis than any other country in the world.

## Single Parenting and Welfare as a Profession

A scourge of American society and a major institutional problem is the single-parent family. It is usually the result of the lack of male responsibility and the curious incentives provided by our social support system, which provides unskilled young women with greater income from childbearing than holding a job. Combined, these account for most out-of-wedlock births. In turn, children born in environments driven by these factors are significantly more likely to

1. become criminals,
2. drop out of school,
3. be social misfits,
4. become a burden to the health care system, and
5. be unemployed or even unemployable.

Welfare has become a profession or a career for many recipients, particularly young welfare mothers. The system of welfare—as now established—provides no incentive for recipients to move toward or lead a productive life. We now spend $301 billion on welfare, or about $1,200 per capita per year.

Welfare is not only easy to get, even fraudulently, but for many has become a right instead of a privilege offered by society to those unable to lead productive lives for health or other reasons. The United States is among a handful of nations that provide welfare to the able-bodied without a requirement to work or provide service in return. In other countries, as during the recession in the United States during the thirties, welfare recipients work on public work projects or provide other services.

Our welfare system has become so distorted that welfare is not only a right of individuals but a responsibility of society. A major reason for this increased dependence of a growing portion of our society on government handouts is the breakdown of the U.S. family, the decline in the family, and, probably most important, the decline of American education, personal responsibility, individual discipline, and a sense of social belonging. An increasing percentage of Americans, particularly among the poor, are alienated and not only do not feel part of the system but are convinced that society and its institutions have failed them and therefore bear the responsibility to care for them.

## America as Moral Leader and Role Model of the World

Since World War II America has served as the moral leader and role model of the free world. Not only was its system of democracy and its legal and market-driven economic system admired, but so was its ability to accommodate people with different backgrounds and cultures and even languages under one system in which individual expression, opportunity, and freedom were guaranteed by a well-established legal system and a system of government that supported the institutions that made it possible.

Not only did America exert a moral leadership, but its culture, policies, and even institutions were emulated as if their adoption would automatically lead to the achievement of an American-like dream.

We are now bystanders and observers of a decline not in U.S. world but moral leadership. This decline affects the influence of America and what the United States stands for—its moral values, personal freedoms, insistence on human rights, compassion for the downtrodden, and effective interracial and interethnic relations.

The greatest threats faced by the world and the United States today are the combined effects of unbridled nationalism, which justifies cruelty, murder, and abolishment of human rights in the name of national interests; and fundamentalism, which has emerged from religious fanaticism into a form of an oppressive cult to justify brutality, suppression of anyone and anything judged, interpreted or accused of opposing the basic interest of those beliefs.

The combined effects of these two forces of evil—which have grown from little brush fires of isolated discontent to massive conflagrations that raze everything in their way to the ground, no matter how valuable or respected—now endanger civilization as we know it, civilization that has taken thousands of years to build and nourish, which, at its center, recognizes the rights and freedoms of individuals to live in peace and practice their customs and beliefs without infringing on the rights of others. These basic tenets of civilization have been dismantled in the former Yugoslavia and some parts of the former Soviet Union, as well as in many parts of Europe, Africa, Asia, and now even America.

The trend is growing. Racial and ethnic conflicts are on the rise and self-serving bureaucracies in government and institutions that control most resources do little to stop the trend. Complacency has become not only an individual but a national obsession. Let us not rock the boat, let us conform, even if we conform with a minority that tramples on our own basic rights.

Complacency has become a worldwide phenomena that allows nations to agree to let horrible things happen in the name of consensus, which gives in to most threats. Today much of the world is governed not by leaders but by followers. We may agree on principles, such as the right of a people for self-determination, only to dismiss the concept in response to a consensus that is only interested in the inviolate status quo and a desire for the lack of confrontation.

Whole nations with all characteristics of nationhood, such as the Kurds, are prevented from self-determination because it would interfere with the political and strategic interests of some nations. At the same time, we make a mockery of these principles by giving some entities nation status that represent neither a national entity nor a coherent national identity, such as language or culture, and which, as a result, offer a threat to the interests of people forced into the unit.

The United States, as the only remaining real superpower, is relinquishing its leadership and drifting into the current of a murky area in world opinion by trying to impose its morals and democracy. It is increasingly more concerned with world opinion and consensus, which it never achieves anyway, than with what is right and just, most important, in its own interest and in line with its moral values. It is often unable to recognize that different people have different cultures, backgrounds, and even values and that these are not necessarily immoral or undemocratic—just different.

A major factor in these developments that has led this country from a nation of principled individuals to one led and largely consumed by unprincipled institutions is our lack of will to stand up for what we as a nation have stood for for so long—our basic moral values, objectives, and concerns. Our Constitution assumes a nation of free men, free to voice their opinion, and stand up for what they believe in without the danger of retribution or interference with their rightful interests. We have allowed our institutions to capture not only our wealth and our economy but also many of our rights. These institutions control not only much of the political process but also increasingly our standard of living and way of life. Instead of serving the public and the public interest, they have largely evolved into self-centered and selfish institutions primarily concerned with the benefits to themselves and their own stakeholders. University executives, doctors, and lawyers who pay themselves 10 to 100 times the income of the average American, including the teachers, nurses, and legal aids serving them, cannot claim to represent or serve the public interest, particularly if their income is the only inviolate issue in any overhead designed to bring the economy of these institutions in line with the general growth in prices.

We preach that increased costs must be justified by increased productivity and performance and therefore value, yet we do not apply the same rationale to improvements in our institutions. The choice is clear. We either restructure and reengineer our institutions to their original purpose of selfless service to the community and into organizations that are responsive to the public and not largely their own interests or we will face a continued decline in the performance of the American economy and world leadership, which will ultimately lead to the destruction of America as a flourishing democratic, multicultural nation and a world leader.

We maintain our economic leadership and our political leadership only through our still formidable military prowess. Yet this may be temporary and of less concern in the future. On the other hand, our moral leadership is increasingly being challenged. Others may accept American popular music and jeans but are less and less willing to accept American moral and ethical standards. We preach human rights to others when most Americans are afraid to walk their streets and mistrust their police, lawmakers, doctors, and government in general. We are similarly concerned with corruption, misuse of public funds, and the honesty of our financial institutions. We have health, legal, and educational institutions that are mismanaged and suck the lifeblood out of our economy. Under these circumstances, who are we to preach to others how to run their affairs?

America—the military superpower of the nineties—may become the declining industrial power and newly developing country of the twenty-first century unless we put our priorities in order. Our preoccupation with military prowess—like that of a surviving dinosaur—may cause us to limp into the next century.

We must stop exerting our military prowess in order to solve every civil disorder, ethnic conflict, military upheaval, or political confrontation, which often have long histories and cannot be resolved by quick military solutions. Most of these do not affect American strategic or economic interests, and we increasingly get involved for sociodemocratic reasons, such as the reestablishment of a democratic government or family relief.

Although many in the world aspire to the American concept of democracy in a multiracial and multiethnic society, most countries do not have our diversity and either are made up of a single people or have a dominating majority. In both cases, the cultural background that affects the concept of democracy and our concept of the supremacy of individual rights, which takes precedence over the rights and well-being of society at large, are not only strange to many other people but often contradict their moral values, such as Confucian doctrine, for example.

Economic well-being or growth depends to a large extent on national morality. Although all industrialized nations have recently suffered economic recessions, their impacts have been quite different or distinct. In some countries, recession was both driven and sustained by speculation and caused a change in business and work ethics, which are hard to alter. It caused large budget deficits, bankruptcies, and decline in savings. In others, though in part driven by greed and speculation, it caused a reevaluation of traditional values and morality. It resulted in the reestablishment of the value and importance of economic growth through hard honest work and not speculation. It made people recognize the need for both effective social and economic balance and the importance of maintaining moral values and even good taste.

In the United States the recession has caused social dislocation and greater social disunity, while other nations have been able to use it as a unifying force that brought people together to recognize their common interests and goals. What we need above all in America now is the reestablishment of moral values and their use in furthering our economic growth.

We must bring some order into our own house. This must start with the restructuring, reforming, and in some way even reinvention of our major institutions. Only then will we regain the economic resources, the moral base, and the will to lead the world. Obviously, reformation of our major institutions cannot be done over the short run. It may take decades to achieve radical improvements in their performance. But it must be done lest our institutions irreversibly drag us into an abyss. The process starts with small steps, which in many cases are not only obvious but have large public support. Reformation must not degenerate into fault finding or vendettas but must become a process of gradual realignment of our institutions with their historic and societal objectives.

## Rebirth of Personal Responsibility

One of the most disturbing developments in American society is the move from personal self-sufficiency, the traditional mark of Americans, to dependence and reliance on government and public institutions for personal needs. As a society we have largely abrogated personal responsibility for health, education, and safety. We have transferred these responsibilities wholly to institutions. We similarly make little attempt even at prevention in these three basic needs of society.

At the same time, American society clamors for less government and a smaller role of government in daily life, as the recent 1994 swing to Republican leadership in both houses of Congress shows. We cannot have both less government and less personal responsibility. They depend and feed upon each other. More personal responsibility requires a more educated and responsible population as well as less intrusive institutions that serve the people and not largely themselves, which are concerned with their contribution to the betterment of society and not just their own standing and the success of a few of their disciplines.

As a nation we want to make our own personal decisions and be free to live our lives in a safe, clean, comfortable, and open environment, but few of us are willing to pay the price of less central government and more local or personal responsibility. We want freedom but not responsibility. We want safety but are not willing to accept discipline. We want things done for us but are not willing to allow others to decide how to do things for us, even when we do not know what we want or what can be done for us. We want without being willing to assume the responsibility for what we want.

We recognize the links between discipline and crime and also between responsibility and freedom. Somehow, though, we feel we are immune from these dependencies and can have our cake and eat it, too. There seems to be a growing consensus that we are exempt, that the rules that apply to others and have been proven throughout human history do not apply to us—that we can have free access to guns without an increase in crime, greater individual freedoms without effect on society, less government without more individual responsibility. We somehow feel that we are exempt from the quid pro quo, the need to pay for what we use. These are dangerous assumptions, as invariably the bills keep coming until we are no longer able to cope or continue the free ride.

## Human Values Are Not Static and Unique

After three hundred years of European world leadership, a growing number of people are looking at the world from different perspectives and associate different value scales and norms with their decisions. Africans' increasing disenchantment with the perceived failure of integration in America and Europe is causing them to develop a particularly African perspective, while East Asians influenced by Confucianism and other ancient cultural values that set moral codes and interpersonal relations, increasingly renounce European standards of behavior and success.

Americans, in particular, who advanced the European type of social standards in a dynamic way are taken aback by these developments. We cannot understand why others would disdain approaches that have served us so well. We ignore the fact that these are all relative measures influenced by history, culture, belief, and the environment.

Our interpretations of fairness, equality, morality, and decency are very different from those of people with a different history, background, and surroundings. We must learn to see our values not as absolute but as temporary and changeable judgments. The concept of democracy advanced first by the ancient Greeks has undergone many changes. Why is it then so difficult for us to understand that concepts such as democracy can and in fact must be interpreted in different ways and change over time as well?

All human values are molded by experience, and each of us has different experiences. Whole people develop histories based on different experiences and build value systems based on these experiences.

## Moral Decline

It is doubtful that the authors of the Ten Commandments, Confucius, or the writers of our Constitution would be able to relate our present value system and its moral interpretations to the codes and articles embodied in their proposals for interpersonal behavior for a balanced and fair society. To some among our society and, even more, its leadership, moral decline is somehow related to a modern interpretation of freedom.

Traditional centers of moral leadership in religion and politics have often become ineffective. People no longer simply accept duties—they assume rights independent of their contribution or duty to society at large or even their close friends and families. In turn, rights generates entitlements, even when the recipient assumes no responsibility toward society or those around him. In fact, if not in words, we no longer vow to stay married "till death do us part" but agree informally to stick together until one party wants out, as legalized by our no fault divorce laws.

Responsible personal conduct, and standards of responsibility and honesty have become the sign of weak tradition, not in line with today's selfish, self-centered, antisocial norms accepted as a right by so many. True, there are still many who live decent, honest lives and care for others, but they are no longer considered leaders but laggards.

In fact, selfishness and lack of concern for others is not only acceptable but a sign of competence and superior ability. Selflessness is increasingly deemed weak and incompetent, if not outright stupid. The increasing lack of consideration for society on the whole and others in private, social, and general, as well as in professional, business, or other transactional relationships or contacts, has made us into a society that cares for the individual in theory and emphasizes individual rights, while at the same time trampling on the most basic individual rights of personal safety, freedom of movement, equal opportunities for all, and protection of the weak.

We use the Bill of Rights more to protect the opportunities for the strong and selfish than the rights of the public of large. We have become a society in which everyone is essentially on his or her own. We protect the rights of criminals as individuals but not of society. We are not concerned with damage to individuals or cost to victims.

## Societal Moral Erosion and Criminals as Victims

The most astounding phenomenon in the American legal system supported by civil liberty organizations is the perception of the criminal as a victim of society, a person who has been wronged and to whom society owes a debt. It does not matter if the crime was premeditated or vicious, if it was based on hate, jealousy or greed. These organizations and others among American society find that the criminal is really the victim and society is at fault. The point is often made that criminals are often disadvantaged individuals who are forced into criminal activity by a system that provides little, if any, other opportunity. This argument is ill-founded, as the degree of criminality does not correlate with income or job opportunity. In fact, many recent immigrant minorities from Asia, who are not only low-income but have difficulties in emancipating themselves in the American culture and confront language barriers have very low crime rates. The problem seems to lie with the role of family and culture and availability or opportunity. Some segments of society value family and contributions to society while others could not care less and feel that society owes them.

There are, obviously, also Asian immigrants who use society. Forty-nine percent of all Cambodian immigrants are on government welfare. Another important fact is that 25 percent of all prisoners in the U.S. federal prisons are non–U.S. citizens. The threat to our society and the breeding ground of criminality appears to be the broken American family. With nearly 20 percent of U.S. babies born out of wedlock and usually deserted by their fathers, many have little opportunity to experience family life and an appreciation of family values.

Another problem is that many of the babies delivered (66 percent in Los Angeles) are born to illegal immigrants who often are not part of our social system and as a result become a disadvantage. As a result, a significant segment of the American population is disadvantaged and does not participate in society.

Today crime permeates every aspect of American life and society. It is prevalent in our homes, our private lives, in business, in our schools, in government, and even in our social and educational institutions. We often talk of crime as being associated with poverty and with lack of education. However, it is also common among the middle class or even upper class and among the highly educated. The crime may be different and sometimes less physically violent, but it is devastating nonetheless. A murder may not be committed with a knife or gun, but it results in death from such causes as a suicide or a heart attack caused by theft of life savings or a person's reputation or other, indirect violation of an individual.

## Institutional Waste

At a time when our major institutions are under financial strain and under constant pressure to bring their cost increases in line with the growth in the rate of inflation and population, we find that little effort is made to eliminate waste, to improve efficiency and quality of service, and to delay unnecessary or readily deferred expenditures. It is more important to do what is right than what is popular or in the interest of an institution. In the long run, doing what is right is in the interest of any institution.

In recent years, our principal institutions have made the choice of doing what is in their short-term interest, which often translates into short-term financial interest. In turn, this frequently causes a reduction in emphasis on the principal objectives or even reasons for being, such as learning and research at educational institutions, health care in medical institutions, and law enforcement as well as public safety in legal and criminal justice institutions.

Many educational and health care institutions face serious financial problems. It is interesting to note that the usual response is to go fund-raising to the private and public sectors. Few efforts are made to significantly raise revenues from new services. On the cost side, the approach has largely been to cut the costs of services. Universities and schools reduce the number of teachers and hospitals reduce doctors and nurses, ignoring the fact that reducing the productive capacity will usually have a greater effect on revenues than on costs.

## American Institutions as Moral Leadership Builders

The American system of democracy has been the moral leader of the world for long. It not only provided the model on how to integrate different people and assure individual liberty and freedom, but it also provided a fair justice system and opportunity for all. The influence of the United States as a social, economic, and moral leader reached its peak after World War II. This was because the United States had become the world's largest economy and technology developer, as well as the most powerful military nation. At the same time, it maintained a great social system and concern for individual rights and opportunity.

It became, and in a way still is, the greatest magnet for people around the world, but for the first time in a long time American moral leadership is being questioned. Other nations and their institutions, educational systems, culture, and economic structure are now increasingly chosen as role models. India, for example, is looking east, not west, as a recent headline in an Indian newspaper suggested. This is not only due to the lack of individual responsibility and ineffective government and institutional leadership, but also to the increasing breakdown of law and order in America. Personal responsibility is increasingly shunned while the interests of society are subjugated to personal greed.

There is growing skepticism that the United States can provide effective leadership and meaningful guidance or examples for the rest of the world. America today is less united than it has been for a long time and appears to have lost the value system that provided guidelines for its moral and economic leadership. It is increasingly blamed for compromising moral values to achieve economic goals and the use of its superpower status to advance its economic objectives.

American institutions in education, health care, and law enforcement used to provide the foundation for American moral leadership—but no more. As we become an increasingly lawless and undereducated society, with a health care system that is perceived as largely self-serving, the moral leadership of our primary national institutions is fading and the rest of the world is looking elsewhere for their role models. This affects not only the status of America in the world but also the terms and conditions of our relations with the rest of the world.

## Is Institutional Self-Correction Feasible?

Whenever our institutions come under attack for ineffectiveness, overpricing, or even corruption, they will advocate self-correction or self-policing. In theory, they all have such mechanisms in place. Legal, medical, and educational associations or boards all advertise their self-policing mechanisms. But reality is different and few are the cases where serious offenses are punished by more than a slap on the wrist. In fact, these bodies act more to protect the interests of the institutions, their components, and practitioners than those of the public.

The most serious area is the organized prevention of complaints and charges. The punishment of whistle-blowers and reporters from within and without our institutions has been the response to exposure by American institutions. Reporting misbehavior, fraud, or simple mismanagement to the public's notice or even reporting it internally is now considered antiestablishment or even anti-American by proponents of our institutions. Instead of praising people who expose waste, fraud, and mismanagement, we more often deride them, fire them, and punish them in a myriad of ways.

Standing up for what you believe in and disclosing the questioned unethical or wasteful practices is considered disloyal and subject not only to reprimand but also to loss of rights, standing, opportunity, and, ultimately, jobs. People within institutions are trained to consider whistle-blowers as a danger to themselves and as adversarial, even if they agree with the whistle-blower and suffer under the facts exposed. This type of unquestioning loyalty, which is fostered by our institutions, is undermining their very function, as well as their ability to improve in an ever more demanding environment.

## Empowering the Customers and Professionals

The major problems of institutional management can be traced to the loss of power by medical, educational, and legal/law enforcement professionals and the customers of the institutional services or the public at large. Doctors and nurses have little say in how hospitals and other health care institutions are run. Faculty and teachers do not set educational policy or control educational institutions and lawyers: judges and law enforcement professionals do not manage the legal or law enforcement systems. Today all of these institutions are largely managed by institutional managers who consider professionals simply hired hands who should have little, if any, influence on policy. Similarly, society has little, if anything, to say about how these essential institutions are run, and if public opinion or outcry is considered, it is usually belatedly and often reluctantly.

In all these institutions the principal concerns are not their effective functioning and performance in the interest of society but a conspiracy to protect vested interests, careers, contracts, and current practices. The interests of society, for which these institutions exist, have very low priority, if, in fact, any at all.

Improving the quality of education, health care, and law enforcement is lip service but, sadly, plays a very small role in how institutions work and how they are managed. Change and reform will only materialize under outside pressure and not from within the institutional systems. It will only come about when society at large insists on empowering both the recipients and beneficiaries of institutional services, as well as the professionals who make it happen.

The self-serving bureaucratic model that has invaded our institutions must be dismantled and control returned to a union of recipients and providers, not bureaucrats and political managers.

Jefferson and Madison recognized that the broader the power of those who control the state and its institutions in granting favors and exacting penalties, the more inbred and self-serving will be their management. It ultimately loses sight of the basic institutional roles and objectives. In most free societies, market forces are ultimately supposed to correct these problems, but if markets set prices on institutional favors, the institutions soon become corrupt.

In American industries hierarchial management is now often replaced by flat organizations in which decisions and responsibilities are delegated to numerous cells and the lowest competent levels, thereby assuring not only timely and competent decision-making but also effective ownership and empowerment. Obviously, such a system of management requires that at each cell or level the required expertise must be available. Considering that younger workers today are usually much better-trained than their older colleagues, this is not a problem. It is interesting to note that alone in the American economy, institutions hang onto traditional hierarchical management, as if afraid that the lower-level cells might preempt their prerogatives. And well they might! Few of our institutions today are headed by the most competent professionals. Few really competent professionals in education, health care, or law enforcement ever get a chance to assume important responsibilities.

Probably the most important void in American institutional management is in leadership. While United States business management has been accused of a lack of leadership, it has recently overcome much of this. Institutions need leadership in management more than most other enterprises because they set standards for and affect the public as a whole. Leaders need commitment, conviction, and a sense of direction, in addition to effective interpersonal and communication skills. They must be able to almost predict the future and have vision and an ability to get things done. They must be able to convince, generate trust, and somehow dare to be different and generate as well as project concepts, albeit unpopular ones.

## Institutions Should Put Customers First

The single most important change required in the way institutions are managed in America is their approach to their customers. They exist to serve society and its needs. To do this effectively, they must develop a customer-first approach and a service orientation. They must provide what people need and want and not what the institutions decide to offer. They must assure continuous feedback from the public and continuous updating of their services to respond to changing needs of society.

Over the years our institutions have increasingly grown apart from those they are supposed to serve. They emphasize services not necessarily wanted and have become more difficult to access—this notwithstanding advances in technology that make it very easy to communicate with customers. Customer-service databases can be readily established, service access facilitated, and continuous customer contacts maintained to assure that services are up-to-date.

By and large, our institutions are not customer-oriented and, in fact, do not even know who their customers are. Similarly, the public has great difficulty in obtaining information on services provided by these institutions and how to access them. Few know how to make full use of legal, medical, or educational systems, what services are available, the conditions or terms attached to their availability, their costs, and other important information. As a result, many are hesitant to use their services.

The administration of many of our institutions is primarily oriented toward internal controls and not customer services. Customers are supposed to identify their needs and request the desired services. Institutions seldom go out and volunteer services or draw in their customers. There are obviously exceptions, particularly in preventative medicine.

It is difficult to understand that these American institutions are going down in disgrace for a lack of the same imagination that built them up as shining examples of what America stood for. It is not for want of demand but for the lack of understanding of the marketplace, technology, and social expectations.

Institutions feel competent to dictate what the market demand should be. They offer services they deem appropriate instead of letting the market or society decide its own needs. For example, society increasingly demands preventative measures and not corrective medicine. Institutions must be customer-oriented and assure that they respond to the real and not perceived needs of society. This means that institutions must become dynamic and responsive organizations.

Our institutions were created to help build and maintain society and to promote family, work, personal ethics, and community building. Instead, they have largely alienated people, both in their personal relations and in their relations with their institutions. People now often consider institutions abstract entitlements and sources of services that are somehow funded and controlled by unknown interests. They do not care who pays for these institutions as long as they serve their interests. Therefore, there is an increasing gap between institutional users and providers. The latter feel that they should determine what the former needs or what the institution ought to provide.

Institutions are designed to serve society, assure responsible behavior by individuals, and provide them with opportunities. Thus, institutions must adapt to changing societal needs and not be cast in concrete or become reflections of special interests, particularly those providing the institutional services. They must first develop an approach that balances the rights of the individual with the needs of society. They must assist community building, which obviously includes family building. As a result, the customer is not just the individual but society at large as well.

## Demand for Institutional Services

By and large, Americans assume that health care, law enforcement, and educational institutions exist to serve them—which is reasonable—but increasingly their demand for these services is unmet. There is a major gap between demand and supply for institutional services not only in the volume of service but in the type and method of delivery of service.

Not only do we expect health care to legitimate ills, but the majority of health care costs are now expended on preventable or self-inflicted ills, like drug abuse, gunshot wounds, and more. Similarly, the majority of law enforcement expenditures do not go to basic law enforcement services for the community but to law enforcement and the protection of a small proportion of society who flaunt the law and the societal norm of behavior.

Finally, much of higher education costs are spent not on providing advanced education to people who need and want it to advance their career and quality of life, but to people who go to college to bide their time and just hang around because that is a "neat" thing to do.

A large proportion, some say as much as one-third, of the expenditures for health care, law enforcement, and higher education could be saved if these wastes were eliminated, with public or free health care only provided to heal legitimate ills, law enforcement only to meet society's needs, and higher education only to those who planned to make use of it.

## Institutional Governance

Most American institutions, particularly universities and hospitals, achieved their reputation for excellence as a result of the selfless contributions of a number of unassuming faculty, doctors, and researchers whose interest was the advancement of knowledge, the betterment of mankind, and the education of a new generation of scholars as well as practitioners who continued to advance these goals. As noted before, tradition was for the governance, and of equal importance the goals and direction of these institutions were to be under the care and responsibility of those who made these universities and hospitals.

The facade persists and most assemble faculty or hold meetings periodically to present involved governance. The exclusion of those who made these institutions from relevant decisions that affect them and their institutions has become the norm rather than an exception. As an example, average participation of faculty at faculty meetings at MIT is a dismal 7.8 percent and only occasionally reached 20 percent in four meetings during a recent ten-year period, and only when other than routine academic issues were on the agenda. During the current fiscal constraints in which most institutions find themselves, close cooperation of faculty/doctors and administrators is required to sustain excellence. However, the opposite is usually the case.

Fewer and fewer faculty or doctors are drawn into the decision-making process, and the administrations appear to "circle the wagons" to exclude others from meaningful and effective involvement in fiscal and administrative policy. Many administrators contend that it is unresponsiveness, unconstructiveness, and lack of proactiveness by faculty and doctors that is the primary cause. However, this pattern so prevalent in the "best" of these American institutions appears to be a case of "learned helplessness," a term coined by experimental social psychologists for when knowledgeable and affected people become unresponsive.

## Institutionalized Corruption

To many Americans recently publicized revelations of widespread corruption in police departments throughout the country came as a surprise. Yet it had gone on for years and in many cases was endemic. Not only was it known to many in the system but, what is worse, is that it was not only tolerated by many in charge but accepted by the public as inevitable. While police corruption is now in the limelight, the situation in the educational and medical institutions is similar in many ways.

Service is no longer the principal motive for its practitioners. Many medical doctors are in it primarily for the money and not to provide a contribution to society, nor are many teachers, particularly in higher education, in it for the satisfaction of teaching or even research. While in some cases institutional corruption is direct and materialistic, it is more often than not indirect, intellectual, or organizational. Money, position, status, and, most important, power appear to have replaced the traditional reasons for an institutional career in law, education or health care.

What is particularly worrisome is the public's acceptance of this situation. By and large, the public claims impotence in the fight against institutional corruption. In other words, it admits that our institutions have taken over not only their but our governance and have in most cases become immune to public concern and criticism. At the same time, the public has learned to live with its impotence.

Institutional corruption not only consists of dishonest bribe-taking cops, dishonest customs officials, teachers who fake grades or plagiarize, and nurses or doctors who misuse drugs, cover up malpractice, or perform unnecessary procedures. It now includes management conniving in institutionwide corruption, with padded contracts or bills, obscene salaries, hidden fringe benefits, and more.

The ineffectiveness, inefficiencies, and corruption of our institutions are due, to a large extent, to selfishness: selfishness that interprets our basic tenet of the supremacy of the individual and his/her rights to include the right to selfish use of the society and the exploitation of institutional powers for selfish motives.

Those in control of our institutions somehow perceive themselves to be the institutions. University administrators think of themselves as the institution, as do hospital and legal institution administrators. Few of these are managed or administered by the cream of the professionals who make these institutions. In fact, more often than not, these are people who did not excel in their profession as doctors, educators, or lawyers or so-called professional educational, legal, or health care administrators.

## Academic Rules and Intellectual Honesty

Universities are perceived as ivory towers with lily white standards for intellectual values. I have spent long periods of my life in industry, government, and academia and conclude that this public perception is far off the mark. In fact, interpersonal relations and intellectual honesty are probably kept to higher standards in government and industry. Interpersonal competition in academia is supreme, and basically any means that advances one's standing or prospects are considered fine. Even academic niceties fostered by long tradition are falling by the wayside. Competing in research proposals was always accepted, but today we have an increasing number of cases of research-idea theft. All of this has led to a change in the academic environment, which has become more oriented toward career and funding than teaching and learning.

As ancient Greek scholars noted, it is not only important what you accomplish but how you accomplish it. This simple standard seems to have been lost in many academic institutions and even more important, to academics as individuals. There has always been healthy competition among academics in R and D as well as in education, but there was always a set of well-respected norms and traditions that assured that the ethical and moral boundaries were not violated. No more.

Today the rules of competition in academic activities surpass inviolate standards of the past. Plagiarism has emerged as a fine art unto itself and something greatly facilitated by computer and communication technology. Similarly, the increasing scarcity of research support and the need for rapid scientific and technological advances to keep pace with the rate of technological developments is forcing more and more academics to use shortcuts to stay ahead and assure that their research results are not made obsolete by other developments. As a result, there are more cases of academic fraud and lack of collegiality in research planning.

## Institutional Honesty

An institution is what it does. If the institution degenerates into unethical practices or allows such to occur, it will ultimately fall prey to its own degeneration. False or exaggerated claims by institutions are no longer the exception but have become the accepted norm. More and more, ethical values are subjugated to the purposes of the bottom line. Institutional leadership is usually the first to relax these norms and thereby induces an aura of cynicism among the staff and those served by the institution. It thereby degrades not only the service of the institution but its own values. Covering up and misleading claims have quite often become accepted practices, and institutions use all kinds of means to discourage whistle-blowers.

Institutions spend enormous sums on public relations and go out of their way to polish their image. This exercise often leads them to believe what they tell the public. As a result, American health care, education, and law enforcement institutions perceive themselves as being the best and without peer. While this is true in some isolated cases, it is far from true in general.

There are superb hospitals and universities as well as legal institutions, but by and large the services rendered by American institutions to the average citizen are well below those obtainable by citizens of many other developed countries. Institutions are increasingly tempted by opportunities and often excuse compromised actions by the uniqueness of an opportunity that required such action.

## Investing in Our Institutions

Reductions in federal budgets for education and health care are said to undermine the American tradition for excellence in education, health care, and research. Many claim that any such reductions threaten the performance of these institutions and, as a result, may cause a move toward loss of leadership in science, technology, and medicine, while at the same time undermining the education and health care of Americans.

Knowledge is the basis for progress, and investment in education and research is the principal method for assuring our leadership in knowledge. In turn, this provides the foundation for the new information age. While there is little argument with the above, there is a serious question of who should invest and how much should be invested in education and health care. Of the utmost importance is the role of government in funding these cornerstone institutions. While as Americans we have always advocated small government, many feel that education, health care, and law enforcement are—and should be—principally a responsibility of our government. But the roles government can assume are many and funding is only one of these roles, and probably not the most important. In fact, we face the curious situation of asking government to monetarily support health care, education, and research but not wanting it to get involved in or even specify the roles or agendas of these institutions. We want government to provide the resources without their involvement or control. But this is not the way things work. Funding, even public funding, automatically involves some degree of representation. Yet our institutions feel betrayed when government reduces funding under a severe budget crunch without feeling an obligation to similarly tighten its belt, improve efficiency, and become more selective in spending. Similarly, these institutions have made only limited and often half-hearted efforts at alternative fund-raising, particularly from sources who directly benefit from the work of these institutions.

## Correctness in Our Institutions

Writing is an exercise in intellectual freedom. It provides an outlet for the mind and soul at a time of increasing complacency and conformity. The expectation of social and political correctness has taken the place of dictatorship of the past. We no longer obey the ruler but the rules set by a vocal minority who assume the right of deciding what is good and proper for us all. These appear to be the major guidelines in today's institutions.

To speak out against or disagree with the correct stand is now a sign of social misconduct. It cannot be tolerated in our conforming society. But what about democracy, freedom of expression, and freedom of speech? Are they all to fall victim to the rules of conformity set by a vocal minority who often control our institutions?

Every year fewer decisions reflect majority opinions. More and more of our personal life is being invaded by correctness criteria. At the same time we continue our hypocrisy in our politically correct postures. We refuse to significantly improve the mileage of our car's drive-per-gallon and our per capita consumption, but we outlaw smoking. While smoking is admittedly harmful, the amount of harmful substances inhaled in crossing one of our congested urban streets is a multiple of those even a smoke-filled room can impose on an individual. We permit sexual freedom and all kinds of sexual perversion, while often punishing innocent and harmless advances as sexual harassment.

We release convicted murderers and other violent criminals on probation after serving a small fraction of their sentence but incarcerate nonviolent offenders against our social norms for their full term. A foreign friend suggested that "in America it is less dangerous to stab than to kiss a stranger." You may even get a shorter sentence, particularly if the stabbing is fatal.

Much of the power that institutional management has attained is the result of their contention that they are purveyors of social and political correctness. They represent what society wants and, more important, needs. Society does not want more efficient, cost-conscious health care, education, and law enforcement but more extensive and accessible services and continued budget increases for these services. Society wants more high-tech services and not more prevention in health care and crime. It is time for the silent majority to let their voices be heard, their interests defined, and considered independent of the minority naysayers.

# 8

# Reinventing Our Institutions for Improved Economic Performance

Our institutions today affect the performance of our economy and our standard of living more than ever before. Their own performance in terms of their productivity and transaction costs also has an enormous social impact. While the structure and development of our society and economy shaped the direction of our institutions in the past, which then provided social incentives and support systems, recent institutional changes have created real dangers of reactive developments whereby our institutions abduct our economy instead of providing a risk-reducing support net for it.

According to Douglas C. North, some economies develop institutions that produce growth while others develop institutions that produce stagnation or worse.[1] In the United States we have benefited from the tremendous contribution of our institutions to our economic growth over a long period. We now seem to be mired in an irreversible trend in which our institutions drive our economy toward stagnation. We now attempt to develop a strategy to counteract the imminent dangers and to reinvent our institutions.

In recent years, American institutions in health care, education, and law enforcement have exploded, and they now consume an inordinate amount of our resources. This is largely due to the lack or loss of a specific culture. Conventions and standards that provide guidelines to institutions are difficult to specify in a multicultural environment such as that found in the United States. In turn, this opens the unregulatable floodgates of institutional growth. Institutional standards and conventions must be based on moral norms if they are to acquire moral force, without which institutions grow like weeds.

Our institutions are no longer agents of economic change and contributors to economic growth, as in the past, but are now net consumers of public assets. The costs of resources consumed now well exceed the value to society generated by them. America had been a multicultural society even in colonial times, when it espoused clear moral norms and standards that gave rise to our unique Constitution and the resulting moral base for the development of our institutions. In recent history, though, the link between our traditional moral norms and standards and our institutions not only has been diluted but is more often than not simply ignored.

The relations between the public and its institutions should be based on contracts of performance. Unfortunately, in the United States such contracts are non-existent, incomplete, and, most important, unenforceable. Only contracts that stipulate performance can provide a basis for enforcement on the supply side. Yet we have basically no performance standards in education, health care, and law enforcement. In fact, nationwide performance of institutions in these fields varies widely, with little rationale for the differences. A high school diploma may be proof of effective education or just completion of twelve years of schooling, with little or no skills or knowledge acquisition. The same applies to medical and law enforcement services.

In any business or other contractual relation, both parties should have an incentive to minimize transaction costs. Not so with American institutions. They seem to maximize their transaction costs without the knowledge and consent of those they serve and who pay the bill. The information and communication technology revolution of recent years was expected to reverse this trend of growing transaction costs by providing low-cost, near-real-time access to information, but this did not happen in our institutions, though it certainly did reduce transaction costs in banking, manufacturing, and most other types of businesses or services.

In theory, institutional transaction costs should be lower in the United States than in smaller or less developed countries because of economies of scale on the one hand and learning on the other. Yet this again is not the case. In fact, it is curious to note that advances in technology have done little to improve institutional performance and, in general, have led to an increase in direct transaction costs, sometimes under the guise of more advanced services, which usually benefited only a few.

Transaction costs faced by users not only are those charged by the institutions in terms of rates, taxes, or fees but also include costs to the user of queuing and lost time, loss of business opportunity, costs of access, and more. In fact, indirect costs that users of institutional services face often outweigh direct service costs and have become a major deterrent to the use of some institutional services such as emergency hospital rooms by people who have a legitimate use for them. In other words, mostly people who have the time or whose time is near valueless make effective and often excessive use of institutional services with high indirect transaction costs. Others who pay for but hardly use such services then face huge direct transaction costs per unit use of services.

While in theory inefficient institutions should be weeded out or fail over time and only efficient ones survive, reality shows that in today's highly politicized and media-driven environment efficient institutions can stay in business and thrive. In fact, inefficient institutions survive tenaciously even under conditions of public criticism and economic pressure. The consequences of inefficient institutional services are known. Socialist economies show that the major cause of poor economic performance is the underlying institutional framework and associated institutional inefficiency. Karl Marx tried to integrate technological and institutional change and assure institutional effectiveness through political doctrines. But it never worked because the incentives for such integration did not and do not exist and people need incentives to improve.

Currently our institutions constitute a net drain on our society and our economy. Their social and economic costs outweigh the social and economic benefits they generate. This cannot continue and we must develop a more positive social and economic benefit-cost ratio in the provision of institutional services if we are to continue to thrive as a nation.

The social and economic rate of return on our investment in education, health care, and law enforcement must improve to justify the tremendous resources devoted to these institutions. Not only must we contain the growth in expenditure for these institutions to, at most, the rate of inflation plus population growth, but we must actually attempt to achieve a zero growth rate by the end of this century and then reduce our expenditure by a few percent per year until we reach the level of expenditure of other industrialized countries, or about 25 to 30 percent of GNP, which is about half of the projected costs of these institutions by 2005–10. This is achievable only if we put our minds to it. This can be done without reducing the availability and quality of service. In fact, services should become more accessible and effective if cost reduction is achieved by cutting much of the burdensome institutional bureaucracy as we must.

## Institutional Organization

In the most basic terms, institutions are constructions of the mind. They represent concepts deemed essential for the meaningful and orderly advance of society. Their organizations have evolved over time and have only become rigidly defined in recent years. Until the turn of this century, education, law enforcement, and health care were largely community services provided by the public for society. Some were established by institutional entrepreneurs. Institutional organizations soon evolved into self-serving organizations, with various segments of society giving different support to certain institutions as they confront or consider problems differently and then allocate different resource levels and human input to cope with such problems. Institutional structure and organization has an increasing impact on the risk that the contract will be fulfilled and the services expected by society will be delivered. This risk has increased significantly in recent years as institutions cut back on services instead of overhead in dealing with budget shortfalls. They do not seem to recognize that lower service levels and greater risks in the delivery of services lower their value to society and the assets or resources society should be willing to assign to them.

Institutional organizations, to be effective, must convey a feeling of efficiency, commitment to quality and service, customer orientation, technical competence, and reliability. They must be stable and yet designed to respond to changing social and economic requirements while fulfilling their assigned responsibilities.

Institutions must instill an incentive structure that rewards superior service in terms of service quality, customer responsiveness, and efficiency in the use of resources. This implies an internal reward system that is not hierarchical and permeates incentives throughout the organization.

Institutional management in the United States must be restructured into flat decision-based organizations in which responsibilities and related decision-making powers are delegated to the lowest competent level—the level that has all the information as well as the training, experience, and competence to make the decision. This applies to professional decisions by nurses, accountants, and laboratory staff, as well as police officers and teachers. They should be given authority to make all those decisions where bringing them to a higher level adds neither information experience, nor competence but only delays and possibly interferes with the decision. Institutional organizations have now grown into largely unwieldy bureaucracies that feed upon themselves. There is little need for many of the so-called middle management levels in institutional organizations to manage groups of professionals who, in this age of high technology, are usually highly trained themselves and more competent to make relevant decisions than professional middle managers.

Institutional organizations have become bloated and, in many cases, unresponsive to their basic service function. American industry in manufacturing and services has largely eliminated middle management and thereby developed a leaner, more effective and responsible organizational structure that in many cases was instrumental in making it globally competitive. The same is needed in our institutional organizations.

The time of institutional empire building is over, and the importance of a position is no longer a function of the number of people reporting to the holder of the position. Today the importance of a position and the reward should be only a function of the relevance, effectiveness, and contribution of the decisions made by the holder of a position. This applies equally to education, health care, and law enforcement institutions. Similarly, checks and balances within institutional management organizations are readily provided by extended information networks and no longer need duplicate hierarchical positions. As a result, very simple flat organizations today provide the most effective management controls for institutions.

In other words, it is no longer necessary to have complex approval and accounting procedures involving several levels in an organization when all the information needed for each decision and the results of each decision are readily available in real time in a management information systems network. In fact, today we are able to essentially eliminate paper from most institutional management functions, such as recording, reporting, evaluation, decision accounting, and funds transfer (instead of billing). Today many large commercial institutions, such as ports, banks, hotels, airlines, etc., are essentially run as paperless operations.

In a typical American hospital or clinic, school or university, courthouse or prison, as many as 30 percent of all staff are engaged in purely bureaucratic functions, such as bookkeeping, accounting, and inventory management. In fact, less than 50 percent, and as often as few as 30 percent of the staff are employed in directly or indirectly providing the services of the institutions. Today most, if not all, of these non-service-related functions can be performed by computers and other electronic technology not only cheaper but also faster and more reliably. The resulting improvements will result not only in major cost savings but also in greater efficiency and productivity, faster and more reliable service, less bias, improved productivity, greater tractability, and better accountability.

Most important, institutional service providers would be able to concentrate on providing their assigned service to the best of their ability and not spend inordinate amounts of time on paperwork and organizational or jurisdictional queries. In other words, in the future institutional organizations should be efficient, lean, customer-oriented, and professional service organizations that concentrate on providing their assigned services with proficiency, quality, and speed at minimum cost to the public by eliminating all unnecessary bureaucracy, management, and other overhead structures.

The task of institutional management should be primarily strategic. It should be concerned with long-range planning, discovery and development of markets, customer relations, evaluation and development of new services to meet society's needs, technology change, planning, and long-term operational management. It should not devote its primary attention to day-to-day operations, which are much more effectively managed by direct service providers. Concentration of management on short-term issues at a cost of inadequate long-term management dilutes and wastes management effectiveness at many of our institutions. It is time for us to reinvent our institutional management and get short-term operational problems out of the board room and the executive suites and back to the service providers. By and large, our institutions have failed in strategic management and provided inefficient operational management.

Strategic and operational management are distinctly different management functions. Both are necessary, but each requires a different approach. Top institutional management substitutes fund-raising and public relations for strategic management, often to meet current operation, budgetary, or image shortfalls. In turn, this results in direct operational involvement, such as short-notice budget cuts or operational changes. Such interference by senior management in the day-to-day operations can be very disruptive and counterincentive, as it presents an image of lack of planning and control. Instead, strategic and operational management should be separated and should complement each other.

To achieve well-coordinated and effective institutional management of our institutions will require a gradual elimination of most layers of middle management, development of a flat operational management structure of professional service providers, and top-level strategic management that interacts with operational management through periodic audits of operational performance against established strategic objectives. These periodic audits are also designed to identify potential threats to and opportunities for the provision of services by the institution and to provide feedback for strategic planning.

Strategic and operational management, though unique, should interface periodically in many functions. For example, while day-to-day purchasing, payroll, and billing is an operational function that should be highly computerized and require little bureaucratic involvement, budgetary revenue and cost controls are invoked by strategic management that audits budgetary performance against strategic budget plans periodically. The same applies to service performance, manpower development, and other functions.

Another issue is quality management, which requires both real-time operational and strategic management involvement. In addition, institutions that serve the public require external controls and sometimes external policing to assure service quality, fairness, objectivity, and public trust. Many of our institutions have adopted self-policing to deal with internal problems of quality and fraud, such as double billing or billing for services not rendered. There are also questionable practices such as fee-splitting referrals, ambulance chasing, nonexistent student registration, and excessive hourly billings, among others, which may require external policing. Our medical and legal professions are now largely self-policing, while in the educational field there is a curious mix of self-policing with some outside review, yet reviewers are usually selected by the institutions to be audited.

As a result, there are no nationwide or even regional professional, service, quality, or even fee standards. In other words, we have largely a free-for-all in most of our institutions and, for that matter, our service providers. They make up their own rules, standards and methods of service delivery, as well as fee structure. This not only causes a lack of institutional responsiveness to public concerns but also increases public mistrust. Our institutions must build effective, unbiased external policing mechanisms that review both strategic and operational management performance in light of the needs and interests of the public.

As an example, boards of trustees at universities and hospitals should not be, or at least not exclusively be, appointed by the management of such institutions. It also is not enough to have a single, well-chosen student or community representative on such boards to quell questions on user representation. Such boards and similar bodies must truly represent the owners and users of the institution and serve as watchdogs of its management and staff performance and not yes-saying representatives of its management. The same applies to various regulatory and review panels or bodies.

## Cost of Institutional Services

The costs of American institutional services are exorbitant not because of the cost of the actual services or their providers, such as doctors, nurses, orderlies, lab assistants, teachers, police officers, etc., but because of the large, unnecessary overhead burden posed by a bloated administration, underutilized or unnecessary high-tech equipment, and related diagnostic, legal, insurance, supervisory, and other activities. As noted before, less than 50 percent and in some cases as little as 30 percent of institutional costs are actually consumed to pay for the direct and indirect costs of providing institutional services.

In most of these institutions, overhead or administrative costs have gone up at more than twice the rate of the direct and indirect service costs. While much of this is the result of inefficient institutional management, the government often shares the blame for adding unnecessary or ineffective regulatory and inspection requirements, which often cause additional staff and other expenses, to perform functions already provided. While major financial institutions, airlines, hotel chains, and others have been able to reduce their bookkeeping, accounting, inventory, reservation, and similar staff by 30 to 40 percent over the last ten years by introducing effective management information systems, hospitals, universities, and similar institutional facilities have moved in the other direction by expanding their staffs in these categories, notwithstanding the fact that most have also introduced modern computing and other electronic equipment.

One reason may be their unwillingness to support standardized hospital or university management software development and adoption. I do not know if this is the result of lack of cooperation, shortsightedness, or concern that it may force exposure of proprietary information or, worse, inefficiency. Needless to say, we have the ability to manage most hospital and university administrative functions, admission, accounting, billing, insurance claim administration, stockkeeping and ordering, room scheduling, shift assignments, and more, by computer. Airlines have done it for years and probably are doing a better job than most of these institutions by using modern electronic technology to manage most of their operations.

While many of our educational institutions and hospitals are private, they are largely run like public-sector enterprises. In a way, it is curious that nonprofit private institutions are often less efficiently run than similar public-sector institutions. On the other hand, similar for-profit institutions are frequently significantly more efficient than their not-for-profit counterparts while providing equal, if not better, service. The nonprofit institution was a good idea in the past and may have worked well under peer management. It does not seem to work well with narrowly focused professional management. It benefited from the active involvement of public-interest, religious, or ethnic groups who often provided the incentives as well as the basic direction for the establishment of many of our educational and health care institutions. Today this involvement is on the decline as is the contribution of volunteers in education and health care. Many of our nonprofit institutions are in difficulty as they must now work in an increasingly competitive environment without the basic support of a traditional interest group.

Many of our health care institutions also face changes in factor input costs. They often compete with lower costs of for-profit health clinics or health maintenance organizations, which often benefit from economies of scale and bulk purchasing powers of large nationwide organizations. In the future, we may see similar trends in education and law enforcement where national associations of for-profit universities or other educational institutions or nationwide for-profit prisons compete with publicly owned or not-for-profit institutions in their field.

Another issue is the increasing interest of the public in preventative and nontraditional health care, areas in which American health care institutions have provided little guidance, or for that matter, services in the past. Preventative medicine has grown from a consequence of our preoccupation with exercise and health food to a real alternative approach to health care by many Americans who now emphasize a healthy lifestyle. Similarly, Oriental and South Asian methods of noninvasive healing, such as pressure treatment and acupuncture, have become serious alternative treatments for many Americans.

This presents a real dilemma for traditional U.S. health care providers and has even forced some health insurers to permit such treatments under their policies. The reason is often public dissatisfaction with the provision, quality, or costs of traditional health care. The cost accounting and pricing methods of many medical and educational services should be reconsidered. The large-scale cross-subsidization by hospitals and universities, where paying users are charged a multiple of the actual costs of services to make up for shortfalls from non- or underpaying users and for the underutilization of facilities, is not only immoral but economically untenable and inefficient. There is no reason why the public or taxpayers at large or the few unfortunate paying users of such services should pay for the bulk of indigent users. This causes an inexcusable distortion of the prices for hospital and university services, which are superimposed on already inefficient systems' cost to cause the often obscene pricing for such services. While a simple cost-based fee system may be difficult to implement and such fee-for-service systems counterincentive, a more equitable pricing system must be put in place that is efficient and fair, encourages use of services when needed, discourages misuse of services, discourages overinvestment in facilities and equipment and other waste, assures effective access of services to all, rewards quality of service, encourages innovation, research, and development in new service, and encourages preventative approaches. While this applies primarily to hospitals and health care providers, much of it also applies to educational institutions.

For example, many HMOs have been able to devise monthly fee-plus-copayment fee systems that achieve many of the preceding objectives, often at a significantly lower total cost to users. It is also interesting to note that many HMOs provide an array of free, no-fee services to seniors over and above those normally covered by Medicare for no added fee and just a small copayment. These quite often also include major reductions in the costs of medication, eye care, and other services. They appear to be able to provide these simply by use of more efficient service administration.

One of the reasons for the economic success of many HMOs is that they usually assign patients to a primary care physician who serves not only as a preventative medical provider but also as a gatekeeper who prevents unnecessary or frivolous use of medical services. There is an urgent need for the introduction of similar preventative providers and gatekeepers in education and law enforcement to reduce the often unnecessary or frivolous use of educational or law enforcement services. In other words we need a system of Educational Maintenance Organizations (EMOs) and Legal Rights Maintenance Organizations (LRMOs), which, for a monthly fee and some small copayment charge, provide primary preventative as well as remedial care in education and legal matters to all citizens. This would include not just primary care (advice) but also college education, vocational training, continuing education, additional skill development, and more.

Such a system would not only easily pay for itself but also assure better use of educational and law enforcement services, greater economic opportunities and major cost savings to society, improvements in intersocietal behavior and tolerance, better educational and skill levels, and greater focus and improved direction in societal development.

Today many of our health care, educational, and law enforcement services are misused, which is a major cause for their excessive costs and ineffectiveness. We must provide a better link between these institutions and society and train people in the more effective use of these essential institutions for which, in the end, we all pay.

## Rationalizing Institutions

Institutions should be the embodiment of people's ideals. They should forever change in line with changing ideals. Instead our institutions have become rigid organizations that force people to conform to their requirements instead of being responsive to those of the people they are designed to serve.

Institutions have become self-serving instead of embodying society's goals. They are usually controlled by laws, regulations, requirements, and rules designed more to safeguard the perpetuation of the institutions than to further the needs and ideals of the people they are supposed to serve. People have become the serfs of their own institutions instead of the other way around. We have to follow rules made by institutions to allow us to use or benefit from these same institutions.

This is equally true in health care, law enforcement, and education and is probably the principal reason for the widening gap and increased lack of confidence between the people and these institutions. Institutions set their own standards and charters and seldom try to make these responsive to the ideals they were set up to observe or the needs expressed by the community they are supposed to serve.

Ideas affect the markets for institutional services, and these ideas are generated by the public, which then makes its choice. The public choice theory indicates that while the public's demand is largely affected by ideas, publicity, advertising, and the media in general, they have a growing influence on public demand for institutional services. Our institutions have learned how to use the media to their advantage and thereby affect not only the market but also public support for institutional policies. While we have long assumed that the public followed the rational actor paradigm in its demand for institutional services, this is now a past dream. Although people think of themselves as rational consumers of institutional services, the reality is quite different as people consider their transaction costs and benefits, in addition to institutional constraints in making their choices. This makes it difficult to determine the total cost of services and, even more significant, consumer choice and demand for institutional services.

## Institutional Quality Management and Benchmarking

Effective TQM has been the major approach towards the reassertion of American industrial competitiveness in the world. After long trials, much of American industry has jumped on the TQM bandwagon and reformed themselves into world-class industries, second to none. Our service industries in class finance, recreation, transportation, telecommunications, etc., are now following suit and are trimming their bureaucracies, improving their service qualities and emphasizing customer responsiveness. It is now necessary to introduce TQM into our major institutions—this notwithstanding the argument that such institutions do not readily lend themselves to standardization, quality management, benchmarking, and quality assurance or control. The facts indicate otherwise. We urgently need standards of education for all levels of education and training, standards for health care and the provision of medical services, and standards for law enforcement and the punishment of infringers of our laws.

In turn, these require standards for the methods used in education, health care, and law enforcement and the qualifications of those administering education, health care, and law enforcement, as well as those to be qualified in or receiving services in these fields.

The International Standards Organizations (ISO) quality standards (such as ISO 9000) are now being redeveloped to include such service organizations. This is expected to lead to quality standards that are equally applicable to health care, education, and law enforcement organizations.

In fact, some hospitals, HMOs, schools, and institutes of higher learning have taken the initiative by developing benchmarking standards as a first step toward an effective TQM approach. This includes standards for the delivery of services, achievement of service results, facilitation of customer access and feedback, cost reduction, and intercollegial cooperation. These standards are based on achievable levels with gradual increases in the benchmarks to encourage and recognize continuous improvement in the delivery of services.

## Parallel Futures

What happens to America when it depends increasingly on the development in and effectiveness of its institutions? Two alternative and parallel futures emerge. One is the continued corruption and ultimate demise of institutional functions and the other a radical change in direction and return to the basic values.

These parallel futures hold the power of deciding the prospects of American and in some ways also Western civilization. We can either self-destruct or move toward revival and growing human development. The choice is becoming clearer every day as our institutions disappoint our society and society responds in kind to justify the fulfillment of the prophecy.

Our institutional systems have become highly politicized and spend enormous sums on public relations, lobbying, and fund-raising. At the same time, they are frequently less concerned with local or customer support or support by those they are designed to serve. Institutional leadership and management, as well as others such as lawyers and judges, have become increasingly isolated from the views of the community.

Many question the feasibility of reinventing our major institutions, particularly in light of the very powerful interest groups that now control them. Considering the growing public concern with the issues of education, health care, and crime prevention that have captured the political agenda of all parties, the time appears to be ripe for a determined effort at reinvention. There is general agreement now that these institutions do not work, and the public is becoming increasingly impatient with the lack of effective leadership and action in making them work.

There is a near-consensus that we should have universal health coverage. We actually have coverage of the very poor and very rich, the very young and very old. What we lack is coverage of the working poor and the independent workers and/or businesspeople who form the mainstay of our economy. Universal HMO coverage would be one-way, and if we include all, including Medicare and Medicaid recipients, but require some copayment or similar misuse disincentive, we may actually be able to develop a universal, yet cost-effective, system in which hospitals are joined to HMOs, excess capacity is eliminated or redistributed, and the overall quality of health care provision is improved. This should also include family as well as home visit care in emergencies.

It is unacceptable to require severely ill people to travel to emergency rooms for treatment. Even in economic terms this makes little sense, as the cost of an ambulance certainly exceeds the value or cost of travel time of a medical doctor to a patient's home. At the same time, a patient's health may be endangered by the transfer.

Elimination of excess administrative cost burdens, the cost of underutilized equipment and facilities, and improving the efficiency of health care institutions and organizing a nationwide system of HMOs with universal access and basic minimum service standard requirements should allow us to not only reduce national health care costs by as much as 20 to 30 percent over a five to ten-year period but at the same time move toward universal coverage, improved health care access and quality, and improved preventative care and general health standards. This would have a tremendous impact not only on the physical but also on the emotional and social state of our society.

Our educational system needs to be similarly reinvented. Not only do we need minimum national standards for primary, secondary, and higher education, but we must also make education more effective, accessible, and meaningful. We must agree on some educational norms and quality standards throughout all schools in the country, starting with preschool and first grade. Standardizing should permit major reductions in local school supervisory staff and administration and thereby costs. Teaching materials could be largely standardized, and resulting economies of scale should save billions nationwide.

At the same time, examination and advancement from grade to grade should be based on gradually introduced national standards that assure equal qualification at any level and ultimate graduation. In fact there should be one national high school graduation standard or examination. We must do away with functionally illiterate high school graduates. In addition, vocational schools and institutes of higher learning will have to satisfy higher national standards in their programs, admissions, teacher qualifications, and graduation or degree requirements.

Programs should be more oriented toward career or professional requirements. Community colleges and universities should get out of remedying ineffective high school education and really become institutions of higher learning, which implies learning that not only educates a person but equips him or her to perform better, do a better job, and better contribute to society. This does not mean that freshmen should immediately start their engineering, medical, or legal training, but the education should provide a meaningful basis for professional or career training. Higher education should not remedy or just entertain but must improve a person's ability to choose and perform a meaningful job for him- or herself and society and build a satisfying life in the area of his or her choosing. Higher education must have direction and purpose and not be just a way to defer hard career, job, or personal decisions.

Today we need much more effective standards for the conferring of degrees, which now are only meaningful when associated with a particular institution. Minimum national standards may have to be developed for degrees in the different areas to make sure that they become respectable qualifications.

Cooperation among professional associations, universities, and state boards or licensing bodies may be required to set such standards. In theory, one can today qualify for an engineer's license, the bar, or other professions without ever attending college or law school, or receiving other formal preparation. The combination of efficient administration of educational institutions assisted by more standardized tests and focused programs should result not only in major cost savings but also in the development of a much more employable graduate body. We must bring the total cost for education down to less than 10 percent of GDP while improving the competence and employability of the people we graduate. In parallel, we should develop a much more effective system of continuing education that assures that people remain technologically up-to-date throughout their working life.

Finally, reinventing our criminal justice system does not require a change in our excellent concept of the administration of justice per se, but the distortions imposed on the system over the last fifty or more years. From a system of justice designed to protect society and assure the freedom of its citizens to engage in lawful enterprise we have now developed a system in which the average citizen has little recourse to justice. The system is increasingly being used to protect criminals and others who use it for their often selfish antisocietal activities.

As in health care, we must emphasize prevention much more than rehabilitation and care. We know that few criminals are ever really rehabilitated, yet we spent hundreds of billions of dollars on expensive prisons and so-called reform programs. Opportunities for crime must be reduced or eliminated and convicted criminals required to earn their keep. Prison should mean not only confinement but also work, which will, frankly, serve rehabilitation better than most of our existing social rehabilitation programs. Prisoners must learn that everyone owes to society and that there is no free lunch. In fact, prisoners should not only work for their own keep but also to contribute to their victims' compensation.

We must begin to stamp out the demand side of crime by severely dealing with drug use and not just punishing drug pushing. Drug users often become drug pushers, and early action can, we hope, treat drug users successfully. The treatment may not be gentle, but it is a much more humane alternative to lifelong dependence and resulting crime or death. We somehow feel that dealing forcefully with the demand side of drug addiction and other crimes is somehow at odds with our overriding concern with the freedom of the individual. In my opinion, this is a convoluted logic akin to concern with sexual freedom when use of condoms is advocated in an AIDS-infected social environment.

Prisons must become places of social responsibility, in which prisoners do not just atone for their crimes but also work at restitution. They owe society and their victims and must not be allowed to forget it. Society deserves to lock them out of contact with civilized, law-abiding people but does not owe them their keep. Other countries have found that making able-bodied prisoners work for everything including restitution, is a better approach to rehabilitation. It could also save large amounts of public money and in the long run even reduce our prison population.

We should also reorganize our legal and justice systems. Our courts are overwhelmed, our administration of justice too slow, our appeals procedures too complex, our parole system uneven and often illogical and dangerous, and our admission of frivolous cases simply ludicrous.

Nearly one third of lawyers' and court time in the United States are taken up by frivolous cases—usually damage claims, which are frequently handled on a contingency basis or as class actions. The rest is largely taken up by criminal cases or economic challenges. The average American, and I mean the vast majority of the population, has no access or recourse to our legal or justice system, no matter what his or her grievance and how badly damaged, unless able to assume a huge financial burden, waste large amounts of time, and show the potential for large financial compensation. The system must be made to work for the average American, who suffers injustices all the time and cannot count on the legal system to address his or her grievances. In other words, the American legal system has really been hijacked and now serves largely to assure justice to criminals and address potentially profitable damage and contractual issues. It serves very little in addressing the legal needs of citizens at large, who are usually the victims. With over 700,000 lawyers and 21,000 judges and another 3 million employees of the legal system, we spend nearly three times as much as any other country in administrating justice, yet justice, like health care, is not universally available.

Reinvention of our justice system should start with streamlining the legal and court system, which uses century-old procedures. Our parole and appeals procedures should be reconsidered to follow uniform and limited guidelines that have defined a set of applications over a specified time period. The public's rights and concerns should weigh at least as much as the criminal's rights in parole and appeal decisions, and when the outcome is in doubt society's rights should prevail.

Technological advances provide our court system and the legal profession with rapid access to much more information than ever before, which, if properly used, should improve efficiency in the administration of justice. To do this may require us to change some outdated procedures. Most important, the justice system must become readily accessible to the average American, organized to administer justice fairly and speedily and consume less of our national resources.

The indirect costs of our justice system in lost time and opportunity probably add hundreds of billions of dollars to the already exorbitant cost of justice in America, which, as we discussed, has failed us miserably in assuring public safety and opportunity. It is time for us to reinvent our justice system and make it a true example of American civilization.

## Opportunities for Institutional Success

For our institutions to succeed and to again provide the basis for the development and growth of our nation requires that they themselves learn to lead and not just respond. To accomplish this, every institution must define its missions and decide which are worth doing. In other words, we must rethink American institutions, their functions, and their programs. We must insist that our institutions be true to themselves and the public they serve, as well as to practice what they preach. In general, the American public has lost trust in its institutions, both public and private. To regain this trust, our institutions will have to

1. recognize that customers are the driving force of success;
2. develop unselfish leadership;
3. make effective use of available and/or required resources, including public resources;
4. develop effective, implementable strategies and business plans that develop new markets, recognize new opportunities, and assure financial viability;
5. understand that institutional success is based on identification of future opportunities, which provide the impetus for movement, as success can no longer be built on the past but on success in the future;
6. learn that institutional success will increasingly depend on technological expertise and understanding of the impact and management of technological change; and
7. get control of deficits not just by curtailing expenditures but by also identifying areas of strength, new markets and opportunities and going after them. The goal is not cost but deficit reduction.

There is a widespread perception that our institutions are more concerned with perpetuating their comfortable status quo than dealing with the increasingly complex problems of our society. In fact, most people have given up on our institutions and consider them to have different cultures, which causes a division between the public and its institutions.

It is evident that most of our immediate problems with our institutions can be solved without cutting services by simply eliminating waste, fraud, and excesses. Each of the three institutions discussed here spends 25 to 40 percent more than necessary to provide the services they now supply. In fact, we should be able to reduce costs in each case to well below 10 percent of GNP while improving accessibility, service quality, and range of services. However, this requires political will and courage as well as re-education of both the service providers and the public.

## Initial Suggestions for Institutional Reinvention

One question in the readers mind may be why Social Security (SS) was not included in our discussion. Well, the reasons are simply that SS, as a self-financing program, should never have been linked to the federal budget. In fact, it had and still has large budget surpluses and is currently financed to the year 2020, by which it will have grown from 4.9 percent of GDP today to 6.7 percent of GDP.

We spent $385 billion on SS in 1993, well below SS revenues. According to *Business Week* federal spending on all entitlements grew from 22.7 percent in 1963 to 51 percent in 1993 and is expected to grow to 58.2 percent by year 2003.[2] SS constitutes about half of that spending today but will constitute 39 percent in the year 2004 and should be removed from the budget altogether.

As noted, the major issues are the waste and fraud in our institution, which could be corrected speedily with sufficient will. According to the *Boston Globe,* $275 million was lost every day in 1994 as a result of health care overbilling, fraud, and abuse ($100b/year).[3] There are not only inadequate federal resources (222 investigators to track $400 billion in Medicare/Medicaid spending), but there is actual foot dragging in pursuing fraudulent hospitals and health care institutions. Similarly, private insurers do not pursue fraud effectively. Our system provides monetary incentives to doctors in hospitals, and fraudulent behavior is seldom punished. For example, doctors are not removed by boards or convicted for fraudulent behavior and whistle-blowing is discouraged. We must introduce severe punishments for medical fraud, which in a way is not just theft but in many cases also affects the health of the public or access to health service by society.

In many cases, waste is not just the result of administrative anarchy or casual, incompetent management but is quite often self-serving and therefore fraudulent. Until these types of white-collar crimes are treated for what they are—theft—no attempt at improving the cost efficiency of our health care institutions will succeed. At the same time, we spend staggering amounts on Medicare ($3830/year per recipient family or 24 percent of all Medicare-receiving family income in 1990). Similar Medicaid payments (32 million recipients) averaged $3,906 per enrollee, with cost for elderly recipients averaging $9,226. Medicare and Medicaid costs are expected to grow from $230 billion in 1994 to over $570 billion in 2004, or 27 percent of all federal expenses, if radical reforms are not introduced. Following are some suggestions:

1. Introduce more free market competition in health care, particularly for Medicare/Medicaid services.
2. Government should stop micro-managing these health care programs and develop an effectively strategic management approach to assure meaningful waste and fraud elimination.
3. Private HMOs should be given greater opportunities to manage Medicare/Medicaid service provisions on a competitive basis.
4. Medicare costs should only be allowed to increase in proportion to the number of seniors covered and the cost of living increase or less than half the current rate of Medicare cost growth.
5. Copayment systems should be encouraged but limited to income and vary from say one to ten dollars per service, except for emergency services, which should be free. The Rand Health Care experiment showed only an indirect link between copayment and unnecessary use of services when fixed copayments were used, but the results indicate that a scaled copayment may have the effect of reducing unnecessary service demands.[4]
6. Overbilling and fraud must be relentlessly pursued and perpetrators convicted. They should be treated as thieves or cheats in the fullest sense of the law.
7. Waste in health care must be eliminated by forcing hospitals to make effective use of equipment and facilities and justify major equipment purchases, manning levels, facilities, etc. Overhead ratios should be tied to tax status, or, in other words, institutions with excessive overheads (more than 20 percent above the mean) should be charged a tax on the excess costs. This should bring down their overhead as well as the mean overhead rate of U.S. hospitals and other health care providers.
8. The monetary flows in the U.S. health care system must be

simplified. At this time there are too many agencies and government authorities involved and the monetary flows are not only complex but largely intractable. Risks are transferred without associated budgetary commitments, and there is little control over the system or any part thereof by any or all the funding agencies.

9. There is an urgent need to standardize allowable costs and procedures among insurers as well as among government agencies. Contrary to statements by insurers, this will not reduce competition in the provision of health care. Adjustment mechanisms to allow competition among insurers affecting "basic or defined" benefits packages can readily be developed and have been found effective when employed.

The combination of the preceding measures, if introduced, should go a long way in bringing our health care system into line with what we need and what we can afford. A study by researchers at Johns Hopkins School of Public Health in Baltimore found that low-cost providers offer the same, if not better, care than higher-cost providers, including HMOs.[5] It reviewed the technical quality and appropriateness of care of 2,024 Medicare patients and concluded that health care providers can contain costs without reducing quality, particularly in primary care. These findings contradict the predictions of doctors, politicians, and health care providers that cuts in health care funding will invariably lead to a reduction in health care quality.

American education has been mismanaged for quite some time. It largely lacks effective management, strategic planning, and most important, customer orientation. The focus is increasingly on isolated budgetary issues, without emphasis on traditional academic values.

Fraud and unethical behavior that undermines academic values are increasingly condoned, particularly when perpetrators contribute to the financial objectives of the institution. It needs to restructure its administrators from being one of uninspired paper pushers oblivious to the financial issues involved to leaders who are also effective user-oriented managers.

American education at all levels must reinvent itself if America is to develop and grow. American high school graduates are often functionally or intellectually illiterate, with little, if any, civic knowledge, who try only to learn what they think they need or are told to study and who readily absorb unsubstantiated biases.

In the twenty-first century, education will have to become a lifelong, continuous process. Few, if any, people today are able to make lifetime use of their professional education. Reinventing our educational institutions requires the following:

1. Restructuring of the educational system and reinvention of the approach to financing and managing of educational institutions. School and university budgets will have to be incentive-linked (based on various success ratios).
2. Elimination of waste and fraud. Administrations must be reduced and direct teaching and other contact persons increased. The costs of overhead and benefits should be substantially below these incurred by industrial firms to be allowable.
3. Making educational institutions become customer/user-oriented and market themselves in a way that proves to customers that the institution offers what they need.
4. Orientation of education toward the continuous requirements of people, including updating of knowledge and skills in line with changing work, societal, and technological requirements.
5. Requirement of national standards for all levels of education. Advancement in the education process from primary school to higher education must be based on the achievement of acceptable standards and not just for graduation with a high certificate or a degree, but school certificate, vocational school certificate, or a degree, but also for advancement from freshman to senior or similar levels. Students who do not achieve such standards should be required to withdraw or repeat the grade.
6. Tying scholarships and other educational support strictly to a combination of both need and scholastic accomplishments, not just one or the other.
7. Developing national standards not only for students' scholastic achievements but also for programs that meet acceptable levels in terms of subject and program content. These standards should be periodically updated by a forum of educators, industrialists, and professionals to assure that subject and program content not only is academically acceptable but also meets the changing requirements of the professional and job environment.

The preceding can be achieved by a determined effort of those who fund and provide education and, most important, those who are affected by it—the students and employers. Without a reinvention of our educational institutions, we not only forfeit our young generation but our future as technological, economic, and political or moral leaders.

More than 35 percent of the cost of education in the United States is wasted on fraudulent expenses. In addition as many as 30 percent of students in so-called higher education programs either do not receive higher education of any value, do not benefit from it, or both. This percentage is even higher in vocational training, which has been plagued by major misuse of funds or outright fraud. Overall we should be able to save as much as 30 to 40 percent of the direct cost of education nationwide. Indirect savings accruing to the economy (and federal tax revenues) would largely be the result of additional productive years contributed by young people who enter the workforce two to four years earlier instead of pursuing essentially worthless higher education.

Finally, summarizing some of the suggestions to reinvent our criminal justice system, we must first start a major program to reeducate our society and convert it from the world's most litigious nation, in which anyone assumes that any accident or assumed accident is the fault of someone else, into a society where people assume responsibility for their own actions. Few of us are aware that we pay a tort tax of probably 15 to 20 percent of the price of most goods and services we procure.[6] We must discourage or even outlaw the so-called silly lawsuits on one hand and the jackpot settlements (which mostly benefit lawyers) on the other hand.

Much of our litigious attitude is, unfortunately, lawyer-driven, which may make it easier to convince the public (but harder to change the system), that a change is necessary because under the present system we have a lose-lose situation where only lawyers win in the end.

While we devote the bulk of our justice system's costs on tort-related issues, violent crime continues unabated. True, some cities and towns have recently experienced a temporary leveling off or even reduction in violent crimes, but the trend continues. Crime in the United States in 1992 cost $425 billion per year (or 8.8 percent of GNP), according to an analysis of all direct and indirect costs of property and violent crimes that includes emergency care, alarm systems, property loss, etc.

At the same time, we only spent $90 billion for our criminal justice enforcement system, including the cost of police protection of $35 billion.

As a result, in only three out of five murder cases were arrests ever made. We have one of the lowest ratios of police officers to violent crimes. To return to the ratio in place in 1960, we would have to add 5 million new police officers. At the same time, our prison population is mushrooming, with 1.664 percent of our population currently in jail, and our violent crime rate continuing at 120 to 180 per 100,000 population per year. Ninety- four percent of inmates are men, and our death row population is growing and now stands at over 3,000.

There is an obvious need for reinventing our criminal justice system. We now spend only about 15 percent of the total cost of our legal system on fighting crime, administering justice, and punishing criminals. As a nation, the bulk of our expenditures on criminal justice are consumed by tort, white-collar, and similar judicial procedures and legal services. In fact, we spend significantly more on property, accident, or service claims than on violent crime fighting and prevention. At the same time, we urgently need court reform to assure speedy justice, curtail rights of appeal, and restrict demands for retrial or mistrial on technical reasons. Trips through courts must be sped up and punishment standardized for vicious crimes. We can improve our justice system but must first reinvent its priorities and put the emphasis and resources on judicial issues of real concern to the nation and Americans as individuals.

This is not to say that white-collar crimes ought to go unpunished but the resources devoted to them should be curtailed by simplifying and reinventing the system while devoting more resources to the reduction of violent crime. Not only does it consume an unacceptable percentage of our economy, but it is now seriously affecting our standard of living and quality of life. We must concentrate more on crime prevention as a cure, as punishment does not work. The cost of crime must be raised to unattractive levels and crime prevention given all necessary resources.

We have nearly as many lawyers, judges, and court officials as police officers, and we spend much more on lawyering than policing. Similarly, the amounts spent on drug use prevention are a pittance compared to those spent on fighting the drug trade. We really must attack the demand side of crime if we want a safer, higher-quality environment. Fighting the supply side is always a losing battle as long as the demand exists. But fighting this losing battle is enormously profitable to many and may therefore be hard to change. But change we must, and not just the principles of our legal system, but the ways in which it is enforced.

# 9

# Our Institutional Future

Institutions mean different things to different people. For the weak and the poor they mean shelter, support, and hope. For the opportunistic they mean order and limits. For the average honest citizen they mean service, assurance, and maintenance of living standards. For those who want to take advantage of society, they mean barriers to criminal or antisocial conduct and sometimes even opportunity.

Institutions have been the foundation of American society and culture since its beginnings. They provided support and hope as well as continuity from generation to generation. They have been and still are the mainstay of American society and form, the basis for the American way of life.

In the past our institutions have always provided stability and formed the major support for our Constitution. They protected, nourished, and guaranteed our freedoms. They were designed to help provide equal opportunities for all and help for those in need.

Health care, education, and law are the principal institutions of concern. For a long time they have represented what is America. They sustained us and provided the guiding lights to all those within and without our borders.

These institutions guarded our values and assured continuity. They were inviolate and needed no change. They embodied the major tenets of our Constitution. However, something happened in the past few decades that caused these institutions to change. They eroded from within and lost public confidence from without. Increasingly the public started to mistrust law enforcement, lost faith in the quality of our health care, and was forced to recognize the deficiencies of our educational institutions. While we were raised to believe that our institutions were second to none, that our public safety and law enforcement were superior to that of other countries, that our health care and educational institutions provided better services than similar institutions anyplace in the world, we know now that our streets are not as safe as those in other countries and that our health care and education have serious problems.

In this book we discussed how and where we have gone wrong and how superbly designed and organized institutions were allowed to disintegrate, sometimes fall prey to selfish and parochial interests, how the public lost faith in the institutions, and how they failed to reestablish public confidence. We discussed the opportunities that are presented to us to reestablish our institutions' competence, credibility, and purpose. There is still time to reorganize or reinvent our important institutions. But this will require courage, vision, will, and commitment.

Various solutions and approaches designed to regain our institutions will now be suggested. All will take a great deal of effort to achieve the needed change. But change is indeed needed if America and the American dream are not to vanish like the Roman Empire. The round table of Camelot has assumed many corners. Opportunities are no longer open and equal. Corruption and deceit run rampant, and ordinary citizens no longer feel part of the system. They feel that the system and their government have let them down and no longer represent them.

Institutions traditionally provided the bridge and the basis for citizen participation and support. Citizen involvement must be reestablished and our institutions truly returned to the people, so as to serve the people's interest.

For America to remain the world leader that can shape the world at large to common advantage requires that it set its own house in order first. While elimination of the budget deficit and reduction of the public debt and the huge imbalance in foreign trade are essential, reinventing American institutions must receive similar attention if the country is to maintain its prosperity, leadership, and influence. Failure to reinvent and restructure American institutions can only lead to an increasingly self-serving, inefficient, and nonproductive society with chaos within and loss of influence without.

It is a difficult problem that affects many powerful and long-vested interests, but it must be attempted if the values Americanism has represented for so long in areas of individual freedom, human rights, and freedom of expression are to continue to influence development worldwide. This does not mean that America should continue to prescribe an American type of multiparty system for every nation and particularly newly independent developing nations. In fact, it will have to curb its attempts at prescribing American systems as a solution for the ills of the world. They worked well in a young, multiethnic, and well-endowed country such as the United States but may be less suited to ethnically homogeneous, resource-poor, or less developed societies. In fact, many including citizens and leaders of economically successful Asian countries, increasingly question the relevance or even appropriateness of Western or U.S. style concepts of the eminence of individual freedoms and rights as expression of democracy.

This style democracy, which makes the individual's rights supreme and ahead of the interests of society, is not acceptable to many, particularly Asian societies, which emphasize socially responsible behavior. The two approaches are not necessarily mutually exclusive and may, in fact, reinforce each other.

American economic, political, and social leadership is now being questioned both within and without the United States. We maintain an unchallenged military superiority, yet many of our political, social, and cultural values are being questioned. The major cause for this is that American institutions, which have historically provided the backbone of the American system, not only are in decline but often fail to live up to their responsibilities. In fact, they have become a drag not only on our economy but also on our social development. They now distort instead of support many of our most cherished values and often undermine some of the basic foundations of our lives.

We must recognize that our constitution was not designed to be a static set of rules but a guide for a developing society. There is a lot to be learned by us from the economic and societal progress of others, as there is a lot to be learned by others from the success of American individualism. There is no conflict between maintaining individual rights and advancing our society's interests. The latter is necessary to guard the first.

Our institutions must be reinvented to assure they focus on society's interests while providing individuals with the opportunities for their own success. But this will only be possible if our institutions reestablish a truly society-oriented commitment and become institutions that serve society and its individuals and not primarily themselves.

To reinvent them will not be a task for politicians, because they think and plan short-term, but for the visionaries among us who are more concerned with the revival of the true meaning of our Constitution and the mission of America than with power and recognition. This will not be an easy task. However, it is an essential undertaking not only to assure our economic survival but also to realize the dream that is America.

The principal strategy to reinvent our major institutions must first be based on, the downsizing of their bureaucracies, in size and control. It is estimated that nearly 40 percent of the cost of health care and an even larger percentage of the total cost of education and law enforcement/criminal justice are spent on administration, paperwork, unnecessary recording, and unnecessary regulations. We can afford world-class health care, education, and law enforcement if these institutions and the services they supply are run more efficiently.

Comparison of similar health care and educational institutions in the United States and other advanced countries, such as Germany, Japan, Switzerland, Israel, etc., show that administrative expenses can readily be halved or more without any effect or with only positive effects on quality and accessibility. Similarly, the major causes of the escalation of institutional costs are the spiraling costs of administration that contribute most of the cost escalation. New technology provides many of the means, and the ultimate goat will have to be paperless institutional administrations.

Reducing these administrative and related costs by 50 percent is not only feasible but desirable. It would save nearly $400 billion (1996) in institutional costs and assure annual increases in costs more or less in line with the rate of inflation and population growth adjusted for the changing age distribution of the population. At the same time, decision-making authority would be returned to the professionals providing the services, assisted by administration and not the other way around. Furthermore, while government should set minimum standards in health care and education, it should not get involved in the administrative details of these institutions and should reduce reporting requirements to paperless (electronic) reporting of only essential information.

Similarly, in law enforcement we need a system with fewer loopholes, less overlap in policing and judicial functions, and greater real enforcement. Most important, as shown, we must move from a remedial to a preventative approach in health care, education, and law enforcement. We can become a great society and retain world leadership, but only if we show the will to tackle the serious deficiencies of our essential institution, which are now dragging us down in social, economic, and political terms.

Today we have the technology to eliminate most traditional administrative functions and assure greater functional productivity as well as improved operational and management control. Hospitals, universities, law firms, courts, police departments, and similar institutional organizations invested tens of billions of dollars in information, communication, and other administrative technology under the guise of expected cost savings and productivity/service/quality improvements. We have yet to see the results or benefits.

In most cases, the new technology was simply superimposed on the old administration, with additional technologists hired to run the added systems. This duplication has caused both added costs as well as large-scale demoralization and lack of performance. It is about time that we not only espouse the virtues of our new technologies but also reorganize their ability and make real use of them, not just for publicity, but for improvements in operational efficiency, performance, and service quality. This will is still lacking, but we will not see a real improvement without it.

## Reinventing Institutions

The need to reinvent our institutions is becoming more and more evident. The public is becoming more vocal in not only its criticism but outright disgust with many of our institutions and their operations. While many of our leaders have suggested numerous improvements in our health care, educational, and law enforcement systems, most of these proposals offer only partial and often disjointed solutions. Universal health care coverage of children or testing of fourth-graders' reading and eight-graders' mathematics skills at a standard level are nice but really constitute only makeshift solutions, as does the federal financing of 100,000 more police officers. What we need are more global and structural changes that address the core issues and not just a few of the symptoms. This obviously requires political will and courage, which few of our leaders exhibit. Yet it appears that, contrary to some politicians' dire concerns, the public not only is ready but supports such changes.

As a matter of fact, health care, crime prevention, and education have become the most important issues and concerns of society and in many cases take priority over economic issues. This trend will continue as unemployment remains at a low level and the economy experiences expansion. Unemployment today is largely a function of education, as more and more high-tech and fewer basic jobs are generated. Similarly, people associate effective, accessible health care and personal safety and freedom of movement with quality of life.

In other words, institutional services play an important role in our daily lives and we are becoming increasingly dependent on them. This is in part due to increased urbanization and resulting personal dependence on institutional services that used to be largely supplied by family, friends, and neighbors.

As we approach the new millennium, we must prepare ourselves to live and work in a new global environment in which people and nations become increasingly interdependent. Our landscape in physical, spiritual, and economic terms continues to change. Frontiers are being demolished while new boundaries are drawn up. People are or at least feel increasingly alone, even when living in a busy, modern city. We stress individuality, which contributes to loneliness instead of encouraging community, family, and togetherness.

We emphasize competition even when cooperation offers greater advantages. We mistrust public institutions and family, yet we want to be connected. Religion and spirituality are assuming new meanings and often substitute for lack of moral roots and leadership.

Concerns with individual rights, which dominate our behavior, must be complemented by obligations of individuals and institutions. To be effective and fair, we need a much more positive attitude and thinking. We seem to be increasingly unable to tap the human potential of our society for maximum or at least enhanced performance, largely because many of us are consumed by ourselves and our needs, in isolation of the larger interests and needs of family and society. We often fail to recognize that if family and society prospers, so will we. Many of our institutions have also become self-centered toward their own and their members' needs more than the needs of those they serve and society at large.

Our new institutions, to be effective and efficient servers of society's needs in education, health care, and criminal justice, must become outward-looking, with the objectives of society foremost in their minds. They could and should be successful not mainly as businesses but as servers of society.

Considering our educational system, for example, we spend an average of $6,525/year per primary and high school student (FY 1995 in Massachusetts, excluding capital outlays and construction expenditures). Given class sizes of twenty-five, the annual cost of a class is $163,125. Direct and indirect teaching and instructor costs (which assume that teachers teach twenty contact hours per week) are less than 42 percent of that amount. In other words, 58 percent is absorbed by administration, etc.

Inefficiencies in providing services are similar or greater in health care or law enforcement. In the next few sections we discuss how the situation can be changed and how these institutions can be reinvented to become truly responsive to society's needs in an efficient manner.

## Interpersonal and Public Relationships

American institutions have fostered use of assertiveness by design to further their economic objectives. Their objectives pertain not only to profit or revenues but also to power and exclusiveness. Civility and polite accommodating interpersonal relations are often interpreted as weakness. Even when civility is encouraged and people dealing with the public are encouraged or even directed to be polite and not confrontational, this is often largely a perfunctory response to perceived legal, political, or competitive pressures and not a recognition of the importance of civility in all interpersonal relationships and particularly toward dependent users of institutional services.

Assertiveness is a focus of our legal, business, and even medical education, and students are trained in the Socratic method of confrontational grilling and humiliation. They are instructed to be confrontational and combative, an experience that greatly affects their later professional attitudes and dealings with the public they are expected to serve. No wonder people are in awe and hesitate to use legal, medical, and even educational services. Domination, not service, is often the principle used by teachers, health care providers, lawyers, and police officers. As a result, people hesitate to ask for help that is rightfully theirs to receive. This will have to change if our institutions are to become truly efficient and effective providers of essential services to the public.

This will only happen if we redesign the way we educate lawyers, doctors, and teachers and other service providers and the way we organize and administer these institutions and, finally, the way we value and reward performance of institutions and individual service providers. At the same time, our institutions excel at publicity overkill. Not only are many negative or even destructive developments buried, covered up, or only subjected to internal review, but even the slightest success is given great publicity, often at large cost to the institution. Public relations have become not only a priority but an art for our institutions, often more concerned with public image than public service. In fact, few of our institutions live up to the premise of their advertisements and public relations pronouncements, which are only designed to improve public perception, not satisfaction.

## Reconstructing Our Education Institutions

As we approach the new century, we must reconstruct our educational system. We are losing our productivity edge in manufacture and services, the mainstay of the U.S. economy, not because Americans work shorter hours, less diligently, with less commitment or interest, but in general because our schools and universities are not providing students, at all levels, with the skills and knowledge required to succeed in the increasingly competitive marketplace.

We lag farther and farther behind other industrialized countries in literacy, and the percentage of school leavers who are functionally illiterate remains obstinately at nearly 18 percent. The result is that a significant proportion of our adult population is incapable of participation in the economic growth opportunities offered by new technology, which dominates our job market. Literacy and education today separate our society more than sex, race, ethnicity, or even wealth. We have allowed a permanent educational underclass to develop, which has formed its own society and rules.

The late T. Bell, a former secretary of education, warned of a "rising tide of mediocrity" in our schools, which increasingly lack

- challenging academic standards based on rigorous courses,
- character education that focuses on discipline, honesty, integrity, and trust, and
- effective classroom teaching, not just academic credentials by teachers.

While these are primarily issues degrading our primary and high school education now, they also affect higher education.

Peter Denning explains that both market and political forces conspire to generate a new design for universities.[1] Yet universities are slow to respond and continue to have obsolete business and curriculum designs. We need curricula that address new issues, concerns, and the real needs of society, an education that recognizes required and not perceived or idealized competencies. An education that affirms the moral values central to our civilization and encourages responsibility and satisfaction of societal needs.

We are entering a knowledge era where knowledge workers will be able to tap and use information technology and add huge value to their work. In *Post-Capitalist Society,* Peter Drucker describes a vision of the education of the future knowledge worker.[2] It is now evident that information technology and the changed work environment and workplace structure are undermining our traditional concepts of higher and particularly professional education. Professional education is no longer a one-shot deal where people acquire lifetime professional credentials after satisfactory completion of a set of courses and programs spread over several years. We now need continuous educational and technical upgrading throughout a lifetime. Similarly content and focus of subjects, courses, and programs must be continuously redesigned to conform to changing requirements.

Also, traditional measures of academic performance of university faculty based largely on scholarly publications may not serve their purpose. We publish annually 2 million "scholarly" papers in the United States in 72,000 journals, read by but a handful of people. The average scholarly article is read by only four to eight people. There is a serious question of the value generated, if any, particularly as these narrow groups of peers often communicate or contribute little to the broader community of peers or potential beneficiaries of their "discoveries." They similarly are seldom concerned with or interested in any possible application or use of their discovery.

Dennis Tsichritzis, pointed out in a recent article that "the value of research lies not in the discovery of ideas, but in the innovation that eventually results."[3] Yet most universities and many governments think that discovery of ideas is the main value, not the innovation that may result. Research should generate new ideas, learning, practices, products or processes, and, finally, business to be of value.

Many of our great research universities have made major contributions to science and technology, yet the link between research and innovation on one hand and research and education on the other hand has become more tenuous. There is no continuous logical progression from discovery to innovation, and discoveries as a result often stay in limbo and often die without making a contribution. It is for that reason that industry hesitates to fund university research at this time of rapidly changing technology. We must develop a new paradigm and relationship that connects the ivory tower to the shop floor. This may require research faculty to spend mandatory periods of time with industry to really learn and understand the innovation process, as well as the feasibility of translating their discovery into a real product.

Similarly, we need a new approach to the integration of research and education. MIT, for example, has a very effective Undergraduate Research Opportunity Program (UROP) in which undergraduates participate in research normally performed by graduate students, other researchers, and faculty. But the process should be even more encompassing. Research should become part of the educational process by substituting traditional laboratory work with actual research participation to instruct students not only in science or technology basics but also in current developments and methods. This, furthermore, assures that teaching faculty will have to adjust their teaching continuously to the latest knowledge requirements. It would prevent them from teaching subjects year in and year out in the same manner and often presenting outdated or irrelevant material.

As discussed before, we must also develop better programs for lifelong knowledge updating. We now educate students in high schools, at our universities, at professional schools, and at other institutions of higher learning but have few programs that cater to the remaining forty years of a person's professional life. In other words, we need effective, possibly mandatory, continuing education. Occasional short courses or seminars are not enough. We require a change in the business design of American universities, a change in their meaning and role. This may include a reevaluation of formal degrees and other professional qualifications. These may have to be renewed periodically and should also substitute for professional licenses.

Education must become truly customer-oriented. The customers are foremost the students, with meaningful reference given to the workplace and the employers. This must start in high school, where values such as responsibility, discipline, work attitude, social relations building, curiosity, and tolerance are affirmed as part of academic teaching. Students must gain not only knowledge but also the ability to use it, to work in teams, to communicate, and to advance their knowledge throughout their lives. They must understand and learn to use social relationships. They must similarly adapt to and learn to use, yet understand, the limitations of ever-advancing technology.

The new educational system for the twenty-first century must be reinvented by both structural changes and a transformation of approaches to teaching. The structural changes are designed to improve the efficiency and integration from kindergarten to postgraduate education. We must introduce nationwide standards to eliminate the need for remedial education at all levels. Now high schools often have to correct deficiencies of primary school education; universities that of deficient high school education; and so on and so forth. Most important, education must become a life experience and not just a preparation for life.

## Needs for Educational Reform

Our educational system must be reformed if we are to meet the challenges of the twenty-first century while maintaining a democratic and equitable society. The late Albert Shanker, former president of the American Teachers Union, wrote as the Teacher's Advocate that tougher standards for all students and higher educational goals are essential if we want to maintain our quality of life.[4] This not only means greater student discipline and levels of education but also continuous education and upgrading tests for teachers.

Reform must start with preschool education, which represents a most important development stage for our children. Preschool must be challenging, taught by trained teachers, and involve real training that excites children's offering opportunities to express themselves, experiment, and experience. It must not be a day care, holding pen type of playtime, supervised by untrained and often unimaginative and unmotivated teachers or kindergarten staff. Preschool must be reasonably structured and, while not subject to a curriculum, should assure content that stimulates children, arouses their curiosity, and allows them to grow intellectually while developing basic social skills. These are the most important development years in a child and largely determine future intellectual development and capacity. This is particularly important in America, where the family structure has disintegrated in many parts of society.

Many preschool programs are designed to simply keep children occupied, but this should not be the purpose nor does it really help or even entertain the child. Intellectual stimulation generates excitement and curiosity even in children as young as three years old and serves to develop not only the brain and memory but also communication skills.

Our primary and secondary (high) schools need complete revamping to improve their performance and efficiency. It is ludicrous to spend on average over $6,000 per student per year for twelve years and end up with a high percentage of functionally illiterates and even more semiducated, unmotivated high school graduates. The problem is perpetuated at the college level, where much time and money is spent correcting these deficiencies. In many cases, the first one or two years of college are essentially devoted to remedial education—in other words, bringing students up to a respectable high school level.

Reforming our primary and secondary schools will require new or superlearning models, a veritable teaching revolution that assures teachers not only are qualified but also maintain their qualifications, a longer school year, and greater emphasis on basic knowledge and skill areas. To accomplish this, it is suggested that:

1. Teachers must be put in charge of curricula, subject content, and teaching methods. In other words, school administrations should administer and provide the support services required but not interfere in academic matters.
2. Teachers should be subjected to periodic testing using a continuous certifier system. Tests should not only concentrate on knowledge and narrow proficiency but also include teaching ability and responsiveness to changing demands of the real world, including technological change and innovation. There must be easier rules for firing incompetent teachers.
3. Education in high school must cater to society's basic needs of safety, health, and social relations, as well as education and not just knowledge acquisition.
4. School years in the United States are among the shortest in the world, and total student/teacher contact hours are even shorter. This is not only a waste of school human and physical resources but also of student time and learning opportunity. We should increase our school year by at least twenty days or 100 contact hours and, furthermore, increase learning opportunities during vacations.
5. Student performance is the only measure of the quality of teaching. Teaching must assure that students not only acquire knowledge but learn to use it. Their performance can therefore

not be measured by stale tests but only by tests that evaluate their ability to use and apply knowledge.

6. Students must be taught pride of accomplishment, entrepreneurship, interpersonal relations, discipline, and self-control and should be motivated to use all their ability. Rewards should be downplayed and team spirit, cooperation, and pride given emphasis. Students must be taught cultural norms, the understanding of realities, and responsibility. Rewards should be replaced by pride of accomplishment.
7. Students must learn that authority can only be exercised if founded on competence and that one can only lead by example, not by assertiveness or bullying.
8. Merit, not seniority, should be the sole measure of performance and ultimately reward. Rewards for teachers should not only be financial, using merit pay, but also include recognition and other pride factors.
9. More resources should be devoted to learning facilities such as libraries, computers, videos, the Internet, etc., and less on activities used by only a few, such as special sports equipment, which may contribute to narrow prestige but little to educational performance.

Teachers should be available to students outside normal contact hours to discuss not only subject material but also other issues and thereby encourage a more collegial relationship. In fact, high school education should become more collegial, with students and teachers joining in social, business, and environmental projects that permit real-world applications of knowledge. Teachers should be encouraged or even required to upgrade their knowledge and experience periodically to assure that they are well acquainted with changes in knowledge, technology, and the social, business, and environmental developments.

Grading should be realistic and fair. Students who fail a required subject must repeat it and if they fail more than half the subjects in any grade must be required to repeat the grade and not be allowed to advance with the rest of the class. This does not benefit them and only holds back the rest of the class.

Considering higher, and particularly university, education, an even more radical change will be required. Universities must truly become institutions of higher learning and not largely holding pens for high school graduates who do not know what they want to do or become and who would like to continue to just hang around for four more years before facing the realities of life, including a choice of profession or career. It is unconscionable to waste four years of a person's life without advancing the person's life opportunities. While some may claim that such undergraduate education helps to mature young people, my experience after forty years of college-level teaching is that students who enter programs that are not professionally oriented may become a little more educated or literate but are seldom better prepared for a professional career. There are armies of overeducated and frustrated secretaries, clerks, administrators, nurse assistants, buyers, and waiters who after years of college had no really marketable professional skills. They seldom make good secretaries, and so forth, as their expectations are unfulfilled and frustration becomes permanent. Colleges should educate and train young people for responsible and meaningful careers and lives and not just defer the time they must declare their maturity. Not every high school graduate should qualify for college. College attendance must be a distinction, a sign of maturity and scholastic aptitude, not one of professional immaturity and desire to defer difficult decisions. While young people may require another year or even two beyond our high schools to focus on their choice and aptitude, four years of floundering becomes a waste. Such deferral usually makes it even harder to focus, as by then the person is years behind those who chose college as a professional development path. A large number of our general education or liberal arts colleges may have to redesign their curricula and offer more professional and life-skill oriented programs, including shorter one- or two-year programs in specific professional fields.

There is a dearth of quality vocational and professional schools in the United States compared, for example, with Germany and other European countries. This is particularly bad because unlike Japan, Korea, and some European nations, industrial and business employees in the United States in general do not offer as much formal in-house professional training. This may change if our colleges and universities as well as community colleges and other one- or two-year programs do not start to develop high-quality, focused professional programs. Major industrial firms as well as large consulting, accounting, and other business firms are already offering high-quality programs that have expanded at a phenomenal rate, as have in-house programs offered by in-house or external staff. This trend will continue, particularly if our colleges and universities do not accelerate their offerings in continuing professional education.

Current trends indicate that budgets for continuing education (lifelong professional learning) and focused professional and skill training will soon exceed the total budgets for state and private colleges, with most of the funding provided by business and not government. Corporate America now (1995) spends about 8 percent of its total budget on training. This amounts to about $36 billion. This amount is growing at about 12 to 14 percent per year and is expected to exceed $66 billion per year by the turn of the century. This growth is driven largely by the inability of American higher education to deliver what employers demand. In parallel new noncorporate providers or servers are offering continuing education to individuals who now pay for this training themselves. These offerings vary from computer skills to interpersonal relations training. While there are no reliable figures available, it is estimated that this growing industry now (1995) accounts for about $18 billion per year. In other words, non–university or college continuing education and training expenditures now exceed $54 billion and are expected to grow to over $100 billion within six years. This is about equal to the budgets of all private four-year colleges in the United States.

Colleges have been slow in developing continuing education programs as well as in adopting advanced electronic and telecommunications technology. This not only is the most rapidly developing market in higher education but may also become the most important ingredient in maintaining high-level undergraduate and graduate programs. Continuing lifelong education provides the most effective feedback to assure the relevance of the programs offered. American universities for too long relied largely on the inbreeding of their faculty and research staff, with little contact with the outside world. While some basic research and theoretical science teaching may still be done in this way, engineering, applied science, management, social science, economics, etc., education and research today requires close and up-to-date involvement with the real world.

Collaboration with industry in education and research is essential for our universities now. The increase in competition from industry, brokerages, and private providers in offering courses, seminars, workshops, and other types of training is growing. In some areas, such as software and network engineering, these organizations now dominate the market. Even in distance learning and virtual education, as well as Internet delivery, universities have been slow in restructuring their curricula as well as course content. There is also a need to develop effective and accepted accreditation of virtual degrees and course completions.

One of the reasons for the lack of responsiveness of our universities is often the lack of practical experience of faculty and administrators. This, in turn, implies lack of recognition of newly important areas, such as internal delivery, biogenetic information management, and more.

Industrial partnerships and international cooperative arrangements are today essential requirements for universities and other institutions of higher education and research. Research must be integrated with education at all levels of undergraduate and graduate study, to teach investigative procedures, discovery, and innovation, as well as realism or feasibility of concepts and approaches. Students must be taught communications skills, effective representation, and team building. Education must satisfy the needs of the students and their expected employers and not be a reflection of the perceptions of the faculty, who often train students in their own image, to repeat their own experience.

Most important, university education must deliver value and enhance the students' ability and marketability. Courses should be shorter with close relationships to use of knowledge. In other words, students must not just acquire but learn how to use knowledge under different conditions and in an ever-changing environment. Learning must be integrated with applications, and while the use of abstract concepts should be taught, students must learn how to translate these into real-world analysis and solutions.

Similarly, learning should always include social and environmental concerns and considerations on the one hand and broader global implications on the other. Students should be taught pride and intellectual as well as personal discipline and not assertiveness and selfishness. Also, learning self-reliance, team building, leadership, and entrepreneurship, in its broader sense, should be part of all, and not just some, business school programs. In fact, scientists and engineers probably need it more. How can this be accomplished by a traditional, largely self serving system of higher education?

## Toward Future Educational Institutions

Our educational institutions must become efficient providers of education and training in interpersonal relations, team building, leadership, entrepreneurial competence, and communications, as well as skill development. They must develop full persons, enhance their personality, and permit each student to recognize his or her potential at every age in school or university. Teachers must be not just knowledge providers but role models who show and transfer not only knowledge but also how to use it and how to recognize and solve problems. To accomplish this requires a new approach that reverses the self-centered and largely self-serving educational process now used.

The major suggestions for change designed to educate our young for the challenges and opportunities of the twenty-first century can be summarized as follows:

1. Schools and institutions of higher learning, as well as vocational and continuing program providers, must be turned over to the teachers. Administration in educational institutions should be a service and not management function. Programs and course content must be under the control of the teachers and professors, the providers, and not some administrators. Teachers must control the schools and the schooling.
2. Programs and course content must be customer (student and future–employer) oriented. They must not only provide for knowledge transfer but also convey the skills to apply the knowledge.
3. Teachers and professors must be role models and train students in interpersonal relations, social skills, leadership, and communications as well and not just dry knowledge.
4. Students must meet agreed-upon minimum scholastic and skill standards to satisfactorily pass a course or subject. Students who fail required courses should be required to repeat them and if they fail more than half their courses should be required to repeat the grade (or, at university level, withdraw).
5. Nobody should be allowed to graduate from high school without passing all essential senior subjects. A high school certificate must become a valid credential and proof of competence and not a joke, which it now represents.
6. College degrees must become proof of professional competence and should over the next ten or fifteen years be combined with professional examinations in professional specialties. It is rather curious that a person with a doctoral degree in engineering (including many engineering faculty) may not be qualified as a professional engineer.

7. Rapidly changing educational requirements impose a need for a change in the tenure system. Tenure was designed to allow teachers and professors to pursue teaching, studies, and research as well as voice or publish opinions without fear of retribution because of political or social correctness. It was never designed to protect incompetence or inability or unwillingness to maintain subjects and teaching as up-to-date and in line with changing requirements for knowledge and education. As a result, we now need mechanisms that allow the disqualification of teachers and professors who do not update their subjects and/or become ineffective teachers. Most important, sabbatical leaves must again be used for professional development and not leisure purposes.
8. As with high schools, college degree standards must be tightened so that college degrees really mean something. Accreditation today is a rather lax process, and nationwide minimum degree standards must be developed and enforced.
9. School and college years should be expanded. School contact hours at all levels should be increased by 10 to 20 percent by both extending school hours and school days. Similarly colleges and other institutions of higher learning should offer courses year-round to permit undergraduates to complete first degree programs in as little as three calendar years, increase the utilization of facilities and teachers, improve the continuity of subjects, and provide students with greater lifetime earning potential. This alone should reduce the cost of a college education by at least 20 percent.
10. Educational technology must play a greater role. Distance learning, Internet instructions, digital libraries, and so forth, will soon make traditional in-person weekly classes outdated. Person-to-person contact should concentrate on skill development, and leadership teamwork training, entrepreneurship, and problem solving, and not on simple knowledge transfer, which is more conveniently and efficiently done by use of advanced technology.
11. Tests, particularly in business, engineering, social sciences, medicine, etc., should evaluate problem recognition and solving ability or the application of knowledge, not test knowledge alone.

12. Similarly, evaluation of teachers, professors, and researchers should not be based on narrowly focused publications that actually devalue the purpose of research and education. The important evaluations should be made of the impact or application of the work of the candidate. The verdict of a narrowly focused clique of experts who perpetuate their narrow interests, without regard to the broader importance of their work, is bound to be biased.
13. Higher and continuing education must be integrated into lifelong learning for each profession.
14. College programs must become truly customer-oriented and train students in the skills the market demands. Universities must play an integral role in the development and delivery of continuing education (lifelong learning), both for the benefit of their graduates as well as to assure continued involvement of their faculty, who will thereby understand and provide feedback on the real needs of the marketplace.
15. While admission of college and higher education should be means-blind, it should not compromise student quality. Disadvantaged students should be given opportunities for remedial education, but standards of admission or education should not be compromised, as this hurts everyone and, most of all, disadvantaged students. Special funding should be made available for remedial education, followed by scholarships for such students. Funding for this should preferably come from a central federally funded "Foundation for the Correction of Historic Injustices to the Disadvantaged." It can readily be shown that the savings in social costs accruing from lifting children from disadvantaged parents toward self- and often parent-supporting individuals would be more than adequate to fund programs that increase higher education for disadvantaged students by 10 percent a year until their percentage of college graduates is equal to the national average.
16. The administration of institutions of learning from primary and high school to college and other institutions of higher learning must be streamlined. They must take full advantage of modern technology, become nearly paperless, reduce or eliminate unnecessary bureaucracy, and concentrate on the primary function—the support of teaching and research. Administration

and overhead may not exceed 40 percent of total expenditures, with practically all the rest spent on direct education-related expenses.

17. Schools and institutions of higher learning should concentrate on their prime educational mission and not devote significant resources on peripheral activities such as intercollegial sports and similar activities that, in recent years, have become largely selective semiprofessional and not really universal activities open to all students.
18. Schools and institutions of higher learning should cooperate in procurement of supplies and sharing of libraries and expensive equipment, and even physical facilities where location permits. Much equipment is duplicated within or without such institutions and often attains very low utilization. This is particularly relevant now, when technology rapidly becomes obsolete and when remote access is efficient and readily available.
19. University administration should be returned to the faculty. Faculties have ceded most of their traditional powers because they assumed power to be degrading and antiliberal. "Power was better given to those who wanted it and were willing to use it." Today campus liberalism has been redefined and often reinterpreted, often by those in power, as political correctness, which in turn is often enforced by subtle and not so subtle means. The result is that faculty have become hired hands instead of serving as the heart and soul of the university. This situation must be reversed. Faculty are still used by administrations for fund-raising and public relations but seldom receive proper credit. Faculty takeover of administration should result in greater faculty responsiveness, academic effectiveness, and ultimately economies, as faculty administrators would usually rotate between teaching and administrative functions. It would also keep administration salaries from the obscene levels that have become common on many campuses.

The preceding changes would go a long way in improving our institutions and preparing them to cope with the challenges of the next century.

## Reinventing Our Health Care System

Our health care system is technologically highly advanced, exorbitantly expensive, inaccessible to some among the population, and highly uneven. The practice of medicine has become more a business than a service. Doctors see many patients per hour and make sure that they fill every hour of their appointment calendar, independent of the amount of time their patients have to wait. Each hospital tries to have the latest in medical technology even when potential utilization is low and other nearby facilities have the same equipment. Our hospitals are overstaffed, have topheavy administrations, and are mired in bureaucracy. The cost of medical care in the United States is now $3,200 per person per year for each man, woman, and child, if we divide the total cost of all health care by the U.S. population. We discussed earlier how others provide equal or better care for a fraction of this cost and make it not only more affordable but also more accessible.

Over the years numerous suggestions for general health care insurance, similar to the Canadian or British systems, have been suggested, but all failed. More recently HMO have proliferated across the country. Many of these provide reasonably effective health care and, in fact, offer many Medicare recipients a package of health care benefits well above the normal Medicare benefits at no extra charge. This shows that efficiently run medical care organizations can provide superior service. But this is not enough, as there are many who are not covered by Medicaid (poor) or Medicare (old) and cannot afford health care. These people either do not obtain care when needed or only use hospital emergency room services, often when their condition is already well advanced.

As the United States is one of the richest countries in the world and the world's largest economy, this condition is unacceptable. Our health care system must be made more affordable and accessible and this can only be achieved by reinventing it. The following suggestions are designed to help reinvent our health care system:

1. A nationwide program in preventative medicine or health care should be mandated. Young and old should be educated in preventative measures, not just diet workshops and formal exercise, which are only used by a small fraction of the population, but healthy food, natural medicines, basic natural exercises,

and noninvasive treatments of ailments. Most illnesses can be contained and healed by basic preventative health care methods, and harsh chemical medication as well as intrusive treatments should be last resorts and not immediate solutions. Even though many Americans exercise, our diet and lifestyle are usually not very healthful and medical services often consider more radical treatments than necessary. We are enamored of our medical technology and are encouraged to make use of it, necessary or not. The main reason appears to be that today we train mainly narrow medical specialists and not enough general practitioners who can take a broader view and are less tempted to use the latest technique or procedure. Preventative medicine starts with lifestyle training. This includes health, natural foods, adequate exercise, calm, nonexciting living, harmonious behavior, simple satisfactions and pleasures, and close friendly relationships. Mental attitudes play as much a role of physical conditions as in preventing illness. Few Orientals ever use psychiatrists, for example. Developing nationwide preventative approaches to health care should be able to reduce doctors' visits by as much as 50 percent, improve the general health, lower health care costs by as much as 20 percent, reduce absenteeism, and improve the feeling of well-being. Preventative medicine should be taught and encouraged, and people should be made aware of natural remedies. In particular, the NIH should take a lead in approving them or at least comment on their safety.

2. Our hospital and health clinic system should be revamped. We have too many full-service hospitals and too few clinics that can take care of most cases and are equipped with all the basic diagnostic equipment, but with an overhead cost that is a small fraction of that of a hospital. Many of our hospitals are overequipped, with only a few sharing expensive, often underutilized, equipment. This results in not only large investments but equally seriously pushing of expensive and often unnecessary diagnostics or treatments. Hospitals should integrate their high-tech services. This is already a developing trend with hospitals merging or affiliating, but it should be made a universal requirement. Such multihospital complexes should also integrate their accounting, communications, pro-

curement, and marketing activity, which again benefit from economies of scale.

3. Most American hospitals are highly overstaffed. A recent investigation found that nonmedical or support staff in American hospitals averaged nearly 3.2 per bed versus 1.2 to 1.7 per bed in equally well-equipped and similar-size hospitals in Japan, Israel, and Germany. This is not only unnecessary but in most cases self-defeating. Job classifications are too narrow and skill requirements often too low. During a recent hospital stay, seventeen different people served my room, excluding medical staff. It is also curious that a hospital stay in a semiprivate room, excluding all medical service costs, is three to four times as expensive as a room at a most exclusive luxury hotel. Servicing a hospital room costs nearly ten times as much as servicing a much more luxurious hotel room. It may be interesting to let large, experienced hotel companies manage the hotel functions of hospitals and have the hospitals concentrate on the medical service part. The cost savings could be of the order of 20 to 30 percent of hospital operating costs. It is recognized that hospital installations are more complex and require access to various types of medical or support services not available in hotels.
4. Hospital management in many cases is inefficient. Hospital accounting has often become not just a joke but a downright prescription for fraud. Not only do few hospitals know their costs, but they invent artificial charges to generate revenues. Aspirins at three dollars per tablet have become a typical outrage. By and large, hospital management requires not just a businesslike approach but also effective budgetary and quality controls. Most hospitals are still either public or supposedly nonprofit-making. As they are tax exempt institutions, their control and reporting is usually much more lax. Directors are usually not shareholder representatives but selected by hospital management. Accountability to boards is often much more lax, and donors seldom require detailed accounting. It is simply now nice to ask "institutions in the public interest" to account for their use or misuse of resources and to question their commitment to the public interest. While most hospital managements are probably honest, there is an urgent need to re-

structure hospital administrations. Leadership of hospitals and HMOs should always be in the hands of a renowned and respected medical professional who can set the priorities, overall objectives, and standards. Administrative functions from personnel, finance/accounting, and procurement to housekeeping and public relations should be supporting functions. Some of these should be farmed out to competent, efficient suppliers. Only by returning the management of health care organizations to health care professionals will our health care institutions regain their focus, priorities, and ultimately effectiveness. Our hospitals and HMOs have been criticized in recent times for their lack of humanity and for putting economics ahead of care. This happened largely because health care administrations have become largely cost controllers or bean counters and not benefit/cost optimizers or effective business people who always put the customer first.

5. Public education in and media coverage of medical issues have become largely news-oriented. Emphasis is given to the most interesting and not necessarily most valuable or effective methods or treatments. High-tech diagnostics or treatments as well as the latest genetic engineering breakthroughs capture the headlines though only a few will ever benefit from them. On the other hand, the average American is more ignorant of basic medical solutions than most people in undeveloped and many in developing countries. The nation is full of rumors of new breakthroughs that soon thereafter are discredited. Basic health care has become more a fad than intelligent application of available medicine. Part of it is the result of often misleading advertising or marketing, but public education and our media carry at least equal blame. Much of it is probably due to a combination of bad business practices more concerned with gaining short-term market share and profits and less with the health impact of new products and the public attitude, which wants miracles and not cures. We must educate the public from an early age in healthy living, remedies for basic and common illnesses, recognition of signs of medical problems, sources for help, and more. It is curious to note that not only are there many Americans who have no family doctor, but also many do not know where to get help when needed.

6. Americans consume many times more over-the-counter medicine than anyone else. We have over-the-counter medication for practically every possible ailment, even for nonexistent ailments. Though the FDA is doing a superb job in assuring the effectiveness and safety of individual over-the-counter and other drugs, most people are not aware of the long-term effects of large doses of different, basically safe, drugs. The amount of chemical materials ingested by Americans may have severe effects, and reeducation of the public as well as more responsible approaches by drug companies are urgently needed.

In summary, we need a more efficient, more compassionate, more accountable and transparent, as well as more open and communicating or educating health care system. We must put much more emphasis on preventative medicine, use of natural remedies, simple procedures, accessible basic health care facilities, and family doctor networks. In other words, we must spend more on curing common ills and less on exotic ones.

We must educate the public not through headlines of high-tech breakthroughs that few will ever need (or could afford) by thorough, well-designed articles and programs that deal with healthy living, prevention, natural remedies, treatment of common ailments, access to medical services, and caution with consumption of large doses of chemical medications.

Our hospitals and HMOs will have to merge and improve their efficiency, effectiveness, accountability, and accessibility. If all this is done and we develop a truly compassionate medical establishment with well-paid doctors and nurses, we should be able to not only contain our explosion of medical costs but actually bring them down to less than 10 percent of GNP, while at the same time improving the quality and universality of health care for all.

## Restructuring the Criminal Justice System

Our legal system has really gone haywire by any standard. We have 20 million (1992) lawsuits/year (or one lawsuit for every ten adults). Twenty-five percent of all civil suits are frivolous or fraudulent. We have 800,000 lawyers and 27,000 state and federal judges, more than the rest of the world combined. Our prison population is the largest in the world and is growing older. We now spend $22,000/inmate/year average and $69,000/inmate/year for those older than fifty-five.[5]

We have a very porous prison system that allows drugs and weapons to infiltrate. Prisons do not rehabilitate and the three-strike laws do not really prevent crime. According to Prof. John Deluho of Princeton, nearly half of the 671,000 parolees and probationeers are caught committing a serious new crime within three years of release. Counseling does not seem to work, and plea bargaining has become a real failure. The rearrest rate of released prisoners is even worse.[6] Seventy percent of those eighteen to twenty-four years of age and 10 percent of those sixty years or older are rearrested in the commitment of a serious crime.

Legal reform has strong support from nearly all segments of American society and is bottled up in Congress under pressure from politically powerful groups, such as the trial lawyers. As 70 percent of all legislators are lawyers, certainly not a fair representation of American society, getting Congress to vote any serious reform of our legal system is nearly impossible. At the same time, the average lawyer costs the U.S. economy $1 million/year in real output of goods and services (1995).

The Common Sense Law Reform Act proposed recently is a compromise and whitewash that certainly does not go far enough in correcting the ills of the existing system. The system must be made more accountable, less self-serving, more just, more transparent, and, most important, more accessible. Currently fewer than 50 percent of all crimes are ever adjudicated, because the system does not provide access, is too expensive, too cumbersome, and unjust, and lacks transparency or is too complex.

The following are a few suggestions to make the system fairer and more effective while reducing its costs to society. They are based on the concept that laws must be enforceable, in the interest of society, and fair to be effective. Unfortunately, many of our laws are no longer, yet Congress is unwilling to change such laws, often because of pressure by interest groups who may represent but a small percentage of society.

1. Our justice system must be streamlined to assure that cases are heard no more than one year or so after the event or crime. Long delays only cost a lot of money but also invariably affect the fairness of the ruling. Obviously, in cases where evidence only becomes available later, the case should be heard within a year after completion of the bulk of the investigation and col-

lection of the evidence. Frivolous and fraudulent cases must be discouraged by huge fines and assessment of costs to both the clients and lawyers to bring such cases to court. Fraud by lawyers should result in mandatory disbarment. Similarly, losers in civil cases should be held accountable for fees and costs of winners to encourage settlements and to unclog law courts. Reducing frivolous and fraudulent cases by 50 percent would reduce court loads and costs significantly.

2. Only criminals who pose a physical threat to society should be incarcerated in traditional secure prisons. Others should receive other types of punishment, including work camps or other forms of separation from normal society. It is unacceptable to have dangerous criminals like Lawrence Singleton, convicted of raping a teenager and cutting off her forearms and accused of murdering a woman, released after eight years. Many violent, often repeat, criminals are walking our streets, while prisons are full of nonviolent drug offenders and others convicted of white-collar or other civil crimes. We must develop systems of work camps and groupings in which nonviolent criminals pay off their debt to society by performing necessary work tasks. Not only will this greatly reduce prison costs and crowding and improve street safety by keeping violent criminals incarcerated for their full term, but experience in other countries and some parts of the United States show that rehabilitation of nonviolent criminals, including drug offenders, is more effective if such people are required to perform meaningful work. They gain in self-worth, personal attitude, and most important, feeling that they have made effective restitution to society. All earnings from such work have to go toward the cost of maintenance and restitution to victims and/or society. A similar approach is advocated for incarcerated violent criminals who as long as physically able should be required to work full-time for their keep and restitution to victims of their crime. It is unacceptable to have society pay for the keep of able-bodied criminals and even provide them with comfort of normal life, such as TV, exercise equipment, libraries, more. They should be provided with nothing but a bare cell with a cot and washing/toilet facilities. Everything else has to be paid for from earnings, including nonbasic food. It is unfair

and unacceptable to have prisoners run private businesses from prison for personal gain while society pays for their keep and the victim gets no restitution. We are nearly alone in our concepts of prisoners' rights, which is not only morally repugnant but societally unacceptable. The argument that prisoners working for their own benefit will change their attitude and rehabilitate them to take their place as normal citizens in society has never been proven. In fact, most "business" activities, particularly of violent prisoners, are related to their previous criminal past. On the other hand, meaningful work in prison may change their attitude and force them to accept a more disciplined, meaningful lifestyle. Society must not be forced to pay for both the crime and the incarceration of the criminal. Such approaches have been put in use in many countries with success, and it is high time for us to admit the failure of the so-called criminal rights or justice system and reestablish a system where criminals truly pay for their crimes. Not only will this improve safety in the streets, but it will also reduce the cost of crime to society.

3. Class action and product liability suits are now out of hand. They are often undertaken not so much to correct a wrong and to compensate victims but to force deep pockets to disburse unconscionable amounts, little of which ends up in the victims' or supposed victims' pockets. Most of these actions are no longer instigated by victims but by lawyers who recognize an opportunity. They know that independent of the merit of the case, defendants will usually try to settle to reduce adverse publicity. Victims, if any, usually receive a pittance from the settlement. We require a uniform, enforceable class action and product liability law and other standards, including limits to both liability for cause and punitive damages. Legal costs may only be fair and reasonable and may not exceed a percentage of damages. The principal beneficiary must always be the victim, not the lawyer.
4. Recent high-publicity cases have shown the unreliability of expert witnesses. Expert testimony should be based on real science to be admissible and expert witnesses should not be paid on a contingency-fee basis.
5. Lawyers should be subject to the same review process as other

professionals in cases of misconduct, fraud, and other misdemeanors. Medical doctors, engineers, and other professionals are not investigated and judged only by their peers in case of negligence, fraud, or other misconduct. They are usually subjected to the legal process. Lawyers, on the other hand, are normally subject to review only by their peers. This is self-serving and unacceptable.

6. Drug-related crime has become the most serious problem in America. For many years we have tried to stem the flow of drugs and related criminal activity by attacking the supply side abroad and in the United States, ignoring the fact that as long as there is demand, supply will be generated at any cost. Apparently, the lessons learned during Prohibition many years ago have been forgotten. We then fought liquid supply and outlawed use. But forbidden demand made supply very lucrative to traders, illegal producers, and a lot of middlemen. In fact, it became kind of respectable activity to circumvent the Prohibition laws. In drugs the situation is similar but more devastating in economic, public safety, and health terms. Some advocate legalizing some drug use to get the criminals out of the supply chain. I do not think this will work because there are so many different drugs and it would be difficult to develop a legal drug supply system. We have to attack the problem on the demand side. We must not only reduce demand but also make it socially and economically unattractive or unacceptable. For too long we considered drug users victims who must be helped at society's cost. I think that habitual drug users must be considered criminals or at least outcasts and made to feel that they are not accepted by society. Severe fines and forced rehabilitation for which drug users must pay through their own work are the only way we will ever reduce demand. Drug users must not be glorified as poor victims but publicized as outcasts who must work to rehabilitate themselves. This approach, combined with very severe punishment of drug dealers, has worked in other countries, and there is hope that it will also work in the United States. There are obviously those who will decry such an approach as inhuman. To those the answer is that allowing lifelong drug abuse to continue with half-hearted attempts to reduce supply is much more inhuman. Drug-related offenses

are today the most serious crime problem in America. We can no longer afford to attack these problems with socially correct solutions instead of addressing the core issues affecting demand. We in America consume nearly 60 percent of the world's major drugs. Drug-induced health problems account for probably 20 to 30 percent of our nation's health care costs. Drug-related criminal justice system costs account for probably a larger percentage. Together the cost of the drug problem to the nation is in excess of $400 billion, or more than 5 percent of the GNP, and growing. This is unacceptable and must be fought at the base, the demand base, even if socially and politically incorrect.

7. Juvenile crime has skyrocketed in recent years and is now the fastest-growing segment in the nation's crime. Much of this crime has advanced from nonviolent and petty to violent major crime, including murder by juveniles as young as ten or eleven years of age. While we blame our media and the decline in family structure for much of it, we, the society at large, are at least equally to blame. We are permissive and not willing to make the hard decisions. Juveniles value freedom, money, driving, and prestige from their peers above all. But all these should be earned. Driving licenses should only be given to sixteen- or seventeen-year-olds who maintain an adequate grade level in high school. Similarly, permission to work or job offers must be dependent on scholastic performance. In other words, employers may only employ juveniles with adequate grades. The grades drop below a certain level, and they lose their job. School hours and supervised homework or study hours must be extended and students required to attend after normal school hours if their grades fall below an acceptable level. This type of approach has been very successful in other countries and would work here, too. Our juveniles have too few challenges, too much free time, and too easy access to money. All of these are counterincentive and have a bad effect on their education and development.

The preceding are just a few suggestions proposed to help deal with the problems in our criminal justice system. They may in part sound radical, but they are probably more humane and effective than the approaches used now. Adding more police officers or prison cells or even judges is not going to do the job. We must attack the root problems and use new methods after failing to stem the problems using traditional approaches for many years.

## Institutional Effectiveness

The most important lesson learned is probably that our institutions no longer deliver on their promises while their institutional transaction and production costs seem to be out of control. Institutions, like other activities, must add value to the economy by providing benefits that outweigh costs. Adding greater value must become the principal institutional incentives, not size or budget. Most institutional transactions involve exchange of valuable resources for taxes,[7] and their impact on economic development must become a key criterion in the measurement of their performance. They must not just be consumers of assets, nor should they be agents of economic exchange. Unfortunately, the costs of resources consumed by our institutions far exceed the value of benefits generated. Our institutions must be required to measure both their transaction costs and the value of the benefits to society and/or the economy generated. Institutional performance can be measured in economic and social terms and effective criteria set which provide benchmarks for value of the benefits to cost terms or benefit/cost ratios. Institutions must be justified by their contributions to society's needs, not for historic or political reasons. Similarly, the cost of institutional constraints must be determined in social and economic and not just political terms.

Instead of constraints and regulations, dynamic informal rules are required to empower institutions. The need for institutional services varies throughout the nation, and social networks not regulations, should define the use and choice of institutional services. Institutions must also learn from their experiences and adjust their services in response to these lessons. Institutional services change the needs of the society they serve and must be adjusted to cater to these changing needs.

In normal business, both parties to a transaction have an incentive to reduce transaction costs. American institutions, though, are different, as they usually attempt to maximize transaction costs without the consent of those they serve. In fact, institutional transaction costs have now grown to unacceptable levels. With a cost-plus culture, there are no incentives to economize and our institutional cultures do not recognize moral norms or conventions to keep costs in check. There seem to be few qualms with regard to the ultimate payers. In fact, institutions in general consider the taxpayer an unlimited source of funds and responsible for the maintenance of institutional funding at the inefficient levels to which institutions have become accustomed. There is no regret or excuse, just an institutional right.

# Postscript: The American Dilemma

Institutions built America but now endanger its fundamental values. The American Constitution relies on the health care, educational, and criminal justice institutions to protect its basic promises. For over two hundred years these institutions evolved in the image of the tenets of the Constitution as bodies that care and protect as well as help people to take advantage of opportunities.

In recent years, though, many of our major institutions have started to deviate from their basic tasks and have become largely self-serving. They similarly are now consuming an inordinate amount of resources that society cannot afford, all at a cost to other essential needs of American society. This cannot continue lest we endanger our own quality of life and future. Our economy is booming now, but there are many danger signs as more and more of it is based on service industries of which health care, education, and law enforcement constitute an increasing and abnormally large portion and of our GDP.

In this book we reviewed the developments and status of our great institutions and provided suggestions for their reinvention. Reengineering as practiced, which consists largely of tinkering with institutional structures, is not enough to turn things around. As indicated, we need a completely new mind-set. We need new commitments. Above all, we need a change in attitude and approach. While institutions should be run in a businesslike manner, they do not primarily exist for business. They may be businesses, but their primary objectives are not to make money or to generate profit but to serve society's essential needs.

The American public has sycophantially nourished the greed and self-indulgence of many or our institutions. Only occasionally has it voiced criticism when things got terribly out of hand. It has been made to feel guilty in questioning institutional policy and excesses. It has learned to accept that these institutions think they know what is best for the American public.

Few actions of our institutions are really transparent, and accountability is resisted or simply distorted by walls of obscurity or silence. Democracy is taught but not practiced by our educational institutions, which, like health care and legal institutions have become increasingly autocratic. The problem is not only that our institutions consume such an inordinate percentage of our economic output, but that they consume so much of our will. We have become beholden to them. They set our standards and our norms. We must regain control of our institutions. We must make then accountable to society, to the people they are designed to serve, and not to their own self-appointed boards. Society and the people must set the standards and rules by which these institutions operate lest we become an institutional autocracy.

# Endnotes

## 1. An American Dilemma

1. C. Nash. *The Culture of Narcissism,* (New York: Norton, 1979).
2. P. Kennedy. *The Rise and Fall of the Great Powers.* (New York: Random House, 1987).
3. D. Cale. *The Imperious Economy,* (Cambridge, Mass.: Harvard University Press, 1982).
4. M. Olson, *The Rise and Decline of Nations,* (New Haven: Yale University Press, 1982).

## 3. The American Health Care System

1. "The U.S. Ranks Low Internationally on Most Health Care Indicators," Office of Technology Assessment, U.S. Congress Report Brief, November 1993.
2. T. M. Terris. "Lessons from Canada's Health Program," *Technology Review,* February/March 1990.
3. According to the American Medical Association, average annual doctor's income is much lower, with general practitioners, pediatricians, gynecologists, and radiologists making \$111,500, \$119,300, \$221,800, and \$229,000, respectively, in 1992.
4. *Benefit Design in Health Care Reform: Patient Cost Sharing,* Office of Technology Assessment, U.S. Congress Report Brief, September 1993.
5. Ibid.
6. Health Insurance Association of America as reported in *Newsweek,* April 5, 1993.

## 4. The Dilemma of U.S. Education

1. *Business Week,* November 15, 1993.
2. This section is based on an article by the author published in the *Faculty Newsletter* of MIT, May 1992.
3. H. Brooks. *University-Industry Cooperation as Industrial Strategy in Managing Innovation and Change,* ed. B. Lungstedt and T. H. Moss, Washington, DC: HASA, 1989.

## 5. American Criminal Justice and the Business of Law


1. J. Sugarman. Executive Director, Violence Policy Center, Washington, D.C., "Want a Gun? Become a Gun Dealer," *Wall Street Journal,* October 4, 1993.
2. According to the American Medical Association (1992), malpractice insurance cost $15 billion in 1970 and $45 billion in 1993. In 1960 one doctor in 100 was sued, and by 1985 the number had grown to 18 in 100. Defensive medicine added another $25 billion in 1991 to the cost of doctors. Legal challenges and liabilities of health care in the U.S. cost 2.5% of GNP, versus .5% of GNP in Europe and Japan. *Journal of the American Medical Association,* June 1992.


## 6. Rethinking American Institutions


1. M. Hammer and J. Champy. "Reengineering the Corporation: A Manifesto for Business Revolution," *Harper Business,* 1993.


## 8. Reinventing Our Institutions for Improved Economic Performance


1. D. C. North. Institutions, Institutional Change, and Economic Performance, Cambridge, Cambridge University Press, 1990.
2. "Federal Spending on Entitlements," *Business Week,* December 13, 1995.
3. "Health Care Fraud," *Boston Globe,* August 2, 1994.
4. "Rand Health Insurance Experiment, 1972–1982," Santa Monica, CA: Rand Corporation, 1983.
5. N. R. Powe. "Study of Medicaid Core—Cost vs. Quality," *Journal of the American Medical Association,* September 1994.
6. Recent studies indicate that insurance costs alone add $300 to 500 to the cost of delivering a baby in New York City.


## 9. Our Institutional Future


1. P. J. Denning. "Business Design for the New University," *Educom Review,* November/December 1996.
2. P. Drucker. "Post-Capitalist Society," *Harper Business,* 1993.
3. D. Tsichritas. "Value of Research," *Educom,* November/December 1996.
4. A. Shanker. "The Teachers Advocate," *U.S. News and World Report,* March 10, 1997.
5. National Criminal Justice Commission, *The Real War on Crime,* Washington, D.C., Department of Justice, 1996.
6. Report by U.S. Justice Department, Bureau of Justice Statistics, 1989.
7. D. C. North. *Institutions, Institutional Change, and Economic Performance,* Cambridge, Cambridge University Press, 1990.

# Bibliography


Becker, Gary S., and William M. Landes. *Essay in the Economics of Crime and Punishment.* New York: Columbia University Press, 1984.

Buchanan, James M., and Robert D. Tollison. *Theory of Public Choice: Political Applications of Economics.* Ann Arbor: University of Michigan Press, 1972.

Cabot, Thomas D. "Is American Education Competitive?" *Harvard Magazine,* Spring 1986, p. 14.

Dowding, Keith, and Desmond King, eds. *Preferences, Institutions, and Rational Choice.* Oxford: Oxford University Press, 1995.

Gingrich, Newt. *Contract with America.* New York: Times Books, 1994.

Hammond, Kenneth R. *Human Judgement and Social Policy.* Oxford: Oxford University Press, 1996.

Israel, Arturo. *Institutional Development: Incentives to Performance.* Baltimore, MD: Johns Hopkins University Press, 1987.

Kennedy, Paul. *The Rise and Fall of the Great Powers.* New York: Random House, 1987.

Krugman, Paul. *The Age of Diminishing Expectations.* Cambridge, MA: MIT Press, 1990.

Lutz, Mark A., and Kenneth Lux. *Humanistic Economics.* New York: Bootstrap Press, 1988.

McCormack, Mark H. *The Terrible Truth about Lawyers.* New York: William Morrow, 1987.

North, Douglas C. *Institutions, Institutional Change, and Economic Performance.* Cambridge: Cambridge University Press, 1980.

Rodwin, Marc A. *Medicine, Money and Morals: Physicians' Conflicts of Interest.* Oxford: Oxford University Press, 1993.

Thurow, Paul. *Investment in Human Capital.* Belmont, CA: Wadsworth, 1970.

———. *Head to Head.* New York: Warner, 1993.

———. *The Future of Capitalism.* New York: William Morrow, 1996.

World Bank. *Bureaucrats in Business: The Economics and Politics of Government Ownership.* Washington, DC: World Bank, 1996.

# Index